The Lure of the Dark Side

The Lure of the Dark Side

Satan and Western Demonology in Popular Culture

Edited by
Christopher Partridge and Eric Christianson

LONDON   OAKVILLE

Published by Equinox Publishing Ltd.

UK: Unit 6, The Village, 101 Amies St., London SW11 2JW
USA: DBBC, 28 Main Street, Oakville, CT 06779
www.equinoxpub.com

First published 2009 by Equinox Publishing Ltd.

British Library Cataloguing-in-Publication Data
A catalogue record for this book is available from the British Library.

Library of Congress Cataloging-in-Publication Data
The lure of the dark side : satan and western demonology in popular culture / edited by Christopher Partridge and Eric Christianson.
        p. cm.
   Includes bibliographical references and index.
   ISBN 978-1-84553-309-0 (hb) -- ISBN 978-1-84553-310-6 (pbk.)   1.
Demonology. 2. Popular culture. I. Partridge, Christopher H.
(Christopher Hugh), 1961- II. Christianson, Eric S.
   BF1543.L87 2008
   133.4'2--dc22
                         2007036372

ISBN-13 978 1 84553 309 0 (hardback)
         978 1 84553 310 6 (paperback)

Typeset by CA Typesetting Ltd, www.publisherservices.co.uk
Printed and bound in Great Britain by Lightning Source UK Ltd., Milton Keynes
and Lightning Source Inc., La Vergne, TN

Contents

List of Contributors

George Aichele is a member of "The Bible and Culture Collective," the group author of *The Postmodern Bible* (1995). His writings include *The Control of Biblical Meaning: Canon as Semiotic Mechanism* (2001), *Jesus Framed* (1996), and *The Phantom Messiah: Postmodern Fantasy and the Gospel of Mark* (2006). His edited/co-edited works include *The Monstrous and the Unspeakable* (1997), *Culture, Entertainment and the Bible* (2000), and *Screening Scripture* (2002).

Brian Baker is a Lecturer in English at Lancaster University, UK, and is the author of three books: *Literature and Science: Social Impact and Interaction*, with John H. Cartwright (ABC-Clio, 2005), *Masculinity in Fiction and Film: Representing Men in Popular Genres 1945–2000* (Continuum, 2006) and *Iain Sinclair* (Manchester University Press, 2007). He has also published more widely in journals and book collections in the areas of masculinities and genre, science and literature, and particularly science fiction, on which subject he is writing a *Reader's Guide to Essential Criticism* for Palgrave Macmillan. He also has forthcoming work on the film *Casino Royale*, and is working on larger projects concerning the Orpheus myth and representations of mobility, space and time in fiction and film.

Charlie Blake is Principal Lecturer in Critical and Cultural Theory, and Head of the Department of Media, Film and Communications at Liverpool Hope University. Formerly a professional musician, who has taught at the universities of Oxford, Cambridge, Oxford Brookes, Hertfordshire and Manchester Metropolitan, he is the founding editor of *Angelaki* (the independent, award-winning, internationally acclaimed Oxford-based academic journal in literature, philosophy and the social sciences) and also of the *Angelaki Series in the Humanities* (which began publishing in 1999). He is the co-editor (with Linnie Blake) of *Intellectuals and Global Culture* (1997) and (with Gary Banham) of *Evil Spirits: Nihilism and the Fate of Modernity* (2000). He is currently engaged in setting up the TransEuropean Consortium of Research in New Media and Culture, and working (with Frida Beckman of Uppsala University, Sweden), on two co-edited collections: for *Angelaki*: *Shadows of Cruelty: Sadism, Masochism and the Philosophical Muse* (two volumes: summer 2009 and spring 2010), and *The Visiotextual Imagination: Space, Time and the Event in the Graphic Novel* (2011); a co-authored monograph on recorded music and philosophy (with Isabella Van Elferen of the University of Utrecht, Netherlands) entitled *Sonic Spectrality: Music, Machines, Hauntography* (forthcoming) and a monograph on Deleuze & Guattari and global media theory: *Media Transversalities* (forthcoming).

Eric Christianson is Senior Lecturer in Biblical Studies at the University of Chester and teaches and researches in Bible and film. He has recently published *Ecclesiastes Through the Centuries* (2007) and (as co-editor and contributor) a volume of essays on film and theology, *Cinéma Divinité: Religion, Theology and the Bible in Film* (2005).

Asbjørn Dyrendal is Associate Professor of Religious Studies at the Norwegian University of Science and Technology. He wrote his PhD thesis on American Evangelicals and the Satanism scare. His research areas revolve around contemporary religion (Satanism, conspiracy theories, neopaganism, UFO religions, fundamentalisms), religion and popular culture, and theory in the study of religions. Recent publications include: *True Religion versus Cannibal Others? Rhetorical Constructions of Satanism among American Evangelicals* (2003); *Demoner* (i.e. *Demons*) (2006); "Satanism as a News Item" (with Amina Lap), in *The Encyclopedic Sourcebook on Satanism* (2008); "Devilish Consumption: Popular Culture in Satanic Socialization, *Numen* 55; "Darkness Within: Satanism as Self-Religion," and "Social Democratic Satanism?" (with Didrik Søderlind), in *Contemporary Religious Satanism* (Ashgate, 2009).

Colin Duriez is author of a literary guide to J. K. Rowling, *The Unauthorised Harry Potter Companion* for Sutton Publishing (The History Press) in the UK and InterVarsity Press in the USA, where it is entitled, *A Field Guide to Harry Potter*. He is author of a number of books about C. S. Lewis, J. R. R. Tolkien and the Inklings, including *J. R. R. Tolkien and C. S. Lewis: The Story of their Friendship*, and *A Field Guide to Narnia*. He has also appeared as a commentator on the extended version DVDs of the *Lord of the Rings Trilogy* (Peter Jackson, director); PBS's *The Question of God*, which compared C. S. Lewis and Sigmund Freud; the Sony DVD *Ringers* about Tolkien fandom and the impact of Tolkien on popular culture; and the "Royal" extended version DVD of Disney's *The Lion, the*

Witch and the Wardrobe. He is currently writing a book on the theme of devilry in the work of C. S. Lewis for InterVarsity Press in the USA.

Crawford Gribben is Senior Lecturer in Early Modern Print Culture at Trinity College, Dublin. He is the author of a number of studies about James Hogg, the literary cultures of Puritanism and the relationship between literature and theology in the early modern period. He is currently working on a history of evangelical millennialism (Palgrave).

Titus Hjelm is a lecturer in Finnish Society and Culture at University College London. His main areas of expertise are sociology of religion, religion and social problems, religion, media and popular culture, and religion in Finland. His latest publications include a book on the construction of Satanism in the Finnish news media and an edited book on Wicca (both in Finnish). Currently he is writing a book on social constructionism (Palgrave Macmillan, 2010) and editing a volume titled *Religion and Social Problems* (Routledge, 2009).

Larry J. Kreitzer is a Fellow at Regent's Park College where he has been based since 1986; he is also the Tutor for Graduate Admissions there. In addition, he holds a Research Lectureship within the Faculty of Theology. He is a member of the Society of New Testament Studies and serves on the Editorial Board for the *Journal for the Study of the New Testament*. His publications include *2 Corinthians* (1996, 2001); *Striking New Images: Roman Imperial Coinage and the New Testament World* (1996); *The Epistle to the Ephesians* (1997); *Pauline Images in Fiction and Film* (1999); *Gospel Images in Fiction and Film* (2002); *Seditious Sectaryes* (2006); *Hierapolis in the Heavens* (2007); and *Philemon* (2008).

Peter Mercer-Taylor is an Associate Professor of Musicology at the University of Minnesota School of Music. Mercer-Taylor's scholarship has been divided between the nineteenth-century German classical tradition—Felix Mendelssohn in particular—and contemporary popular music, including the work of the Bangles, Elvis Costello, Bill Staines, and They Might Be Giants. He has spoken at numerous conferences and symposia, and been interviewed on the BBC radio program *In Tune* and on National Public Radio's *Weekend Edition*. His articles have appeared in a range of journals, including *19th-Century Music, Popular Music, Music & Letters, The Journal of Musicology*, and *Popular Music & Society*. Mercer-Taylor is the author of *The Life of Mendelssohn* (2000) and the editor of *The Cambridge Companion to Mendelssohn* (2004).

Christopher Partridge is Professor of Religious Studies at Lancaster University, UK, and Co-director of the Research Centre for Religion and Popular Culture at the University of Chester. His research and writing focuses both on contemporary religious belief and also on popular music. He has a particular interest in the relationship between popular culture and religion. He is the author of *The Re-Enchantment of the West*, 2 volumes (2004–2006) and the co-editor of the series "Studies in Popular Music" (Equinox). He is the editor of several volumes about religious belief in the contemporary world, including *The World's Religions* (2005), *Encyclopedia of New Religions* (2004), and *UFO Religions* (2003).

Anthony B. Pinn is Agnes Cullen Arnold Professor of Humanities and Professor of Religious Studies at Rice University. After ten years at Macalester College (St. Paul, MN), he joined the Rice faculty in 2004. He is the author/editor of sixteen books. Professor Pinn's research and teaching interests include liberation theologies, African American religious thought, religion and popular culture, and African American humanism.

William R. Telford is Senior Lecturer in Religious Studies (New Testament) at the University of Durham. His research interests include Christian origins, the New Testament, the Historical Jesus, the Gospel of Mark, methods of biblical interpretation, and the Bible in literature and film, and he has published on these subjects in a variety of journals and edited works. His books on the New Testament and the Gospel of Mark include *The Barren Temple and the Withered Tree* (1980), (ed.) *The Interpretation of Mark* (1985/1995), *Mark* (1995); *The Theology of the Gospel of Mark* (1999) and *The New Testament: A Short Introduction* (2002). His most recent publication, as co-editor and contributor, is *Cinéma Divinité: Religion, Theology and the Bible in Film* (2005), and his *Writing on the Gospel of Mark* (Guides to Advanced Biblical Research; Blandford Forum: Deo Publishing; Norwich: SCM-Canterbury; Winona Lake, IN: Eisenbrauns) is shortly to be published.

Introduction:
A Brief History of Western Demonology

Christopher Partridge and Eric Christianson

This collection of papers has its genesis in a 2006 conference on demonology organized by the Research Centre for Religion and Popular Culture (University of Chester and St Deiniol's Library, Hawarden, North Wales[1]). While we were very much aware of the interest such a perennially fascinating topic would provoke, we were delighted by the response. Although a further couple of chapters were commissioned following the conference, the volume indicates the breadth of scholarly interest in the topic and, more broadly, in popular culture *per se*. From testimonies of encounters with demons in early modern Scotland to contemporary Satanism and Norwegian black metal, and from the manifestation of evil in Thomas Harris' Hannibal Lecter to the demonic in Harry Potter, this collection provides a tour de force of the demonic in Western popular culture. For those angelic souls unfamiliar with "the dark side," the following introductory essay provides a brief history of Satan and Western demonology.

In the Classical Greek *daimon* (meaning "spirit")—from which "demon" is derived through late Medieval Latin—was used of any malevolent or benevolent spirit (*agathos daimon*), deified hero, demigod, or ancestor spirit that mediated between the transcendent and temporal realms. Over time, however, such demons gradually came to be understood as malevolent. Hence, by the late Greco-Roman period, the term *daimonia* was specifically applied to evil spirits, the main work of which was to frustrate, to harm, and particularly to tempt humans into sin (see Russell, 1977: 34, 142; Forsyth, 1987: 293). Indeed, the Stoic systematization of late Platonic demonology, which understood the *daimonia* to exist at an ontological level between the gods and humanity, is reflected in 1 Enoch 15 and 2 Enoch 29:5, where fallen angels are described as hovering in the lower air (see Galloway, 1951: 25; Russell, 1977: 191ff.; Forsyth, 1987: 160–81). It is this understanding of the term *daimonium* that is adopted in the Septuagint, the New Testament, and the early church. Moreover, it should be noted that, whilst some reference to evil demons can be found in the Hebrew Bible—e.g. *Aza'zel* (Lev. 16:8–10), *lîlîth* (Isa. 34:14) (see Trachtenberg, 1970: 27; Baker, 1974: 19–21), the *shédîm*, to whom people sacrificed their sons and their daughters (Ps. 106:37), and, of course, the Satan figure (1 Chron. 21; Job 1, 2; 1 Zech. 3.1; see Nielsen, 1998; Forsyth, 1987: 107–23)—and whilst some of the basic characteristics of a good–evil dualism can be traced back to Iranian Zoroastrianism, it is not until the second and first centuries BCE that a sophisticated demonology began to evolve within Jewish theology.

As to the differences between early and late Jewish demonology, firstly, in the later demonology, the chief characteristic is not that demons physically harm humans, but rather that they spiritually interfere with them, tempting them into sin and thereby disrupting their relationship with God. More specifically, whereas some heavenly messengers sought to reveal to individuals the nature of humanity in relation to celestial realities, its origins and its divine destiny, the *daimonia* seek to deceive with false revelations, to pervert true divine revelation, and to confuse. Secondly, and far more importantly, in Jewish apocalyptic demonology there evolved the notion of a single source, or unitary concept of evil. This latter point is particularly significant, in that there was a "movement of thought away from the explanation of evil in terms of numerous capricious spirits operating at random, towards an explanation in terms of a hierarchy or unified body of evil [which] reaches its climax in the New Testament" (Ling, 1961: 9). Whilst, originally, the term *satanas*, meaning "adversary" or "opponent," could be used of any adversarial demon, and thus could also be used in the plural, in apocalyptic literature, and particularly in the New Testament, the term is focused on a particular *satanas*, "Satan"—also called the Devil. (In a way related to the early usage of *satanas*, English also permits the plural "devils" for lesser "demons," keeping "the Devil" for Satan.) That said, it is important to note that, because of the strength of Christian monotheism, Satan and God are never understood in terms of an absolute dualism, in the sense that Ahura Mazda and Angra Mainyu (or Ahriman) are in Zoroastrianism.[2] Good and evil have never been two equal and co-eternal adversaries in the Christian faith. Principally because God alone is the creator

> in the apocalyptic writings the evil powers remain quite clearly subject to the authority of God. He has the supreme power…and finally it is he who will punish the evil spirits. Satan and his subordinates are free to operate on Earth only until the day of judgement… Satan as the archfiend, or representative leader of all evil, is regarded at most as a leader of rebel forces, a would-be, but unsuccessful, usurper of God (Ling, 1961: 10).

Indeed, the Assumption of Moses 10 looks forward to the ultimate demise of Satan as God finally establishes his rule (Barrett, 1987: 331–32). Likewise, in Christian theology the death and resurrection of Christ firmly exclude any possibility of demonic supremacy, let alone victory. As Gustav Aulén persuasively argued many years ago, because of the popular preoccupation of early Christianity with demons and the demonic, the defeat of Satan and the forces of darkness was understood to be one of the central accomplishments of Christ's death and resurrection (1931). In the New Testament and the writings of the fathers, Jesus is *Christus Victor*: "He disarmed the principalities and powers and made a public example of them, triumphing over them in him" (Col. 2:15). "The reason the Son of God appeared was to destroy the works of the Devil" (1 Jn 3:8). Of course, as several chapters in this volume indicate, in some contemporary Satanist demonologies, the perceived balance of power is reversed and Christ has become a victim and a symbol of weakness and defeat, as suggested by, for example, Akercocke's 1999 debut album *Rape of the Bastard Nazarene*.

We have noted that the Satan figure appears in the Hebrew Bible. However, even the casual reader will quickly discover that he is portrayed differently than he is in the New Testament (see Kluger, 1967). Indeed, he is one of the "members of the court of heaven," one of the *bene 'elohim*, a "son of God" (Job 1:6). The Book of Job in particular describes him as a being who works closely with Yahweh as his agent in the testing of Job (Nielsen, 1998: 59-105). To put it another way, in Job the Satan can be read as a provocateur who meets with little opposition from the Lord God. Indeed, it is from the mouth of the Satan that one of the Hebrew Bible's most incisive and modernist questions comes: "Does Job fear God *for nothing*?" It is the Satan who makes possible the book's existential probings into the integrity of Job.

According to Russell, Satan as a son of God has his origins in Canaanite religion:

> In Canaan these "sons" are gods, manifestations of the divine principle. Clearly, the original idea in Hebrew religion was that Yahweh was surrounded by a pantheon comparable to that of Zeus or Wotan. The idea of a pantheon was displeasing to strict monotheism [a phenomenon incisively explored by Aichele in this volume], and the *banim* (*bene ha'elohim*) became shadowy figures. Yet they retained an important function of separating the evil aspect of the divine nature from the good (1977: 184).

Kirsten Nielsen explains the relationship between God and Satan more literally in terms of father and son:

> At the beginning father and son are together, but at a certain time their
> paths separate. Satan in the book of Job [is] the son of God who for some
> time roamed the earth. He lived among the other sons of God, close to
> his father. There is nothing to indicate that he was denied this position
> after he had tested Job, neither was there a revolt against his father or any
> fall from the heavenly to the earthly (1998: 156).

Only in later Jewish legend do we find Satan banished from heaven.
Although Rabbinical Judaism reacted against apocalyptic thought and
minimized the role of Satan (demonology *per se* becoming peripheral in
later Jewish theology), in Christianity Satan continued to be understood
as a rebel angel who challenged the rule of God and led other angels,
now fallen angels, into a like rebellion. It is this figure, of course, that has
become central to contemporary popular demonologies and, as Dyrendal's, Blake's, and Gribben's chapters show, a provocative and powerful
symbol of transgression and chaos.

   As to the origin of demons, widespread in Jewish literature and clearly
stated in 1 Enoch 15 (see also 6:2ff.) and Jubilees 5:1 is the belief that
they are to be identified with the *nephilim*, which are the product of
a union between angels and human women. Much of this theorizing
focuses on the enigmatic story in Genesis 6:1–5 (often read as justification for the flood in Gen. 7):

> When men began to multiply on the face of the ground, and daughters
> were born to them, the sons of God [or sons of the gods] saw that the
> daughters of men were fair; and they took to wife such of them as they
> chose. Then the Lord said, "My spirit shall not abide in man for ever,
> for he is flesh, but his days shall be a hundred and twenty years." The
> *nephilim* were on the earth in those days, and also afterward, when the
> sons of God came in to the daughters of men, and they bore children to
> them. These were the mighty men that were of old, the men of renown.
> The Lord saw that the wickedness of man was great in the earth, and that
> every imagination of the thoughts of his heart was only evil continually.

Tracing this story back to Canaanite mythology, Claus Westermann argues
that it belongs to a distinct cycle of relatively common narratives that deal
with the sexual union of deities and humans (1994: 369). While there is
much scholarly debate as to the meaning of "sons of God" in Genesis 6,
the oldest and most common interpretation within the Christian tradition is, perhaps not surprisingly, that of "angel" (see Westermann, 1994:
371–72; Clines, 1996: 33–46; Nielsen, 1998: 156–83; Russell, 1977:
174ff.). Or, because of the particular baggage that that term carries,
Gordon Wenham prefers the more ambiguous term "spirit," recognizing
that such "sons of the gods" may be benevolent or malevolent (Wenham,

1987: 140). Less convincing are the arguments of those such as Umberto Cassuto, who insists that the term should be interpreted as "angels of a degraded type" (cited in Westermann, 1994: 372). This understanding simply reflects post-apocalyptic Christian interpretations. Justin Martyr, for example, is very clear that they were in fact "fallen angels" and that demons are the product of their unnatural union with human women (see Kelly, 1977: 167). Martin Luther likewise reiterates the early Christian belief that the "sons of the gods" are fallen angels and the *nephilim* demons (Luther, 1955: 10–12). Indeed, whilst it would be interesting to analyse the significance of gender in these relationships, it is also worth noting the identification of the demonic with the erotic, which is a prominent theme within Western—and Eastern—demonologies, and, of course, central to the demonization of the witch in the early modern period and also to the development of contemporary popular Satanist discourse. Roman Polanski's *Rosemary's Baby* (1968) is a good example of this, in that, central to the narrative is the sexual union of the demonic and the human, concluding with the birth of a hybrid being—the Antichrist. Again, the theme is also central to vampire fiction.

These ancient demonologies are clearly influenced by apocalyptic speculation. One of the most influential early apocalyptic accounts of the fall of the *bene 'elohim* and their *nephilim* progeny appears in 1 Enoch. Whereas in Genesis it is not clear that these beings are particularly evil, in the apocalyptic literature they reveal their evil nature in their lust for human women. Referred to as "the Watcher angels," 1 Enoch also identifies their leader, Semyaz (1 En. 6:3). The decision takes the form of a conspiracy, in which they enter into a mutual obligation under the leadership of Semyaz. Their leader is well aware that their plan is contrary to God's will. He therefore wishes them to undertake a mutual obligation, so that the others do not suddenly abandon the plan and leave him on his own, and "I alone will become responsible for this great sin." Then all 200 angels take an oath to stand together as concerns responsibility, and they descend to the summit of Mount Hermon, divided into units of ten, each with its leader, as if they were about to embark on a campaign of war (Nielsen, 1998: 161). We are told that, having had sexual intercourse with human women, the "angels" teach them magic charms and incantations—a point which, again, has not gone unnoticed by those in Christian history who seek to construct a demonology of the witch. We are told that the offspring of the *nephilim* who were a race of giants, eat all the food gathered by humans, leaving them to starve, and, eventually, turn on the humans themselves in a cannibalistic rampage. Furthermore, *Aza'zel*, one of the Watchers, who is later identified with Satan, teaches humans to make weapons of war and introduces them to jewellery, costly gems and dyes, all of which lead to greed, violence, and vanity. Eventually, God responds by sending the four archangels—Michael, Uriel, Raphael, and Gabriel—to slay the giants, although their malign spirits remain to "afflict, oppress, destroy, attack, do battle, and work destruction on earth" (1 En. 15:1). Raphael is also instructed to bind *Aza'zel* and to cast him into an outer darkness, where he is to remain until the day of judgment, when he shall be "sent into the fire" (1 En. 10:5–7). It is also in the apocalyptic writings that we see pride ascribed to the Devil. Enoch applies Isaiah's satirical song about the King of Babylon—the "bright morning star" now "fallen from heaven" (Isa. 14:12–15)—to Satan, who has been cast out because of the sin of pride. (Hence he acquired the name Lucifer—meaning "light-bearer"—a name used of the morning star.) The distance between God and the Devil gradually widens in apocalyptic literature. No longer is Satan God's agent in the world, accusing and harming humans with divine permission. Unlike the Hebrew biblical tradition, which does not problematize God's close association with evil (e.g. 1 Sam. 16:14–15; Job 42:11; Jer. 12:1–5; 18:11; 31:28), apocalyptic developments push towards a dualism in which God is wholly dissociated from evil, which is exclusively the Devil's business. "The Lord is closely associated with ethical good, and the Devil with ethical evil. The Devil is the personi-fication of sin, and he commands at his right and left hands the spirits of wrath, hatred and lying. He is lord of fornication, war, bloodshed, exile, death, panic and destruction. He tempts humankind into error. He rules over the souls of the wicked" (Russell, 1977: 209–11). While in later Jewish thought, as Joshua Trachtenberg comments, the Devil "never played a very prominent role as a distinct personality," being "little more than an allegory, whose moral was the prevalence of sin" (1943: 19), in Christianity his role was much greater.

The apocalyptic writings provide substantial foundations for the con-struction of a complex demonology. All the key themes, from the sexual sin of the *bene 'elohim* to the pride of Lucifer, from the imprisonment of demons beneath the earth in the pit (or in the "lower atmosphere") to their continuing interference with humans in order to tempt them away from God, and, finally, to their demise "at the end of the world when the Messiah comes" (Russell, 1977: 207) are carefully developed in Christian demonology. Yet, Jewish apocalyptic demonology is respon-sible for a shift away from the prophetic insistence on interior human responsibility for one's own sin, to an exterior source other than God. Jewish apocalyptic provides a way of explaining human evil which does not require God as its source, and yet, which does not need to explain any ills that befall individuals as the consequence of sin. As Bernard McGinn's study of the history of the Antichrist shows, although there is an external–internal polarity throughout Christian history, more attention is given to the notion of an external foe (1996: 4). Indeed, although many Christian thinkers, certainly in the modern period, have tended to focus on the interior nature of evil, as this volume demonstrates, the perennial human fascination with an objective source of evil still persists—and, as Crawford Gribben's chapter argues, has been an important device within fiction. Certainly central to much early and medieval Christian theology was the belief that, although all are responsible for their own sins, they are also continually subject to the advances and corruption of personal demons—all of which operate as the agents of Satan. This view is, again, clear in the theology of Justin, for whom devils and demons were understood to be "swarming everywhere, [obsessing] men's souls and bodies, infecting them with vice and corruption" (Kelly, 1977: 167). Likewise the Desert Fathers, whose influence continued throughout the Middle Ages, believed that hordes of malign demons populated the world, taking every opportunity both to obsess human beings—to attack and influence them from without—and to possess some unfortunate individuals—as Augustine puts it, to "inhabit their bodies" and seize them from within (Augustine, 1945: 326). According to Athanasius' *Life of Antony*, Antony, believing the desert to be the abode of demons, went there "to do battle with the powers of evil" (Russell, 1981: 172–77). Alone in the desert, he was "attacked by demons, who tried various devices to distract him from the holy life" (Hall, 1991: 174). Similarly, in the tradition of the Desert Fathers, Evagrius wrote *Antirrhetikos*, a survey of eight evil thoughts related to eight demons that obsess monks. That is to say, particular demons were attached to the following eight sins: gluttony, lust, love of money, grief, wrath, sloth, vainglory, and arrogance (Hall, 1991: 181). Again, as Gribben demonstrates so clearly, things had not changed a great deal by the early modern period. James Hogg and his contemporaries were very familiar with the wiles of the Evil One. However, whilst all manner of harm to humans and animals, as well as natural disasters, were understood to be the result of demonic activity, a demon's ultimate aim was to corrupt the soul, to tempt, and to disrupt a person's relationship with God. Temptation is, as one theologian has put it, "the invasion of Satan's power into the world of creation. [It is] seduction, leading astray" (Bonhoeffer, 1955: 24).

Hence, Jewish apocalyptic demonology, which was subsequently developed in the New Testament and systematized in early Christian

thought, eventually shaped Western demonology in general. Distinguish-
ing it from Pagan religions, of particular significance is the clear understanding that "Satan embodies the ultimate truth behind the profuse
demonology of popular thought" (Ling, 1961: 12). This led to the incor-
poration of folk beliefs that were not specifically Christian into a systematic demonology (a process evident in several of the chapters of this
volume). For example, Karen Louise Jolly notes in her study of popular
religion in England in the tenth and eleventh centuries that

> amoral creatures such as elves were gradually "demonised" to fit the
> Good–Evil paradigm of the Christian moral universe. This process en-
> hanced their similarity to demons. Their invisibility, their malicious attacks,
> and the need to "charm" them away all took on new meaning in Christian
> eyes so that elves began to resemble the fallen angels who seek to inflict
> internal and permanent harm on humans and their works, demons for
> Christian ritual to exorcise (Jolly, 1996: 136).

Furthermore, individual events and disturbances experienced on the plane
of history are, on the one hand, understood as particularized demonic
activity, and, on the other hand, are projected into eternity, being fundamentally related to cosmic, demonic principalities and powers and the
satanic attempt to thwart God's ultimate, salvific purpose.

As demonology evolved through the Middle Ages, and as is clearly
evident in Heinrich Kramer's witch-hunter's manual of 1486, the *Malleus Maleficarum*, "*Hammer of Witches*," Christian demonology focused
increasingly on obsession, possession, and demonic alliances with humans.
As well as being the source of evil, as Jean La Fontaine comments,

> Satan and his demons were believed to have human allies and servants…
> One of the ways in which devils, or the Devil, were believed to associate
> with human beings was in lending them extra-human powers to perform
> acts that were beyond the range of human beings… By the Middle Ages,
> learned magicians were suspected of summoning and using demons by
> their magic in order to exchange their souls for magical powers in Faustian
> contracts (1999: 85).

It was such beliefs in swarming hordes of demons obsessing and pos-
sessing individuals, and in the notion that certain of these individuals
were able to summon up and utilize demonic power, that led (particularly in a period stretching roughly from the fourteenth century to the
seventeenth century) to witch-hunts and witch-trials. As Robin Briggs
notes in his comprehensive study of the social and cultural context of
European witchcraft, the witch is, in this period, "an incarnation of the
'other', a human being who has betrayed his or her natural allegiances
and become an agent of evil" (1996: 3). That said, it is important to

note that, whilst this could be true of witches in many cultures, in that witchcraft is in no sense limited to European thought, it was only in the Middle Ages that, as Keith Thomas argues, "a new element was added to the European concept of witchcraft which was to distinguish it from the witch-beliefs of other primitive peoples. This was the notion that the witch owed her powers to having made a deliberate pact with the Devil" (Thomas, 1973: 521). She (and alleged witches usually were female, the significance of which is not lost on Michel Foucault) was not just an incarnation of the "other," but was so by virtue of being fundamentally allied to the ground of Otherness, the Devil. This widespread idea that witchcraft or *maleficium* involved a pact with the Devil, and thereby constituted a Christian heresy, was initially the work of the Church, "whose intellectuals rapidly built up a large literature of demonology, outlining the manner in which the witches or Devil-worshippers were thought to conduct themselves, and laying down the procedure for their prosecution" (ibid.). This new teaching about heretical, Devil-worshippers making pacts with Satan and meeting to carry out abominable rites was, as Thomas observes, "developed in a series of edicts culminating in the Papal Bull, *Summis desiderantes affectibus*, of Innocent VIII in 1484, and the compendious treatise by two Dominican Inquisitors, the *Malleus Maleficarum*" (ibid.), which became an immediate best-seller, second only to the Bible. Pacts with the Devil, it was claimed, led to the acquisition of certain powers, including the ability to harm individuals, animals and crops, influence over the weather, and, more rarely, the ability to fly and shapeshift—and, of course, as Pinn and Blake discuss in relation to the Robert Johnson legend, virtuoso musicianship and subsequent influence on the history of music (not least, the Devil's own rock in all its varied forms). In the medieval and early modern periods, descriptions of shapeshifting, for example, "are found in many areas of Europe. Here... one may suspect traces of ancient shamanistic ideas, readily assimilated into the folklore of witchcraft. Greases, special skins, incantations and the direct action of the Devil were all invoked to explain these transformations into animal form" (Briggs, 1996: 105). (This, of course, has close links with the demonologies of vampirism and lycanthropy.) However, while such exciting powers might have attracted many to experiment with a little Devil-worship, they were dissuaded by a well-known downside. Because it was commonly assumed that "witches had crossed a hidden boundary when they gave allegiance to the Devil," and because Satan was understood to be a deceitful, macabre, and cruel master, the consequences were often severe. He could, for example, "coerce them directly, beating them and even threatening to kill them" (ibid.).

In effect, the human servant of the Devil becomes an ill-treated slave. "Witnesses," says Briggs, "sometimes alleged the accused had shown physical signs of mysterious beatings or been heard crying out. They plainly implied that they had been maltreated by their master, so the idea that witches were to some degree the miserable dupes of the Devil was widespread" (ibid.). Again, thinking of Genesis 6 and the confluence of the demonic and the erotic, it is perhaps not surprising that, particularly in the *Malleus*, there is much discussion of demons (i.e. incubi and succubi) engaging in sexual intercourse with witches and producing devilish offspring.

If belief in demons in the modern period has significantly retreated before the forces of rationalism and empiricism, as this volume argues, it has not disappeared entirely. Indeed, interest in the demonic is experiencing something of a revival. Even if demons no longer seem credible to many in the West, particularly as most of their various works can be explained quite easily by modern science and medicine, the belief and popular interest in Satan in particular has continued. Although the modern period has seen the detraditionalization of the demonic, an internalizing shift, in which the emphasis has moved from obsession and possession by external demonic forces to internal spiritual battles, there are still a great many in the contemporary West who understand there to be external forces of evil operating in the world. For example, the French historian Robert Muchembled, in his analysis of the changing perceptions of the Devil in Western history since the Middle Ages, notes the upsurge in exorcists and exorcisms. In France, he writes,

> exorcists numbered a mere fifteen, very unevenly distributed between dioceses. They were particularly thin on the ground north of a line running from Le Havre to Chambéry, excluding Alsace; they were absent altogether from the bishoprics of Champagne and Lorraine and from most of those in the Paris region, with the exception of the capital itself and Pontoise. South of the line, few bishoprics were without an exorcist; some had two or even three, in particular in the west and south west (Bayeux, Coutances, Angers, Le Mans, Angoulême, and Agen), Montpellier and the Lyonnais. At Autun, Father Lambey, appointed president of the French Association of Exorcists in 1977, believed that the irrational had made spectacular advances since he had started work in the field in 1955. He now saw up to three "bewitched" persons a week, compared with about twenty a year in the past. Their real problems began, he said, when they became convinced that someone had cast a spell on them; this produced a feeling of deep anxiety at the impossibility of effectively counteracting it... They first went to a "spell-breaker," faith healer, or clairvoyant... Since January 1999, the number of exorcists in France has spectacularly increased, from fifteen to 120, as if in response to the dramatic escalation

of anxiety in society and to the challenge posed by the Catholic Church both by the slump in religious observance and the proliferation of sects (2003: 231–32).

Neal Milner, who has analysed the contemporary resurgence of exorcism within the Church of England, refers to an "official revival of a theology that accepts the existence of poltergeists, ghosts, and the Devil" (2000: 248). Moreover, as Muchembled demonstrates, far from this being simply a phenomenon amongst the uneducated, as some would have us believe, "no social category, no cultural stratum, and no power has been spared." Indeed, "many beliefs in the paranormal demand a degree of culture" (2003: 232). "Out of a sample of 2,350 persons questioned in 1981, more from the upper eschelons than from the middling ranks believed in telepathy (54 per cent), horoscopes (30 per cent), spells (23 per cent), and table-turning (22 per cent)... Of Montpellier University students surveyed in 1988, 24 per cent accepted the existence of the devil" (ibid.). Again, whatever the reasons for such beliefs, the point is that they continue and are increasing in Western societies, even amongst the educated.

Surveys of religious belief elsewhere have produced comparable figures. In Australia, for example, surveys have found that not only do two thirds of Australians declare spirituality to be important to them, but 33 percent believe in the existence of the Devil.[3] More significantly, recent polls in America have found much higher and rising levels of demonological belief. In 1968, for example, 60 percent believed in the literal existence of Satan. In 1994 it had risen to 65.5 percent and in 2001 a Gallup poll found that it had again risen to 68 percent. A 2003 Harris poll found that the number had remained stable at 68 percent (Waldman, 2004). However, a more recent Gallup poll shows that while the proportion of North Americans who believe in God has remained relatively steady at upwards of 90 percent, increasing numbers of Americans believe not only in heaven, hell, and angels, but that belief in Satan is currently at its highest since pollsters began to inquire. During the last decade, it has grown from 65.5 percent in 1994 to 70 percent in 2004—70 percent of women and 69 percent of men are believers. Albert Winseman, Gallup's religion and values editor, concludes that the evidence suggests that, "as science, technology and rational explanations uncover and explain more and more about the known world, Americans are likely becoming more intrigued by the unknown" (Eckstrom, 2004a).

As to who believes in the literal existence of Satan in America today, the strongest belief was found among rural dwellers (78 percent), followed by those living in urban areas (66 percent), and then suburbanites

(64 percent). More interestingly, however, belief in the reality of the Devil varies less across age and education: 70 percent of adults (aged 30–64); 66 percent of young adults (aged 18–19); 70 percent of high school graduates; 68 percent of college graduates; and 55 percent of people with postgraduate degrees (Eckstrom, 2004b). These statistics are significant. As Gallup contributing editor, Jennifer Robison, comments, "we might expect belief in the Devil to have largely evaporated... It hasn't. Regardless of political belief, religious inclination, education or region, most Americans believe that the Devil exists" (ibid.). While North American belief in the Devil is higher than in other Western countries, the evidence suggests that such beliefs are particularly resilient and fascinating to Westerners. It is perhaps not surprising, therefore, that, as Milner has shown, the Church of England has officially revived its commitment to exorcism (see Milner, 2000). Similarly, in 1999 the Roman Catholic Church issued a new ritual of exorcism and increased the number of priests assigned to deliverance ministry, which, in France, Muchembled notes, was from 15 to 120. He also makes the rather sensational point that, accompanying the rise in belief in the Devil, "Satanist sects have become firmly entrenched in a number of countries, especially the United States and England. The Devil has made an impressive comeback" (2003: 1). Although there is little evidence to suggest that he ever really went away, it is certainly true that widespread fascination with the diabolical and the dark side continues in the West—encouraged, to a significant extent, by popular culture. Hence, while, of course, many Westerners would look for more human and mundane reasons for the existence of evil in the world, there still appears to be a widespread unease about the dark side. Moreover, as Muchembled points out, it is important to remember that society is not

> a homogenous whole. It would be mistaken to claim that all the inhabitants of the Catholic countries have rid themselves of the ancient fear of the Devil, as the activities of exorcists make plain. Also, the ludic demonic culture is consumed at very different levels. For some it is a means of relaxation, while others believe everything they read or see on the screen (2003: 228).

Such belief in demons has a dark fascination, for, as Gerardus van der Leeuw argued, it "does not mean that chance rules the universe, but rather that I have experienced the horror of some power which concerns itself neither with my reason nor my morals; and it is not fear of any definite concrete terribleness, but vague terror of the gruesome and the incomprehensible, which projects itself objectively in the belief in demons. Horror and shuddering, sudden fright and the frantic insanity of dread, all receive their form in the demon; this represents the absolute horribleness of the world, the incalculable force which weaves its web around us and threatens to seize us" (1986: 134). Moreover, the Devil and the demonic are significant in that they are, as Foucault has argued, markers of *alterity*, manifestations of "the Other" in religious discourse (1999: 75–84). This reliance on the monstrous other, the demonic foil, whilst neglected in many systematic theologies, lies close to the heart of contemporary Western cultures. Indeed, the demonic has gradually become iconic. The satanic other, flourishing beyond the boundaries of institutional religion and respectable culture, is becoming increasingly attractive to many contemporary Westerners. One only has to peruse the shelves of video and book stores, or consider the content of some of the most successful films and television series, to discover evidence of the phenomenal popular fascination with the demonic, iconic other. Whether we consider Johann Heinrich Füsseli's disturbing painting *The Nightmare* (1782), which depicts an incubus squatting on the stomach of a sleeping woman, or satanic moral panics and the persecution of "the other" in Western societies (e.g. Victor, 1993; Briggs, 1996; Richardson, Best and Bromley, 1991), or explicit Satanist beliefs, or Satan films, or malevolent screen aliens, such as Ridley Scott's *Alien*, or the compositions and activities of black metal musicians and their fans, modern Western artists, writers and religionists have drunk deeply from the well of Christian demonology (see Partridge, 2004; 2005). Ideas that can be traced back to Jewish apocalyptic thought provide basic concepts that run like continuous threads from incubi to malevolent space demons.

Arguably the most conspicuous example of this celebration of the other-than-Christian as both demonic and iconic is the figure of the vampire in contemporary culture, the popular interest in which has soared in recent years. That said, Titus Hjelm argues in Chapter 6 that there has been a significant shift between the "old paradigm" and "new paradigm" celluloid vampires. There has been, he claims, "a transmigration of the vampire soul," in that "whether we look at the depictions of the nature, the motivations, or the ways of destroying vampires, the role of mysticism and religion—Christianity in particular—has decreased to the point of being completely obsolete, only to be referred to as a meta-fictive 'myth'." While it might still be argued that the traces of Christian demonology are still evident in vampire fiction (just as they are, Gribben argues, in Iain Banks' *The Wasp Factory*, and just as they are reworked, as Baker traces in his chapter on Hannibal Lecter in fiction and film), the emphasis is now pathological rather than explicitly spiritual. Hence, for example, in the *Blade* trilogy (1998, 2002, 2004), *Underworld* (2003), and *Underworld Evolution* (2006) the myth of the vampire is less to do with Western demonology and more to do with genes and viruses. This, to some extent, of course, mirrors broader religio-cultural shifts in contemporary Western societies—the most significant being the shift away from traditional Christian culture and the consequent demise in the power of its symbols. Hence, for example, crucifixes are often impotent (see Kreitzer, 1999). Vampire killer Whistler makes this point very clearly in *Blade*: while "crosses don't do squat…vampires are severely allergic to silver." Moreover, "feed them garlic and they'll go into anaphylactic shock." Nevertheless, as Gordon Melton observes, because the vampire is a "cultural rebel, a symbolic leader advocating outrageous alternative patterns of living in a culture demanding conformity" (Melton, 1999: xxiii), it is not difficult to identify its demonological genesis.

Likewise, within contemporary fantasy literature, Colin Duriez cogently argues that the portrayal of evil in the Harry Potter stories by J. K. Rowling—as with, of course, the fantasies by C. S. Lewis and J. R. R. Tolkien—leans heavily on Christian demonology, particularly Augustinian theology. For example, understanding evil to be the privation and perversion of the good, the dark arts, representing evil, are explicitly condemned as a perversion of magic—a central organizing principle of the stories and, unlike the understanding of magic in the early modern period, an aspect of goodness. Interestingly, some parallels might be made between vampire films and fantasy. Not only does Voldemort—the evil manifestation of the transformed Tom Riddle—have a hemic appetite, but more significantly, just as Hjelm argues that there has been a shift in filmic portrayals of vampires, from supernatural explanations of the genesis and cure of vampirism towards more technological and pathological understandings, so Duriez makes the point that, for both Lewis and Tolkien, the modern form of magic is technology, the dark arts being the misuse of it. In other words, there are lessons to be learned about humanity's use and abuse of technologies, from genetic to nuclear. Gribben makes a parallel point about literary secular demonologies in his chapter.

Adopting a more demonically explicit stance than either Voldemort or the vampire, perhaps the most conspicuous capitulation to the lure of the dark side in Western culture, one which cultivates a liturgical discourse about Satan within popular culture, is black metal, a subgenre of heavy metal. Indeed, while early academic apologists for the genre, such as Deena Weinstein, sought to argue in the early 1990s that it was not fundamentally anti-Christian or "against Jesus," following the church burnings and graveyard desecrations of the late-1990s, as well as explicit transgressive slogans such as "Jesus is a Cunt" and "Support the War Against Christianity" and band names such as Impaled Nazarene or Rotting Christ (see Chapter 4), this became a rather more difficult thesis to defend. The anti-Christian rhetoric and the celebration of the other-than-Christian is explicit. Indeed, as Peter Mercer-Taylor points out in his fascinating musicological analysis of the music of the British band Cradle of Filth,

> poetically, black metal is largely defined through its orientation around apocalyptic conflicts in which the forces of good, generally Christian ones, are proved powerless to save humanity from the grim designs of alternative cosmic agents. The victory sometimes goes to Satan himself, sometimes to deities of sketchily recovered Scandinavian Paganism, sometimes to forces more like Lovecraftian "ancient ones" with scant theological credentials of any kind.

If there are scant theological credentials in such demonologies, Asbjørn Dyrendal's chapter suggests that there may also be scant Satanist credentials. Based on thorough empirical research, Dyrendal's insightful chapter provides a thoughtful analysis of black metal in Norway, the country which has seen some of its most extreme developments, including the burning of Bergen's ancient stave church. Indeed, his chapter is particularly useful, in that it introduces Satanism and compares it to Satanist discourse within black metal. In particular, he examines the belief system as it was developed by its most influential theorist Anton LaVey, author of, arguably, Satanism's principal sacred texts, *The Satanic Bible* (1969) and *The Satanic Rituals* (1972). As far as LaVey was concerned, when is comes to "satanic music" the true Satanist should consider the marches of John Philip Sousa rather than rock music. Similarly, the current High Priest, Peter Gilmore, turns, not to Back Metal, but to the more contemplative strains of classical music. That said, he concedes (in correspondence with Dyrendal) that "music that moves one's emotions is music we consider satanic" and that, of course, can be black metal. And, with reference to the articulation of Satanist ideology, there are, shows Dyrendal, few better "hymns" than the self-oriented "My Way."

Mercer-Taylor's chapter provides a thoughtful and revealing musicological analysis of the Cradle of Filth song from 1999, "From the Cradle to Enslave." Those readers who have only a peripheral familiarity with the genre will benefit from reading this stimulating chapter by a musicologist known more for his work on Mendelssohn. In particular, he argues that the work is more complex than it initially appears. Beginning as a hymn and, apparently, an exposition of genuine eschatological conviction—the first stretch of which Mercer-Taylor convincingly compares to Charles Wesley's "Lo, he comes in clouds descending"—it progresses toward "an overt fictionality whose referent might best be understood as a casual conflation of cinema, literary fiction, drama, and opera. This dynamic process," he argues, "eludes tidy categorization according to customary metrics—authenticity, sincerity, sell-out, irony—of popular music hermeneutics." That is to say, what we are presented with in the song is not a "selling out"—which the band have been accused of by many within the black metal community—nor, indeed, pure black metal, à la Mayhem, Emperor, or Deicide, but rather "a reflexive exploration both of the genre's capacity to arouse moral anxiety and of the terms through which its dangers can be brought toward social regulation, or at least toward mainstream comprehensibility." In many ways, the work of Cradle of Filth, while not particularly frightening, does satisfy the musical appetite of the contemporary fan of cinematic horror—the crossing point between the two genres being, perhaps, their graphic music videos.

From a more overtly theological perspective, Anthony Pinn's discussion of African American music explores the influence of Christian demonology. In so doing he provides an insightful overview, from spirituals, through blues, to hip-hop. He shows that, whereas, for example, spirituals demonstrate an explicit struggle against the demonic and an embracing of the angelic—which is understood to be "good" for the community—there is more ambiguity in the blues. Indeed, he makes the point that "whereas the boundaries between these forces and their effectiveness in human life are clear and based on the Christian faith for those singing the spirituals, for those motivated by the blues there is a more utilitarian approach—one that allows for flirtation with both angelic and demonic forces depending on which might offer the most efficient assistance." Some blues artists, rather than giving thanks to God for their extraordinary abilities encouraged ideas of a Faustian pact. The most conspicuous, of course, is Robert Johnson, who transformed a mediocre talent into the conspicuous, awe-inspiring skill for which he is now known. This was done at the crossroads of highways 61 and 69 outside Clarksdale, Mississippi, where, in a transaction with the Devil, he exchanged his soul for his ability, thereby becoming, as Charlie Blake comments, "the most important avatar of the darker side of rock and roll." Bearing in mind the early development of this demonology and, indeed, some of the themes within black metal, it is interesting that, as Pinn notes, the alliance with the demonic is, to some extent, a voice of resistance to a dominant Christian culture: it served as a modality of resistance to staid and reified notions of morality and ethics tied to what these blues men considered the hypocrisy of the Christian faith. They, in dealing with the Devil, signified the claims of the Christian faith (its doctrine, theology—particularly its theodicies) to the sources of the good life in ways that centred on the validity of the desires and wants Christianity condemned roundly—erotic desires, material good, and revenge.

Again, this "inverted spiritual arrangement" can be traced through the child of the blues—rock—to the dark offspring of rock—black metal. Darkness, death, the material, and the body are privileged over light, life, the spiritual, and the soul. The rebellious, the outcast, and the demonic join forces in the blues, in black metal and, argues Pinn, in rap.

> While rap tends to avoid a direct appeal to demonic forces for the development of musical abilities and other markers of success in a troubled world, rap is not devoid of references to sensitivity to the presence and workings of demonic forces. Yet, rather than joining league with them actively, some rappers simply work in ways that seem influenced by the negative tendencies and character of the demonic, while others step through the world seeing the demonic lodged firmly around them.

With the above in mind, Blake's carefully argued discussion of what he refers to as "gothic capitalism" makes interesting reading. Drawing largely on the work of Jacques Derrida, and especially Georges Bataille, he begins by making the point that while much popular music has been motivated ostensibly by an aesthetic of dissent, it is invariably content to function within the capitalist regime that enables its promotion and encourages media deification. In this sense, he argues,

> deviance and defiance in Western popular music is generally diverted away from overtly political objectives and directed towards more ambivalent cultural targets. And in some cases—particularly within the genres of death metal, black metal, doom and alternative country—the target has sometimes become explicitly religious, and indeed, theological. In other cases, however, what might be called the "Luciferean" or "Satanic" element in certain strands of African-American blues has combined with a closely related element in the European artistic and literary traditions conventionally associated with certain aspects of the Gothic, to generate a subterranean discourse of deviance and defiance that, once exposed to the light of rationality, not only decomposes into its constituent elements, but also, reveals through its process of decomposition a *via negativa* through which the atheology of postmodern or late capitalism can begin to be mapped.

James Hogg's *Private Memoirs and Confessions of a Justified Sinner*
was written within a very different context. Indeed, it can be compared
to much of the contemporary anti-Christian discourse of extreme metal
and contemporary horror films. While it can be understood as a religion of oppression and fear, it teaches a theology of predestination that
encourages an antinomianism, which, under diabolical influence, can
lead to extreme depravity. The protagonist, Robert Wringhim, after con-
verting to just such a Calvinist sect, encounters a character, who happens
to be his doppelganger. Under the influence of this individual he is led
to commit a series of crimes, including rape and murder. However,
there is some uncertainty and, therefore, debate about the nature of
the demonic character. Is it a projection of Wringhim's own dark side,
à la Dr Jekyll? That is to say, is the sinful self externalized? Or is it, as
Wringhim comes to believe, an encounter with an external diabolical
entity? Interestingly, Crawford Gribben argues that this is how it should
be understood, namely, as a story about an encounter with Satan. This
understanding is supported by an analysis of the novel's demonological
background. As noted above concerning early Christian theology, "a fascination with demons was typical of standard descriptions of Scotland's
'worlds of wonder' in the late seventeenth and eighteenth centuries,
and the demon that haunts the *Justified Sinner* emerges from and visibly
reflects these earlier traditions of the Presbyterian occult... The Devil was
no stranger to early modern Scotland." And, as we have noted, Gribben
argues that even in the secularized Scotland of Iain Banks' Gothic tale,
The Wasp Factory (1984), new demonologies are being constructed.
"Scottish authors have repeatedly turned to the image of the demonic
'other' to articulate their sense of the proper location of evil. Demonology has provided metaphors that writers have used for social and cultural critique, a means of pin-pointing their sense of the origins of evil."
Just as Hogg referenced popular Calvinist demonologies to alert readers
to the dangers of uncritical religious zeal, so, he argues, demonology
has continued to function as "a cultural barometer of social threat in the
literary culture of Presbyterian and post-Presbyterian Scotland."

In a similar mode of investigation, drawing especially on the work
of Gilles Deleuze and Felix Guattari, George Aichele is intrigued by the
dualism long established by the development, and as Aichele would
have it, overwhelming force, of monotheism within Judaism and Christianity. Aichele finds support for his thesis on the spectacular failure of
monotheism—and its implications for the role of the *daimones* in popular
culture—from a range of fascinating sources, including the fiction of Jack
Miles and China Miéville and the *Buffy the Vampire Slayer* series. Aichele

persuasively argues that the polytheism that can so easily be traced in the Hebrew Bible reflects a tradition of tolerance that lost out to the drive of monotheism to, among other things, account unambiguously for evil. For Aichele, the implications for postmodernity are clear: "as modernism disintegrates in the world today, the biblical canon's synthesis of many gods into one begins to unravel–that is, not only God but the Bible becomes schizophrenic–and the many *daimones* appear once more, albeit transfigured into more contemporary forms." Perhaps most audaciously, Aichele suggests that the monotheistic tradition has long been aware that it is fatally ill-equipped to relate to the Other, particularly in the form of non-Judaeo-Christian belief. Aichele shows how this awareness has been present in the cultural by-products of Judaeo-Christian tradition, such as Tolkien's *Lord of the Rings* mythology. In polytheism, with its many gods, demons and angels, Aichele sees a more robust and tolerant form of relating to the world, which may account for its viability and popularity as a movement within postmodern culture. In this new cultural configuration, the god of Christianity is repositioned, an "ancient god transformed" among a host of other dead, though now newly resurrected, gods, angels and demons, to populate a new polytheism.

Also interested in the opposition between the demonic and the divine, particularly as it developed in Romanticism, Brian Baker assesses the cultural life of Hannibal Lecter, and exposes its roots in Christian demonology and conceptions of evil. Baker shows, as do many authors in this volume, that the articulation of a popular cultural work with Christian demonology runs far deeper than we might suspect. Drawing on Lecter's characterization in Thomas Harris' novels (and less so in the films), Baker demonstrates the degree to which it is constructed from the remnants of Christian discourse, particularly of Dante's *Inferno* and Milton's *Paradise Lost*. As Harris draws him, Lecter participates fully in the Romantic characterization of the demonic as flamboyant, full of artifice and beauty, and crucially, in the mold cast by the Romantics of the Miltonic Satanic hero, "rather than as God's 'evil adversary'." Once again, the Other is a feature of the critical discourse as Baker examines how Lecter comes to represent the Other as Monster, but who is simultaneously a signifier of the Self, which Baker argues is not so much to be understood as a contradiction as a valuable insight. Through his appropriation of biblical discourse and his contrived enigmatic aura of mystery, Lecter is "every inch the Gothicised Romantic hero." As such Baker's insightful spadework reveals Lecter to be at odds with the well-established fictive serial killers of popular culture, who possess "fractured, unstable, transformative or unmasked subjectivities." We can recognize a certain serendipity in Aichele's focus on the travesty of the monotheistic drive to a single, hegemonic truth and Baker's observation that the Other in the discourse in which Lecter is situated represents "the boundaries of rational discourse: the incommensurability of the Other to reason is the point at which these texts point towards 'evil', the monstrous, and the discourse of religion; but also that serial killer fictions signify the limit-case of representations of normative subjectivity and gender roles in contemporary Anglo-American popular culture." In other words, Lecter stands as a critique of the unitary Self of monotheism (though Baker also observes that Lecter is at once a figure of attraction and repulsion—perhaps a sign of popular culture's reluctance to release itself from the tyranny of monotheism).

Two essays concentrate more exclusively on the representation of the demonic in visual culture: William Telford's survey of the Devil in Christ films and Larry Kreitzer's taxonomy of biblical demonology in apocalyptic films. Telford very helpfully overviews representation of the Devil in cinema from its earliest expressions and further relates these to the Devil's much earlier reception history in religious and other popular discourses. As Telford demonstrates so well, the figure of Satan forces filmmakers to pursue their representative figurations through a wide range of rhetorical choices, from figurative to literal to allegorical. As we might expect, these choices say a great deal more about the ideology of producers and audiences of the films than about the biblical traditions they rework (contrast Donald Pleasence's subtly consumptive Devil of *The Greatest Story Ever Told* to the black-robed, villainous whisperer of DeMille's silent *The King of Kings*). Telford brings into discussion the most recent and perhaps most culturally influential of Christ films, *The Passion of the Christ*, and reveals Gibson's very eclectic direction to be sourced from horror films to classical Christian iconography. Telford's discussion, along with the very useful appendix of the Satan figure in film, provides an insightful guide to the development of Satan in cinema.

Larry Kreitzer's inventive taxonomy of biblical discourse in apocalyptic film (as timepiece, talisman and tattoo) provides a helpful index to the influence of Christian demonology in an area of popular culture enjoying increasing academic attention. Kreitzer sees that one of the features that defines apocalyptic films is the use of language from the Book of Revelation. That language is commandeered by filmmakers (in a manner not unlike Harris' construction of Hannibal Lecter from Christian discourse, as identified by Baker) not only to signify the chronology of events (timepiece: namely of the last days) and the detail of characters and events within the film text (tattoo), but to lend filmic monsters a kind of demonic gravitas that can function as protective power (talisman). Of course the films draw equally from other cultural phenomena, such as Hal Lindsey's *Late, Great Planet Earth*. Kreitzer's case studies range from classic horror (*The Omen*) to action thriller (*End of Days*) to low-budget pulp (*Revelation*), showing the pervasiveness of the demonic and apocalyptic in film. His essay is a good illustration of cultural texts that feed into one another to produce a swell of imagery and discourse that becomes a surrogate for biblical demonology. As such it raises the question of whether cultural discourse now generates its own demonology to the extent that little recourse (beyond the most basic exposition) is needed to the primary texts that enabled its development.

Notes

1. For more on St Deiniol's Library—Britain's only residential library, founded by the Victorian statesman and Prime Minister, William Ewart Gladstone (1809–1898)—see http://www.st-deiniols.co.uk.

2. Mani (216–c. 277 CE) taught a similar, later form of dualism, which attracted Augustine prior to his conversion to Christianity. The Manichaean religion taught a cosmic conflict between the primordial powers of good and evil, light and darkness, a conflict which brought the universe into existence.

3. Figures are taken from the Australian Community Survey. See the NCLS Research website: http://www.ncls.org.au/default.aspx?docid=1761&track=21517.

Part I
Music

Chapter 1

Satanism and Popular Music

Asbjørn Dyrendal

In the popular imagination, few products of popular culture seem to connote so strongly with Satanism as heavy metal music. Within that genre, *black* metal, particularly *Norwegian* black metal, has been more closely associated with Satanism than any other subgenre. This is not merely due to the lyrical content or the musical and sartorial style. More than anything else the image of Norwegian "Satanic" metal revolves around the willingness among a few of the early, ground-breaking bands to carry their torches where their lyrics claimed they belonged—directly to old Norwegian churches to instigate arson and "make war" on Christianity.

In this chapter, I shall look briefly at the phenomenon of black metal and its articulation of Satanism. The virulent anti-Christianity and explicit imagery of satanic worship in the lyrics alone make it an interesting case. However, my scope will be broader. I shall compare and contrast black metal ideology with the Satanism constructed by Anton LaVey, founder of the Church of Satan. We shall see that those who had a certain prior claim to defining Satanism have long had their own philosophy of music, and their musical preferences may differ widely from what is popularly seen as "satanic." I shall present this philosophy briefly, and argue that although black metal partakes, to some extent, of the Western demonological tradition, its lyrics are bad examples of Satanist ideology. I will then propose that a better entry to understanding Satanist ideology through popular music is to be found in a less obvious place.

My primary sources for this article are interviews, lyrics, published texts, Internet discussion boards,[1] and personal discussions with insiders concerning Satanism, satanic philosophy, and popular music. With regard to black metal, I will focus on Norwegian bands and the Norwegian situation during the first half of the 1990s. With regard to satanic philosophy, I view Anton LaVey's *The Satanic Bible* as the primary starting point, and to the degree I depart from his texts, I focus mainly on contemporary discussions among Scandinavian (mainly Danish) and American Satanists.

Black Metal "Satanism" and its Demons

In the title song of *De Mysteriis Dom Sathanas* (1994), the seminal album by the groundbreaking Norwegian black metal band Mayhem, the protagonists, thirteen in all, sacrifice a goat to demons. The rite is read from a book "made of human flesh" and the deed is committed in a graveyard. Blending traditional demonological fantasies with horror fiction, the song places the demonic out in the open, explicitly thematizing satanic worship.

Seemingly, the Satanism of the more prominent bands was openly professed as well. Their lyrics often much more than hinted at Devil worship and an unhealthy interest in macabre themes, such as murder or necrophilia. In addition the band members frequently articulated the same themes beyond their musical output. In interview after interview, they would be quoted in a way that made them sound like actual "Devil-worshippers." They also looked the part, in that, at a fairly early stage, the dress code of black metal settled on black denim and leather, with long spikes on jackets, belts, boots, and wristbands. A white facial (sometimes also bodily) make-up called corpse paint,[2] although rarely worn off-stage, completed the grim look of a scene where members seemed never to smile. When their explicit anti-Christianity was connected to the spate of church burnings, violence, two murders, and allegations of rape, their role as "Satanists" was cemented in the public imagination.

There was, however, a limited amount of truth to these claims. To some extent, they were reacting to—and, in their symbolism and discourse, explicitly transgressing—the symbolic boundaries of a complacent, secularized social democracy, in a country where the state church mainly serves as ceremonial locus for rites of passage. In addition, state Protestantism is allowed access to elementary schools in many different ways and, moreover, teaching children to become "good Christians" is still one of the aims of the school system. Thus, the mainly teenaged black metallers inverted dominant cultural themes within Norway. Against the liberal left public—and perhaps equally important, the radical left-wing politics of the Norwegian punk scene—they adopted both the images and the rhetoric of the far right. Against both Christians and secularists, they often adopted an inverted, fundamentalist reading of Christianity in their public discourse. Some, like Mayhem's Euronymous, the central figure within the Norwegian black metal scene, stressed that they *wanted* church burnings to revitalize a stronger Christianity in order to spread both misery and rebellion.

The internal and external discursive constructions of black metal as satanic and fascist served to separate them out from other scenes and was also a process of self-identification. However, the emphasis and seriousness varied between individuals and over time. The external discourse could at times be tongue-in-cheek, but like the grim, anti-fun attitude promoted, it could also, from an emic perspective, be taken very seriously. The stress on transgressive practices, and the internal "competition" over transgression that amplified deviant practices, may (at least to some extent) show how seriously it was taken. However, it is difficult to assess how much the behavior stemmed from ideology and how much it was an effect of the particular dynamics within a rather small group of individuals. The problem with judging when the "attitude" was meant literally, and the degree to which it was, is compounded by what Keith Kahn-Harris has dubbed the "reflexive anti-reflexivity" discursive style within the scene (Kahn-Harris, 2007: 141–56).[3]

While the question of "authenticity" is of limited interest,[4] we shall concentrate on something a little more easily assessed, namely how the subject of the satanic and demonic is treated within black metal lyrics.

Norwegian black metal bands were obviously not the first within heavy metal to use imagery of the demonic and Devil-worship. Indeed, similar lyrics were already explicitly evident from the early 1980s. Evolving from a form of music more akin to death metal, Mayhem was among the ground-breaking, early representatives of what is commonly called the *second* wave of black metal. As such, the use of satanic and Devil-worshipping imagery was always part of what has retrospectively been identified as a subgenre. Black metal's *first* wave included bands such as Venom, which was then perceived to belong to the "new wave of British heavy metal." As early as 1981 they were singing proudly (although not sincerely) about being "In League with Satan," a song that superficially celebrated Christian demonological themes: the protagonist obeys the heretical deity's commands, sits at his *left* hand, and commits deeds of carnality and violence in Satan's service.

That was not the only tradition they drew on. Among their songs we also find black metal classics such as the eponymous "Black Metal" (which Mayhem has subsequently covered), where the musicians follow in the footsteps of Satan as the recorder of "the first note," and lay down their souls to play the Devil's music. In this lyric, Satan as the first musician inspires the rebellious to "rock 'n' roll" (which is also a common theme within some streams of Christian fundamentalism). From one perspective, this continues the mythology of the blues which describes— most notably in the story of Robert Johnson bargaining with Satan at the crossroads—the relation between music and Satan (in itself continuing much older folklore). This is, however, not the place to recount that history (see Moynihan and Søderlind, 1998; Baddeley, 1999; Pinn, in this volume). It is simply noted here as an antecedent to contemporary black metal. Hence, while Venom, in one sense, may be said to have been the pioneer black metal band and was certainly amongst the principal promoters of a satanic image at this early period, the genre had, by the late 1980s, moved on to something bleaker, more destructive.

The second wave of black metal was more aggressive both musically and lyrically than the first. Lyrically, both the lurid and juvenile sexuality—still present in some early black metal—and also the stereotypical rock 'n' roll clichés receded into the background.[5] To the degree that sex was still part of black metal discourse, it was more often presented in the context of violence, rape, and necrophilia—themes one also finds in death metal, the genre which many Black metal musicians began their careers playing. Moreover, while the demonic was usually primary, within Norwegian black metal there was another theme, namely "nature" (e.g. Mørk, 2002: 99–100). Landscapes, particularly landscapes that are bleak, cold, barren, and hostile—which often serve as a backdrop for the violence of the protagonists—became prominent within the lyrics. Generally, agents, story, and landscape tended to draw on imagery similar to the comic book adaptations of *Conan the Barbarian*, which were popular in Norway. However, unlike the Conan stories, the warriors described in black metal lyrics fight under the command of and on the behalf of the dark forces, not against them. This is particularly typical of one cluster of motifs, where the lyrics describe fantasy-inspired, mythic landscapes, where demons rule, and warrior heroes torture and kill their weak and godly enemies. An example from the "Black Circle"— the core of the early scene, centred around Euronymous and his record shop in Oslo—is the lyrics to *Emperor*'s "Into the Infinity of Thoughts." Here, "frozen Nature chilly" is more than the scene for the antagonist's brutal deeds of hatred and violence; it reflects both psychological ideals and the deeper reality of life.

While, in this particular song, the demonic realm is described merely as "the Shadows," the same album, *The Nightside Eclipse*, also features several songs naming the demonic as literally "demonic." Generally, the demon's relation to brutal nature, "red in tooth and claw," is made clear. This is evident, for example, in "Beyond the Great Vast Forest," where a dark Lord and his "Devils of Darkness" haunt a similar landscape, draining the blood of living creatures. Not least, the album also includes "Inno a Satana." This is one of their most "conventionally religious" songs, in that the lyrics praise the "Lord of the Night" who is "master of beasts," compassionless bringer of everything destructive and hateful. The song ends with an oath that the singer forever will praise Satan's name, serve him, and fight for him in the certain knowledge that "thou shalt forever prevail."

It is once again clearly evident from the lyrics that hatred and strife are among the central "virtues" and the beasts of prey are typical symbols for the favored side. Again, we are presented with key themes from Christian demonology. Topics such as the agent's willingness to "serve" and "praise" a nether power are not uncommon in black metal lyrics. Although the relation to "nature" may at times lend itself to a version of Paganism, particularly that of Norse religion, this is a relatively simple inversion of conventional Christian beliefs and attitudes, along with elements taken from horror movies. As such, it constitutes one of the typical "satanic" stances from the black metal scene. Indeed, as well as in some lyrics, in interviews members of the scene sometimes adopted an Christian eschatological narrative, in which they take Satan's side.

In addition to these treatments of Satan and the demonic, however, we find a more conventional, romantic Satan in other parts of black metal. In these narratives, he is portrayed as a proud rebel against servitude, oppression, and conformity. Unlike the readings in romantic poetry (e.g. Schock, 2003), the Satan of even these black metal lyrics more often tends to be explicitly destructive. He despises the weak and encourages their destruction. It is this revised romantic, rebellious Satan that comes closest to the Satanism constructed by some of the followers of Anton LaVey and the Church of Satan.

Satanism and Black Metal

The relationship between black metal and Satanism is complex. From LaVey's side, Norwegian black metal artists often appeared "as essentially Christian," at least in the sense that they were "defining Satanism by Christian standards" (in Moynihan and Søderlind 1998: 234). That there was no love lost between them is evident from the fact that key members of the early Norwegian black metal scene claimed that they despised LaVey as just another humanist. Deathlike Silence Productions, the extreme metal label founded by Mayhem's Euronymous, sometimes featured a picture of LaVey in a circle with a line drawn through it—similar to conventional "no smoking" signs. At least one production carries the term "anti-LaVey." It would seem that whereas LaVey's Church of Satan espouses "nine parts respectability to one part outrageousness," the discourse and ethos of transgression in the early black metal scene inverts the proportions. Indeed, while the Church of Satan, like the extreme metal scene (e.g. Kahn-Harris, 2007), values transgression as well as control, only a few individual Satanists, many of which are marginal, would value transgression to the extent implied in black metal discourse.

But, as noted above, the relationship is somewhat more complex than may be gathered from this mutually expressed distaste. There is, firstly, a certain amount of common ground between LaVeyan Satanism, as interpreted by many Satanists, and the ideology of black metal. Both LaVeyan discourse and black metal share related themes of elitism, misanthropy, individualism, non-conformity, and transgression. An admittedly impressionistic comparison of the treatment of these topics suggests that black metal discourse is more extreme. Not only do few Satanists go as far as black metal discourse, but LaVey himself seemed to have varied widely in his degree of misanthropy, with the early LaVey appearing almost optimistic compared to some of his later writings. With regard to contempt for "herd conformity," they may seem more alike—but with important differences between individuals. While the combination of conservatism and transgression can be found in both Satanist and black metal communities, again, Satanists seem to focus differently on what counts as transgression and to what degree they are willing to transgess.

Although both parties claim to feel naturally alien in mainstream society, one can also make a case for alienation in Satanism sometimes being more strategic. Some consciously take on the role of "accuser" as part of what has sometimes been termed "creative alienation." Consciously taking on the role of "acccuser" involves going against the mainstream by contesting what currently functions as "holy." That said, there are similar elements in play in extreme metal as well.[6]

Moreover, the symbolism of transgression can also take on some of the same elements, with anti-Christian blasphemy and Nazi aesthetics being among the principal areas of continuity. Again, however, Satanists are, generally speaking, much less interested in these elements, seeing anti-Christianity as something to transcend, it being merely an unhealthy obsession with another religion, and the Nazi elements as immature foolishness or worse.[7]

Bearing in mind these common elements, it comes as no surprise that there are more than a few LaVeyan Satanists on the black metal scene.[8] Even with regard to the Norwegian black metal scene, we find several who currently profess or have in the past subscribed to a LaVeyan type of Satanism. My impression, however, is that these are typical within the least transgressive streams of black metal, both with regard to ideology and to their lifestyle. While there are bohemian elements within the lifestyles of many, in actual fact regular employment, marriage, "family values," and moderately conservative politics are far from uncommon (see Kahn-Harris, 2007: 61ff.). This personal impression fits well with what is otherwise known about organized Satanism (e.g. Lewis and Petersen, 2007). To adopt Kahn-Harris' vocabulary, LaVeyan Satanism seems generally more devoted to *mundane* subcultural capital than to *transgressive* subcultural capital (2007: 122–39). Furthermore, the emic ideological stress on worldly success tends to support this thesis. Indeed, unless one holds to the mistaken belief that Satanists worship the Christian Devil and attempt to be the evil opposite to Christian congregations, there was never much reason to hold a different view.[9] That is to say, the Satan of LaVeyan Satanism is a far cry from the popular cultural horror-style demonology of much black metal. To the degree that Satan resembles anything from the history of demonology, as indicated above, it is principally the romantic and decadent reception and transformation of that transgressive symbol.

To those readers unfamiliar with contemporary Satanism, it is a tradition that can, broadly speaking, be divided into three different groups: (1) LaVeyan, rationalist Satanism; (2) esoteric Satanism; and (3) reactive, paradigmatically conformist Satanism (see Dyrendal, 2004; cf. Petersen, 2005; Schmidt, 1992). For the first group, Satan is usually seen as a symbol and their worldview tends to be materialistic, atheistic, and encourages an attitude of rational inquiry—without necessarily eschewing "the occult" completely (see Barton, 1992). The second group includes more theistic approaches. These tend to be inspired by Paganism and learn from the Western occult tradition as well as drawing inspiration from other religious and magical traditions, such as, for example, the Indian religious tradition (see Flowers, 1997; Schreck and Schreck, 2002). Both of these are primarily "self-religions" (Harvey, 2002; Dyrendal, forthcoming). Only the last category adopts elements of Christian mythology. This is what the German historian of religions, Joachim Schmidt, has dubbed "paradigmatically conformist" Satanism. The "reactive" element of such satanic belief and practice is the rebellious inversion underlying what is often an adolescent expression of Satanism.

The categories are not discrete and there has always been substantial movement between them. However, unlike the personal powers and active forces described in black metal lyrics, one looks in vain for such interesting demonologies in Satanism, particularly LaVeyan Satanism. While individual "demons" are referenced during some of the ritual chants constructed by LaVey, most Satanists seem to rarely perform personal rituals and collective ritual performances are even less common. Indeed, as might be expected within a predominantly atheistic tradition, demons within LaVeyan Satanism seem to be primarily understood as fictional or psychological symbols. That is to say, references are not to be read literally. Since "Satan" is most often viewed as a symbol of the vital nature of humankind, or sometimes as the "dark power" underlying the universe—passive and impersonal, thus uncaring, yet fueling the whole of life—it would indeed be strange if the demonic played a larger role.

LaVeyan Satanism is presented as a skeptical, Epicurean, atheistic philosophy of life. "Religion" *per se* is condemned as an elaborate scam (LaVey, 1969: 31, 39). The reasons why religion has prevailed, argued LaVey, include, not only human gullibility, but the fact that they have played on human need for spectacle (ritual) and story (myth). Thus, Satanism in LaVey's tradition has sought to address the same needs as a tool for liberation and the good life.

Since life is to be valued as it is—there being nothing beyond death—carnality and emotion are valued highly. This also holds true within music. A versatile and skilled musician himself, LaVey gave music and the aesthetic in general an important role. Moreover, he gave instructions about how to use music within the ritual chamber (1992: 79ff.) and suggested uses of music in both lower and higher magic. These suggestions are primarily concerned with how music can be used, for example, to heighten emotion and promote introspection. He focuses particularly on notions of universal or, as he puts it, "human type" reactions to certain types and combinations of sound. Thus, his understanding of music commonly played for "the herd" is slightly sinister:

> Music commonly piped into public areas is generally programmed so as to exert an influence on the hearer even though he is not listening. This type of music is utilized for lesser magical purposes (maintaining production flow, including eating and drinking, stimulating shoppers to buy, etc.). The music's provider employs it towards magical ends; those who hear it are controlled by it, rather than using it to control (LaVey 1992: 79).

"Satanic" music, on the other hand, is in accord with the individualist Satanist agenda: "The key element of Satanic music can be revealed in the question, will it appeal to you on an individual rather than herd basis? It's evocative, emotionally charged" (LaVey in Moynihan and Søderlind, 1998: 239). If it is produced for the herd, in order to control them, it is not likely to be deemed satanic.

Thus far, the musical ideologies of black metal and LaVey have something in common. However, much of this similarity evaporates when

LaVey celebrates the marches of John Philip Sousa or discusses "satanic" music: "Simplistically speaking, it's the kind of music you can walk away whistling or humming—thematic" (ibid.). There are a lot of things to be said about early, second-generation black metal, but it is notoriously difficult to whistle or hum.

When LaVey presents examples of music he deems particularly satanic, he refers to classical music (Barton 1990: 151–55). He repeatedly laments, in both interviews and his own essays, that contemporary adolescents only know the kind of sound made by different kinds of rock music. This does not, however, mean that LaVey is consistently adversarial to black metal or to popular music in general. Railing against the American "satanic panic," its proponents, and its consequences, LaVey writes:

> I wanted to tell your children what was RIGHT about Satanism: encouraging sensuality with achievement, outrage with justice, nonconformity with wisdom. Instead YOU provided media saturation informing them what "real" Satanists do, what kind of noises they make when possessed. YOU encouraged them to rebel by the aesthetic standards YOU provided, and still you grouse when they gravitate to Slayer, Ozzy, Electric Hellfire Club, Mercyful Fate, Deicide, Marilyn Manson, Acheron, Morbid Angel.
>
> Do you know what? I think those bands are great. I would also like your kids to listen to Liszt, Borodin, Saint-Saens, Dvorak, Ketelbey, Wagner, Puccini, von Suppe, Rossini, Romberg, Kern, Friml, Al Jolson, Russ Colombo, Nelson Eddy, Nat "King" Cole, and the marches of John Philip Sousa. But you never gave me the time to explain THAT to them (LaVey 1998: 6).

Since those opposing Satanism have been beguiled by the horror stories promoted in popular culture and have been less inclined actually to study Satanism, they have created a particular image of Satanism that is often at odds with the reality. Indeed, the aesthetics and sounds of extreme metal, as well as its apocalyptic images, tend to be constructed as a direct, transgressive response to the taboos of Christian culture and the moral panic mentality.

Having noted this appreciation of classical music and initial skepticism concerning rock music, LaVey later acknowledged that death metal and black metal brought a lot of people into contact with *his* kind of Satanism (see Barton 1990: 147–48). Thus, his opinion of the music he appears to have initially dismissed is later revised. However, LaVey foretells a time when the same kids "come walking in the door with a *Satanic Bible* in one hand and a CD of Mussorgsky's *Night On Bald Mountain* in the other" (1998: 7). Then the *real* nightmare will begin.

Satanism and Popular Music

Having noted his ambiguous relationship with rock music, it's important to understand that LaVey was no enemy of popular music *per se*.
Indeed, he appreciated songs, often from "Tin Pan Alley"-era compos-
ers of the late nineteenth and early twentieth centuries. Moving into the
middle of the twentieth century, the picture emerging from the lyrics of
some of his favorite "demon songs" is very different from those of black
metal. Among his favorites, we find songs such as Wayne Shanklin's song
"Jezebel," Irving Berlin's "Get Thee Behind Me Satan," and "That Old
Black Magic" by Harold Arlen and Johnny Mercer—a hit for several performers, including Sinatra and Sammy Davis Jr.

Typically, "the demons" in these songs belong to a distinctly earthly
realm: The lyrics of Wayne Shanklin's "Jezebel" are about unrequited
love—a paradise promised but never delivered—and a woman so fair
as to be likened to an angel, but obviously fallen, both for her charms
and for the torment love delivers; the "witchcraft" and "black magic" of
Mercer's lyrics is again that of love and desire, the physical effects "when
your eyes meet mine"; and the command to Satan to "get behind me"
in Berlin's song seems at best a half-hearted protest against the powerful temptation of a lover one "mustn't see" but cannot resist. "Get thee
behind me," the protagonist exclaims to temptation, because "the moon
is low, and I can't say no."

Carnality, temptation, love, "the blues"—elements of human life,
body, and psyche—these are the principal demonic elements within
some of LaVey's favorite songs. Black metal's explicit "Devil-worship"
is not mentioned. However, this does not mean that he was unable to
appreciate or commend the anger and sentiment of black metal. As
noted above, he had listened to and, reportedly, even said he liked some
of the bands.

How does the above discussion extend to other Satanists? Do they also
ideologize musical preference? The current High Priest, Peter Gilmore,
is particularly clear about his preference for classical, thematic music,
stating that he does not listen to popular music. He stresses, however,
that this is a personal preference. When considering whether music is
satanic, he, like LaVey, puts weight on both individual taste and the
power to raise emotion. No Satanist, he says, can determine another's
aesthetic choices, hence "Satanic music" is whatever moves a Satanist's
emotions (Gilmore, personal correspondence).

The attitude, although not the taste, seems to be reflected among
both younger and more established Satanists. Listening to the music on

the satanic web-radio, Radio Free Satan, one is exposed to a bewildering variety of music, ranging from classical to country to disco to extreme metal.[10] On discussion boards and Usenet groups a similar pattern is evident. Although the taste frequently runs in the direction of heavy metal, personal taste matters most. This may be one of the reasons why the discussions are most often free of the rancorous debates over "sell-outs" that so often crop up among metal fans.

Examining the boards and news groups, the limited overlap between the extreme metal scene and Satanism becomes much more visible. The few who identify themselves with both scenes become more visible in specific discussions which betray a Satanist point of view.[11] Younger Satanists dominate discussions about music. In expressing what kinds of music they are motivated by, or of what they are currently listening to, black metal references are ubiquitous. These references, of course, also serve as strategies for identity performance. The younger Satanists usually have a better grasp of and more interest in popular culture than in Satanist ideology. Their common references serve as a connection, informing others that they have something in common. Thus, it is little surprise that events of common interest—metal concerts—are among the principal occasions at which they meet, something which happens rarely with regard to most online communities.[12]

A Satanic Hymn?

Even on the discussion boards themselves, heavy metal is not the only kind of popular music that is valued. Following the same, satanic ethos of non-conformity and personal preference, other bands and tastes crop up. However, the typical contrast to metal in such online discussions seems not to be other forms of popular music, but classical music.[13] One exception was made by an older member on the forum "Letters to the Devil" (http://www.satannet.com). He was seemingly annoyed at all the fan-reports, particularly for Marilyn Manson, and instead promoted his own idea about what constituted a really good satanic song, namely "My Way." In discussions with senior Satanists, I have found that most tend to agree that this song is a far better example of a satanic "hymn" in popular music than anything ever composed by a heavy metal band.

Ideologically, it is easy to understand why this might be the case. From the title to the lyrics, "My Way" expresses some of the core elements of Satanist thought. The title itself reflects central Satanist themes. Indeed, the phrase is regularly used in discussions among Satanists. For example, one of the members on "Letters to the Devil" stated the following, when faced with standard questions concerning personal success and the standards by which he lives: "I'm doing my li'l respective proj-ects my way. I consider myself to be a success. My standards determine this." The emic idea of Satanists being an elite—"the alien elite"—is not necessarily dependent on success according to dominant societal values, but rather depends on the individual's own values, talents, and interests. One member of the forum put it this way: "If the herd heads North, one may be at the lead, but he's still traveling with the herd." All is permit-ted, as long as it is done according to the individual's true will. Once worldly success takes on the aspect of "keeping up with the Joneses" it becomes herd conformity and transgresses the Satanist injunction to do things "my way."

The lyrics may be read as reflecting further elements of Satanist ideol-ogy. The voice in "My Way" has led a full life, charted and planned the course, taken its share of both pleasure and pain, but weathered it all. To an outsider, this might seem to contradict the expressed Epicureanism of Satanist ideology. In fact, the opposite is true. Whereas the Epicu-rean elements of Satanism are normally equated with hedonism, this is a common mistake with regard to both Epicureanism and Satanism. While Epicurean thought values pleasure, it is considerably less hedonistic than most Satanist thought. However, they do share a materialist foundation and an emphasis on "balance." Pleasure and virtue are, at least to some extent, interdependent in Satanism as well as in Epicureanism. While LaVey preaches "indulgence, instead of abstinence," he also stresses "indulgence, not compulsion." There is a necessary *balance*, if one is to stay in control. Thus, it is important to plan "each charted course, each careful step along the byway," to map a course through troubles in order to get the best out of life. Indeed, this is—to some extent—what lesser magic is for.

With regard to the troubles that life invariably encounters, LaVey is often quoted as saying that "Satanism is the worship of life, not a hypocritical, whitewashed vision of life, but life as it really is." This atti-tude is generally shared within the Satanist community and has less in common with Epicurean thought than it does with a vitalistic philosophy of "hard masculinity" that seems to permeate much of LaVey's writing. It is related to the "Satan" of Satanism through a hidden or overt appeal to the romantic, rebellious Satan and his towering pride. The Satanist should recognize that he may, at times, "bite off more than he can chew," but that should not be an occasion to complain. The ideal is to "face it all and stand tall."

Pride is a Satanist virtue, in that self-reliance and self-appreciation play a central role in getting the best out of life. The Satanist should recognize that what s/he gets out of life, depends on himself or herself. Bending knees in prayer is pointless. It may be Satanist and ego-focused in intent, but it is useless in practice and wrong as an attitude. What you have is yourself, your pride, your abilities, and your own integrity. Few things, then, could be more appropriately Satanist than to declare triumphantly, as "My Way" does, that: "The record shows I took the blows and did it my way!"

High Priest Peter Gilmore, who prefers the version of the song by one-time member of the Church of Satan Sammy Davis Jr., says that it is "the proper combination of music and lyrics with a committed and talented vocalist that completely project the essence of satanic individualism and self-godhood." No heavy metal song comes close, he insists. It is a far cry from the demonological horror fantasies projected from both heavy metal musicians, their fans, and their detractors, but as an introduction to what contemporary Satanism really values, this unsuspected "hymn" is better than most.

Notes

1. I have focused on the following discussion boards: the Danish "Satanisk Forum" (http://forum.sataniskforum.dk/); the Norwegian "Det norske satanistiske samfunn" (http://www.satanisk.com/forum/index.html); and the Church of Satan-affiliated forum "Letters to the Devil" (http://www.satannet.com/forum/ubbthreads. php?ubb=postlist&Board=27&page=1). I have monitored these for long periods of time and, with the exception of "Letters to the Devil," believe I have a relatively comprehensive overview of the relevant threads.

2. Historically, "corpse paint" seems to have evolved from the use of make-up by KISS and, later, from the make-up worn by first wave black metal musician (and LaVeyan Satanist) King Diamond of Mercyful Fate. One of several emic mythologizations claims that the vikings wore similar body paint into battle.

3. Different statements by key black metal "satanists" from different periods and in different contexts yield a varied and often inconsistent picture.

4. The topic is treated most interestingly and convincingly by Mørk (2002).

5. Having said that, in the last few years such clichés crept back in black metal lyrics.

6. On black metal, see the discussion by Mørk (2002) and Kahn-Harris (2007). The emic literature on transgression in Satanism is relatively large (e.g. Schreck and Schreck, 2002; Baddeley, 2005). For an etic description, see Farren's analysis (2006).

7. For a similar observation on the British scene, see Partridge's comments (2005: 223).

8. Peter Gilmore, the present High Priest of the Church of Satan, is listed as a former keyboard player for the American black metal band, Acheron. However, he claims to have no interest in rock music, does not participate in the scene, and says of his own recordings with Acheron that they were "composed and performed by

myself, and they are bombastic orchestral music, realized with synthesizers, that could be likened to the brief expressive pieces composed by Gustav Holst in his orchestral suite 'The Planets' " (Gilmore, personal correspondence).

9.   The leadership has historically complained, with some justification about the lack of responsibility among local groups (see Aquino, 2002). However, they also complain about the lack of transgressive elements in both thought and deed among Satanists as well as the lack of ideological interest. These complaints have, for instance, been aired by members of the leadership in the Danish network "Satanisk Forum," which recently ceased having local group meetings for largely the same reasons as the early Church of Satan did.

10.   I played the station almost continuously, night and day, for a week and a half. When I first tuned in I was surprised to encounter Johnny Cash and Abba. Indeed, it took a good 45 minutes before I heard my first heavy metal song. That said, at other times, heavy metal is almost continuously played.

11.   In several senses it may be problematic to refer to Satanism as a "scene," but I will refrain from leading that discussion here. In one sense, where it becomes most *like* a scene, is online.

12.   Organized rituals, which in anti-Satanist lore are thought to play a vital role, are actually relatively uncommon.

13.   Similarly, the contrast to popular novels is rarely other popular literature, but "high art" novels, philosophy and science.

Chapter 2

Between Hymn and Horror Film:
How do we Listen to Cradle of Filth?

Peter Mercer-Taylor

God is dead,
Satan lives,
Hail Satan!

O mighty lord of the night...
forever wilt I praise thy dreaded name.

The two foregoing quotations are not dissimilar in their basic thrust. Indeed we might be hard pressed to determine, at first blush, which of these pledges to the forces of evil would prove more objectionable to the fuzzily Judeo-Christian western moral mainstream. In this case, however, context is everything.

The first passage is spoken by a lackluster cadre of late-middle-aged Satanists at the climax of Roman Polanski's 1968 film *Rosemary's Baby*. Thus these words are received by the great majority of twenty-first-century viewers as harmless role-playing. If cinematic representations of evil may once have enjoyed a veneer of genuine moral transgression, those days have largely passed; the controversy surrounding William Friedkin's *The Exorcist* (1973) had died out before most present-day movie-goers were born, and has not been repeated.

The second quotation is a different story. These lines occur in the 1994 song, "Inno a Satana" ("Hymn to Satan"), by one of the leading creative forces in Norway's black metal explosion of the 1990s, the band Emperor. Emerging first as an impulse within the thrash metal scene of the 1980s—through the work of Venom, Mayhem, Hellhammer, Merciful Fate, and others—black metal crystallized through the next decade into a genre bent on pressing heavy metal's persistent fascination with the dark side to a distinctive extreme. Poetically, black metal is largely defined through its orientation around apocalyptic conflicts in which the forces of good, generally Christian ones, are proved powerless to save humanity from the grim designs of alternative cosmic agents. The victory sometimes goes to Satan himself, sometimes to deities of a sketchily recovered Scandanavian Paganism, sometimes to forces more like Lovecraftian "ancient ones" with scant theological credentials of any kind. While we are clearly not obliged to take seriously the religious convictions put forward here in Emperor's "Hymn to Satan," the transgressive energy at the core of both this song's entertainment value and its power to appall—insofar as the two can be distinguished—lies in the fact that it gives us no reason not to take it seriously. It stands up and walks like a real hymn.

In this sense, the two quotations above inhabit altogether distinct spheres, inviting two very different registers of moral judgment: one is regulated by the logic of cinema, the other by the logic of hymnody; one lays claim to the conventions of fiction, the other to the conventions of doxology; one speaks from the comfortable mainstream of the film industry, the other from a subcultural fringe. And that fringe remains a deeply contested territory.

The first great flowering of heavy metal scholarship in the early 1990s was marked by sustained attempts to defuse popular panic surrounding the genre's perennial entanglements with the forces of darkness. Echoing a theme sounded repeatedly in Deena Weinstein's foundational sociology of heavy metal (Weinstein, 1991), Robert Walser's 1993 *Running with the Devil: Power, Gender, and Madness in Heavy Metal Music* argued articulately and compassionately for a view of metal's poetic and iconographic flirtations with Satanism and the occult as a theologically neutral invitation to fans to "participate in an empowerment that is largely musically constructed, but which is intensified by ritualistic images that sanctify the experience with histori-cal and mystical depth" (Walser, 1993: 154; see, too, Straw, 1990: 108 and Harrell, 1994: 95–97).[1] Since the time of Walser and Weinstein's writing, however, black metal has wrought an intensification of metal's counter- and anti-Christian subject matter that has not made the would-be apologists' task any easier, and has only fueled public anxiety. (The most thoroughgoing existing historical account of Emperor and their black metal colleagues, Moynihan and Søderlind's 1998 *Lords of Chaos: The Bloody Rise of the Satanic Metal Underground*, is densely researched, historiographically graceful, and remorselessly lurid, dwelling in consid-erably greater detail on the church burnings, murders, and suicides that punctuated the early days of the Norwegian black metal scene than on the music itself.) While Weinstein's reassuring assessment—"Metal lyrics do not attack God and certainly do not malign Jesus" (Weinstein, 1991: 260)—may have seemed plausible in 1991, it is difficult to support in the face of, for instance, that moment in a 2004 Cradle of Filth concert (Minneapolis, 10 December) that found lead singer Dani Filth lifting a middle finger skyward for the final word of his growled line, "What use are prayers to that 'God'…?," before a crowd of youngsters wearing, in many cases, the band's notorious "Jesus is a Cunt" T-shirts.

This last *Gegenbeispiel* is not chosen at random. For Cradle of Filth's case is a highly significant one, not so much in the intermittent severity of their anti-Christian rhetoric, which is not hard to come by, but in the fact that this British band has done more than perhaps any other act in black metal's history to bring the genre toward the popular mainstream. Since their 1991 formation, Cradle of Filth's steady rise in popularity—built upon some ten albums and a scattering of EPs[2]—has far outpaced the bulk of their competitors in the genre. Their 2001 contract with Sony, though dissolved after only a single album (*Damnation and a Day*), constituted the first major-label signing of a black metal band; *Damnation* and the 2004 follow-up, *Nymphetamine*, became the first and second black metal albums in history to enter Billboard's Top 200 charts; the band even found themselves nominated, in 2005, for a "Best Metal Performance" Grammy Award (for "Nymphetamine"—they lost to Slipknot's "Vermilion").[3] Rockdetector.com proclaims them, in sum, "[w]ithout doubt the foremost exponents of British black metal and one of the very biggest names of the genre in the international scene" (http://rockdetector.com/artist,1928.sm).

For purists, it is unclear what sort of victory this comprises for black metal *per se*, as not all are convinced that Cradle of Filth is a card-carrying black metal band at all. While much of the band's poetic and visual imagery, together with the high, shrieking style of most of the vocal delivery, are consistent with the genre's defining conventions, Cradle of Filth are practitioners (if hardly the sole ones) of a metal style marked by glossy production, frequent synthesizers, the occasional orchestra, and intermittent soprano back-up vocals (from Sarah Jezebel Deva) by no means to the liking of all within the black metal community. More troublesome is the band's pervasive tendency, as Ian Christe puts it, to "[wash] down its blasphemy with a typically British sense of camp…" (Christe, 2003: 288). Jon Fine, writing in the *Village Voice*, lumped Cradle of Filth together with shock-rocker Marilyn Manson in his blanket dismissal of the idea that any real threat was to be found there: "at base they're candy bands putting on goofy costume shows that could only be threatening to clueless parents" (Fine, 1998: 130).

While the "goofy costume" charge is not misplaced, Fine points here only to the tip of what is in fact an intriguing aesthetic iceberg. For Cradle of Filth have proven endlessly inventive in what might be thought of as the cross-pollination of black metal's basic (pseudo-)theological premises with mainstream fictional modes, film in particular. While many of the topics encompassed in their diverse subject matter—Faust, Countess Bathory, H. P. Lovecraft's sundry casts, vampires, and, of course, Judeo-Christian narratives concerning the struggle between good and evil—can be found elsewhere in the black metal repertoire, their very proliferation in Cradle of Filth's work, together with a strongly narrative poetic impulse and an unapologetic theatricality in visual presentation, tend to efface black metal's defining sense of cosmic despair in favor of something more like harmless cinematic spectacle. "They wore the requisite Black Metal corpsepaint, but began to cultivate an atmosphere befitting of Hammer horror films rather than the one-dimensional 'evilness' projected by other groups" (Moynihan and Søderlind, 1998: 282–83). Cradle of Filth's lyrics are prone to sprawling tales—reaching an extreme in their two narratively cohesive concept albums, *Cruelty and the Beast* (1998) and *Damnation and a Day* (2003)—that occasionally go so far as to accommodate sound effects (the creaking door, for instance, of the 1996 "Funeral in Carpathia"). Two albums have featured brief speaking roles for actual horror film actors, '70s veteran Ingrid Pitt on *Cruelty and the Beast*, and Doug Bradley (who portrayed Pinhead in Clive Barker's *Hellraiser* movies) on the 2000 *Midian*. This has proven a two-ways street, as Dani Filth, the singer/songwriter who has led Cradle of Filth from their inception, took a leading role in the 2001 horror film *Cradle of Fear*, directed by splatter film vet Alex Chandon.

In interviews from the late nineties onward, Dani Filth tends to evince complete apathy on the topic of the band's credibility in black metal circles, occasionally voicing the desire for a label that would more accurately reflect their leanings toward horror genres writ large. In a November 13, 2000 interview with e-zine *Lords of Metal*, when asked whether he saw Cradle of Filth as a black metal band, Dani responded:

> Nobody gave a fuck when back in the days when we were young and wanted to be Black Metal so passionately, nobody gave a fuck back then so I don't think we should give a fuck and call us whatever we want now. Quite frankly, I consider Black Metal as a theology, an atmosphere, an achievement of things, you know, a philosophy…in that respect, yes, we are Black Metal… But you wouldn't necessarily say: "Hey, they're Black Metal," in a respect of the current trend. And if Black Metal is only an image or a like the current trend [sic], then I guess we're not Black Metal. I'd rather have people say we're Cradle of Filth, and if that's too pretentious, than call it Horror Metal or just a fucking Metal band (http://www.lordsofmetal.nl/showinterview.php?id=130&lang=en).

Cradle of Filth tend, in short, to lodge themselves somewhere between the poles represented by those two quotations with which this essay began.

On the one hand is black metal's inflammatory capacity for sensational theological transgression, whose force depends on at least the plausible illusion that it comprises, in essence, a body of hymnody underpinned by sincere belief. On the other hand is overtly fictional role-playing, the logic of cinema—or rather of narrative fiction generally—in which theological conviction plays no role, all being securely subsumed under the aesthetics of the horror genre.

In the discussion that follows, I examine a single Cradle of Filth song, the 1999 "From the Cradle to Enslave," in terms of just this dichotomy, arguing that self-conscious engagement with the question of the frame of genre reference—hymnody or fictional horror—emerges as the crux issue of the song's structural conception, both poetically and musically. Briefly, I want to suggest that the song begins as a hymn, firmly lodged in black metal's most theologically treacherous terrain. But beginning around a third of the way through its length, "From the Cradle to Enslave" undertakes a series of incremental steps toward the cinematic, or rather toward an overt fictionality whose referent might best be understood as a casual conflation of cinema, literary fiction, drama, and opera. This dynamic process eludes tidy categorization according to customary metrics—authenticity, sincerity, sell-out, irony—of popular music hermeneutics. For what Cradle of Filth offer here seems a bid neither for the status of pure black metal nor for the genre's selling out, but a reflexive exploration both of the genre's capacity to arouse moral anxiety and of the terms through which its dangers can be brought toward social regulation, or at least toward mainstream comprehensibility.

In an effort to warn listeners and critics away from taking the satanic, intermittently neo-fascist subject matter of his band's songs too seriously, Slayer's Kerry King once observed, "I describe my songs as horror movies on music, it's a fantasy world" (Harrell, 1994: 96). This simile functions, in King's hands, less to shed light on distinct stylistic conceits, compositional decisions, or narrative strategies internal to Slayer's work than as a blanket plea neither to scorn too strongly nor to confide too much in the worldview the music puts forth. In "From the Cradle to Enslave," I shall argue, Cradle of Filth take on the task of enacting just this sort of exculpatory maneuver within the song itself.

*   *   *

The two texts shown in Figure 1 have a great deal in common. The first is Charles Wesley's "Lo, he comes ,with clouds descending," based on the passage from Revelation that appears below it (Young, 1966: 364). This may be the best-known English-language hymn on the subject of the apocalypse (unless the American "Battle Hymn of the Republic" counts, which it probably should). Next to it is the opening stretch of "From the Cradle to Enslave."

Charles Wesley **'Lo, he comes, with clouds descending'**	**Cradle of Filth** **'From the Cradle to Enslave' (opening stanzas)**
Lo, he comes with clouds descending, Once for favored sinners slain; Thousand, thousand saints attending Swell the triumph of his train; Hallelujah! Hallelujah! Hallelujah! God appears on earth to reign.	Two thousand fattened years, like maniacs, have despoiled our common grave, Now what necrophagous Second Coming backs from the cradle to enslave? Sickle constellations stud the belts that welt the sky,
Every eye shall now behold him, Robed in dreadful majesty; Those who set at naught and sold him, Pierced and nailed him to the tree, Deeply wailing, deeply wailing, deeply wailing, Shall the true Messiah see.	Whilst the bitter winter moon prowls the clouds, dead-eyed, Like shifting parent flesh under silk matricide. Watchful as she was upon Eden, Where every rose arbour and orchard she swept, Hid the hissing of a serpent Libido In an ancient tryst with catastrophe soon to be kept.
The dear tokens of his passion Still his dazzling body bears; Cause of endless exultation To his ransomed worshipers. With what rapture, with what rapture, with what rapture, Gaze we on those glorious scars!	Hear that hissing now on the breeze, as through the plundered groves of the carnal garden a fresh horror blows, But ten billion souls are blind to see the rotting wood for the trees.
Yea, amen! Let all adore thee, High on thine eternal throne; Savior, take the power and glory, Claim the kingdom for thine own; Hallelujah! Hallelujah! Hallelujah! Everlasting God, come down!	This is the theme to a better Armageddon, nightchords rake the heavens, PAN DAEMON AEAON! And what use are prayers to that god, As devils bay consensus for the space to piss on your smouldering faith, And the mouldering face of this world, long a Paradise Lost?

Behold, he cometh with clouds; and every eye shall see him, and they also which pierced him: and all kindreds of the earth shall wail because of him. Even so, Amen.
—Revelation 1:7 (King James Version)

Figure 1: Charles Wesley, "Lo, he comes, with clouds descending" and Cradle of Filth, "From the Cradle to Enslave" (opening)

The parallels are numerous. In both, the first-person perspective is articulated only in plural form, reflecting on a general human experience rather than that of any single individual ("our salvation," "our common grave"). Both put forward present-tense narrations of second comings, linking these to episodes in ancient narratives (the crucifixion on the one hand, the Fall on the other). Celestial phenomena factor prominently in both, and both make prominent use of calls to attention ("Lo," "Hear"). While neither invites the onlookers into any direct participation in the unfolding events, both are essentially celebratory in tone ("This is," as Cradle of Filth put it, "the theme to a better Armageddon"). Both even make reference to the music with which the phenomena at hand might most fittingly be greeted, including brief bursts of what amounts to diegetic song: "Hallelujah!" in the first instance, "Pan Daemon Aeon!" in the second. Thus far, the Cradle of Filth song gives no suggestion of critical distance, no suggestion that it does not function, like Wesley's hymn, as an expostulation of an actual eschatological belief system.

After the excerpt offered here, however, the ground begins to shift for Cradle of Filth. From this point in the song onward, so closely is the logic of the lyrics bound up with that of the music that it is worth pausing for a sidelong glance at the song as a structural whole, sketched out—with remarks on salient musical features—in Figure 2.

Intro	0:00 / 1 16 bars	synth alone	
Prelude	0:26 / 17 16 bars	drums & bass in	**Two thousand fattened years, like maniacs, have despoiled our common grave,** **Now what necrophagous Second Coming backs from the cradle to en**slave?
Ritornello	0:52 / 33 16 bars	guitars in; first sounding of catchy 'ritornello'	Sickle constellations stud the belts that welt the sky, Whilst the bitter winter moon prowls the clouds, dead-eyed, Like shifting parent flesh under silk matricide. **Watchful as she was upon Eden,** where every rose arbour and orchard she swept, Hid the hissing of a serpent Libido in an ancient tryst with catastrophe soon to be…

Episode I	1:18 / 49 24 bars	snare strokes in double-time; new groove in guitars & bass	...kept. Hear that hissing now on the breeze, as through the plundered groves of the carnal garden a fresh horror blows, But ten billion souls are blind to see the rotting wood for the trees. This is the theme to a better Armaged- don, nightchords rake the heavens, PAN DAEMON AEAON! **And what use are prayers to that god,** As devils bay consensus for the space to piss on your smouldering faith, And the mouldering face of this world, long a Paradise Lost?
Ritornello	1:58 / 73 16 bars	back to music of ritornello	**This is the end of everything.** *Hear the growing chora that a new dawn shall bring.* Danse macabre 'neath the tilt of the zodiac, now brighter stars shall reflect on our fate. What sick nativities will be freed when those lights burn black? The darkside of the mirror always threw our...
Episode II	2:24 / 89 8 bars	initially operatic vocals; piano & synth strings	...malice back. I see the serpentine in your eyes. **The nature of the beast as revelations...**
	2:38 / 97 48 bars	blast-beating on drums; guitars back; general chaos	...arrive. Our screams shall trail to Angels, for those damned in flames repay. All sinners lose their lot on Judgment Day. We should have cut our losses as at Calvary, But our hearts like heavy crosses held the vain belief, Salvation, like a promised nation, **gleamed a claim away.** **This is the end of everything you have** **ever known.** **Buried like vanquished reason, death** **in season,** **Driven like the drifting snow.** Peace, a fragile lover, left us fantasising war on our knees or another fucker's shore, Heiling new flesh, read, then roared to a crooked cross and a Holy Cause, What else to be whipped to frenzy for?

| Ritornello | 3:57 / 145
64 bars | back to music of
ritornello | This is the end of everything.
Rear the tragedies that the Seraphim shall
sing.
Old adversaries, next of Eve, now they're
clawing back.
I smell their coming, as through webbed
panes of meat.
Led by hoary Death, they never left,
dreaming sodomies
To impress on human failure when we've
bled upon our knees.
Tablatures of gravel law shall see Gehen-
nah paved
When empires fall and nightmares crawl,
from the cradle to enslave.
This is the end of everything. (x2)
This is the end of everything. (x4—reg-
isters freely intermingled throughout)
This is the end of everything.
This is the end of every— |
| Outro | 5:41 / 209
32 bars | synth alone | |

Figure 2: Cradle of Filth, "From the Cradle to Enslave"

As the cues running down the left column show, "From the Cradle to Enslave" begins and ends with an intro and outro for synthesizer alone, bookending a song whose structural elaborateness is by no means atypical of black metal. The load-bearing sections of the song are the three soundings of what I call the "ritornello," a term used in classical music to designate, essentially, "a little something that keeps coming back." These cannot properly be called "choruses," as words and melody are not what they have in common; they share, instead, an instrumental groove, the catchiest material of the song. We break from the first ritornello for the comparatively brief "Episode I." After the ritornello's return, we enter the much more extensive, more profoundly disruptive "Episode II," followed by a lengthy return to the ritornello.

The text is presented in Figure 2 set in three different formats (bold, roman, and italics) demarcating sharply distinct vocal styles, which will prove crucial to the present analysis. Italics appear only twice, for two lines sung (multi-tracked into a small chorus) by soprano Sarah Jezebel Deva. The rest of the song is delivered by lead singer Dani, but in two quite different registers. The regular type represents material delivered in a high, shrieking scream, the archetypal vocal sound of black metal. Bold print is used for moments at which a very different register is present, the inhumanly low, pharyngeal growl more strongly associated with death metal, which Dani does as well as anyone. Dani's alternating high and low registers mirror the "scooped midrange" of the instrumental backdrop—again, standard-issue black metal—which pits the lowest notes of the five-string bass against the overtone-drenched distortion of the guitar. There is more than one vocal track, and some of these bold passages include both Dani's high and low registers (as in the song's opening two lines). These two registers participate cooperatively, as Figure 2 shows, in setting forth the song's hymn-like opening stretch.

If, as I have suggested, the song sounds like a hymn up to the end of its first episode, a critical shift begins at the outset of the second ritornello, as the growling register takes over for the line, "This is the end of everything." From a musical standpoint, this moment is a structurally privileged one, comprising the first large-scale return of a musical idea from which we have made a sustained departure (it is, to reiterate, the instrumental backdrop making the return, not the vocalist). The line is also highly distinctive where the vocal part is concerned, as we see in Example 1, which takes up the vocal line just before the entry of the ritornello.

Example 1: Cradle of Filth, "From the Cradle to Enslave," excerpt ("x" pitches very approximate)

To begin with, the phrase "This is the end of everything" brings with it a dramatic, unprecedented rest on the first beat of the bar; the first two systems of the example are emblematic of the song's almost invariable pattern, up to this point, of dedicating the down-beat of each bar to a word or syllable poetically worthy of such emphasis: "devils," "space," "smouldering," "mouldering," "world," "Lost." At the same time, when the words—"This is the end of everything"—set in, the pace of the poetic delivery abruptly slows, as the tripping, quaver-dominated rhythm of the song up to this point (exemplified in the first two systems of the example) is ironed into even crotchets.

The result of these considerations, in hand with the abandonment of the high vocal register for the lower one and the authoritative finality of the poetic sentiment itself, brings with it a powerful sense of rupture in the integrity of the speaking persona, as though the narrator who has carried us up to this point has abruptly put someone else on the phone. With this rupture, the illusion of hymn begins to give way to something quite different. For the growl suddenly begins to sound, as it had not before, like the speaking voice of an actual character in the drama. This sense becomes all the more forceful in light of the fact that the cheerless poetic line itself sounds much like a paraphrase of the sentence thundered forth by another terrifying, mysterious agent of super-human power at the chilling climax of Revelation's narration of the seven angels' pouring out of the seven plagues: "The seventh angel poured his bowl into the air, and a loud voice came out of the temple, from the throne, saying, 'It is done!'" (Revelation 16:17; May and Metzger, 1973: 1507).

If this line marks the abrupt intrusion of dramatic role-playing, the point is driven home in the next by the actual female chorus that enters to announce the appearance of the "growing chora" (see Example 1). Quite abruptly, the song has stopped sounding like a hymn at all, but like the gathering of *dramatis personae*. Dani returns, shrieking, to take up the narration once more, but shortly finds that he is himself to be summoned into the sphere of the dramatic.

This summons comes at the outset of the extended central section I have labeled "Episode II," which begins with the final two words of the line "The dark side of the mirror always threw our malice back."[4] The sense of musical rupture attending these words—pointless to attempt capturing in transcription—is multivalent and complete. To begin with, the pounding sonic wall of guitars, bass, and drums that has accompanied the entire vocal portion of the song since the first ritornello vanishes abruptly, the instrumental texture giving way, for eight bars, to quiet synthesized strings and piano. Dani abandons both his shrieking and his growling registers, too, breaking into nine words' worth of plaintive, pitched melody ("...malice back; I see the serpentine in your eyes").

The abrupt arrival of this new sonic world is underpinned by a striking development in the song's harmonic adventures as well. Example 2 surveys the harmonic events of the song up to this point (outside of the introduction, which is rooted entirely on D), offering a rhythmically simplified digest of the bass-guitar line anchoring the chord progressions whose repetitions make up each section of the song in turn.[5]

a.

b.

c.

Example 2: Cradle of Filth, "From the Cradle to Enslave" (simplified bass lines)

    a.   Prelude
    b.   Ritornello
    c.   Episode 1

    D remains the anchoring pitch throughout, sounded at, or very near, the beginning of every four-bar cycle. Local departures from D prove, however, to be quite broad-ranging from a harmonic standpoint; as Example 2 shows, by the time we hit "Episode II" we have heard chords rooted on all but two pitches of the chromatic scale (i.e. D, Eb, E, F, F#, G, Ab, A, Bb, and C#); only B and C remain untouched. It is into this void that we are jarringly pitched at the outset of Episode II, as the synthesizer passage brings with it an abrupt turn to the key of C minor, in which palpably remote territory we remain until the episode's midpoint (through the word "away").

    If a central musical rupture of this kind is not, in itself, uncharacteristic of the black metal genre, I suggest that it is here put to a highly distinctive use, completing the shift in the song's frame of genre reference from hymn to drama. For it is at this moment that the subject housed in Dani's screaming register awakens to his own unenviable role as a member of the dramatic cast whose introduction began in the previous ritornello. Critical here is the song's first use of the word "I." From the hymn-like epic narration that governed the song's opening stretch, we suddenly find ourselves faced with a human figure dramatically enacting an individual subject position (such a move would have been incomprehensible in the Wesley hymn we have examined). Indeed, the individual speaking subject seems to awaken for the first time to the fact that it is his own fate we are talking about; as we eavesdrop on his confrontation with that fate in real time, the shrieking Dani passes from something like a religious celebrant to a real, suffering human being.

The moment is cinematic in several senses. The "I" versus "you" configuration of this revelatory sentence—"I see the serpentine in your eyes"—offers the song's closest approximation to the shot/reverse shot structure so crucial to the visual vocabulary of horror cinema (though it is, of course, entirely possible that his own reflection comprises the "you"). And the superimposition of an actual hiss on the final "s" of "eyes" marks the first intrusion into the song of genuine sound effects, as we literally hear the sound of that hiss alluded to several lines earlier.

At the same time, the image of the serpentine eye itself taps into one of the most familiar visual tropes of literary and cinematic horror. It is with her first glimpse of her child's eyes that Polanski's Rosemary understands just what sort of so-called baby she has given birth to, and through the altered appearance of Father Damien's eyes at the climax of *The Exorcist* that we understand him to have drawn the demon from Regan into himself. Such gestures were a cliché even by this point. Despite Truman Capote's over-arching concern with keeping evil mundane and glamourless in his non-fiction masterpiece, *In Cold Blood*, he cannot resist tapping into just this vein in introducing the damaged physiognomy of one of the book's two central culprits:

> …the lips were slightly aslant, the nose askew, and his eyes not only situated at uneven levels but of uneven size, the left eye being truly serpentine, with a venomous, sickly-blue squint that although it was involuntarily acquired, seemed nevertheless to warn of bitter sediment at the bottom of his nature (Capote, 1994: 31).

More broadly, the physiological mingling of the serpent and the human is a trope whose roots run deep in narrative, non-biblical imaginings of the encounter between humanity and the forces of evil. This forms the site of one of the most disturbing images of Dante's *Inferno*, for instance, as one of the damned is mounted by a six-legged serpent whose body is entirely enfolded with his own:

> Ivy was never so rooted to a tree as the horrid beast entwined its own limbs round the other's; then, as if they had been of hot wax, they stuck together and mixed their colors, and neither the one nor the other now seemed what it was at first (Alighieri, 1970: 263)

[Ellera abbarbicata mai non fue
    ad alber sì, come l'orribil fiera
    per l'altrui membra avviticchiò le sue.
Poi s'appiccar, come di calda cera
    fossero stati, e mischiar lor colore,
    né l'un né l'altro già parea quell ch'era... (Alighieri, 1970: 262)]

Just such a mingling finds a triumphant recent cinematic manifestation in the 2005 *Harry Potter and the Goblet of Fire*, in the serpentine visage of Lord Voldemort's newly corporeal self (played by a nearly unrecognizable Ralph Fiennes).

As if to ratify our central character's awakening to dramatic role-playing, no sooner is this pivotal line out of Dani's mouth than his growling alter ego-cum-tormentor returns, speaking of "the nature of the beast" with the beast's own dramatic voice. When the shrieking Dani resumes—together with the wall of guitars, bass, and drums, hammering away at the song's closest approach to utter chaos—the poetry begins at once to move in a new direction. Where the horrors glimpsed in the song thus far were greeted, as I have argued, with an affirmative tone evocative of the religious celebrant (convinced that this was, after all, a "better Armageddon"), all sense of celebration vanishes from this point onward. As if speaking now as a living, breathing participant in the action, our unenviable protagonist suddenly owns up to the fact that the torments he has been describing are actually going to hurt ("our screams shall trail to angels"), wailing his way toward something that begins to bear a suspicious resemblance to repentance, or at the very least regret. Indeed we soon arrive at a profoundly ambivalent encounter with the possibility of Christian redemption, one that seems calculated to maximize ambiguity on the subject: "We should have cut our losses, as at Calvary." If our understanding of the black metal genre and its customs does not permit the possibility of a genuine Christian message at this moment, anti-Christian interpretations of this line are certainly available: we might imagine, for instance, that Calvary's lesson was to nip supernatural forces in the bud when they try to come to earth—Jesus was killed, according to this logic, before he could do any real harm, and these latter-day forces of evil might have been destroyed in the same way. Yet a frankly Christian interpretation of the line is perhaps more plausible, according to which the lesson of Calvary was that, yes, humans are sinners, but they can occasionally be offered the possibility of redemption. Some seized on that opportunity in acknowledging Jesus, in his death, to have been the Son of God, and we might, if we had had the foresight, have turned toward Jesus again before the onset of these end times. Thus, if the turn from the realm of hymn to the realm of fictional horror can be understood as an exculpation of the song's own engagement with evil, this exculpatory effort is mirrored in our protagonist's press toward forgiveness.

It is too late, of course. The beast scoffs upon its return, elaborating slightly on its grim earlier pronouncement: "This is the end of everything you have ever known, / Buried like vanquished reason," and so forth. At this prompting, our protagonist—bringing his confessional impulse to a dramatic culmination—owns up to our collective culpability in the most egregious of human crimes, those of the Nazis, whom we apparently followed out of the sheer human love for being whipped into frenzy. Words are spat out faster than ever, as if from the mouth of one begging for his life: "Heiling new flesh, read, then roared to a crooked cross and a Holy Cause, What else to be whipped to frenzy for?"

If the opening of Episode II marked a moment of signal importance, the opening of the final ritornello comprises another. The ritornello is set off from what came before by a chasm of silence, a brief glimpse over the edge of the abyss, then initiated with a noise not even remotely related to song, sounding like nothing so much as a good, cathartic vomit (a sound heard not infrequently across the black metal repertoire). This final ritornello kicks in with the same line that initiated the second one—"This is the end of everything"—which we have now heard twice from the mouth of the beast (this transition is shown in Example 3). But it is now the screaming register that takes the line. This is no longer the voice of the beast itself, but of the human being whose capitulation to the will of the beast is displayed as complete; the frantic rhythmic vitality of the confession that came immediately before is trammeled into even quarter notes, any hope of redemption through repentance abandoned in the resigned acknowledgment of the fate higher cosmic forces have dictated. As with many moments of structural recapitulation in classical music's "sonata-form" movements (see, e.g., Rogers, 1981 and Webster, 1950), this line articulates the song's golden section, falling just after the four-minute mark of this 6:36 song[6]:

Heil - ing new flesh, read, then roared to a crook - ed cross and a ho - ly cause,

What else to be whipped in fren -zy for? [vomiting] This is the end of ev' -ry - thing!

Example 3: Cradle of Filth, "From the Cradle to Enslave," excerpt

The dramatic logic here runs directly parallel to that of the operatic duet, particularly that vibrant strand that might be called the duet of musical seduction, in which one character must be persuaded to adopt the musical and lyrical material of the other. In the celebrated opening duet of Mozart's *Marriage of Figaro*, for instance, Figaro is systematically persuaded to abandon his own strapping melody for his bride's lilting strains. Mozart's next opera, *Don Giovanni*, includes a duettino whose climax encapsulates this process in a most concentrated form (Example 4). Don Giovanni has spent the first two minutes of this number trying to persuade the peasant girl Zerlina to come away to his house with him. When she capitulates at last, the moment is dramatized musically around the word "andiam": "Let's go." Don Giovanni sings it twice, and we know Zerlina is lost completely at the moment she proves willing to sing it herself.

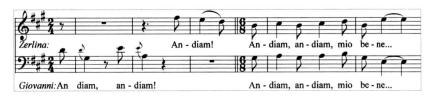

Example 4: Mozart/Daponte, *Don Giovanni*, No. 7: Duettino (vocal lines), excerpt

It is precisely this logic at work as the beast's twice-sounded line is heard, at last, from its victim.

Of paramount importance here is just what this scream can be said to signify. Through the opening stretch of the song, the hymn-like portion, the screams make what amounts to musical sense, as the symbolic musical inversion of the ideal of vocal purity with which traditional sacred music is so thoroughly shot through. Yet as Dani screams, "This is the end of everything," the entire semiotic context has shifted. This scream is not musical, but cinematic; this is not the traditional heavy metal scream born of the fantasy of power (in Walser's persistent analysis),[7] but the horror film scream of terror and despair. The song closes with a series of exchanges on this line, traded between the high and the low registers. Cinematic to the end, Dani utters his final line in something like a strangled cry, evidently prevented by a real-time tryst with catastrophe from completing his last sentence.

* * *

In a 2003 interview, Dani Filth posed what he evidently took to be a rhetorical question concerning the metal artist's right to that realm of fantastic horror unreservedly available to authors of fiction: "If Stephen King, Anne Rice and J. K. Rowling can bring the dark arts to literature, why not to the whole musical genre?" (Muir, 2003: 7). If the foregoing reading of the song is accepted, "From the Cradle to Enslave" offers as powerful a musico-poetic emplotment of this process of appropriation as could be asked for, marking, in incremental steps, passage out of the forbidden garden of anti-Christian hymnody toward the socially sanctioned sphere of fictional role-playing.

That is not to say, however, that there are not perfectly good answers to Dani's question. For there is in fact a range of reasons that the whole notion of "horror metal"—conceived in direct analogy to horror fiction and film—might feel less instinctively tenable than the notion of the hymn-like affirmation of faith for which black metal tends to be taken, explicitly or not, by its detractors. I close these remarks with a glance at the ways in which horror, if it is to be accepted at all as the principal point of genre reference for Cradle of Filth's work, must be accepted in what we might term an aesthetically reduced state.

At the heart of the matter is one seemingly inescapable hurdle: "From the Cradle to Enslave" isn't all that scary. Indeed, when critic Shawn Jam Hill describes one vampiric undertaking on Cradle of Filth's 2006 *Thornography* album as "hell bent on creating an evil image that is about as startling as a kid in a Chewbacca costume" (Hill, 2006: B2), he points to what is in fact a systemic issue in the band's claims to the status of "horror." Frequent critical charges of "camp" contain more than a kernel of legitimacy, but do not really get to the heart of the issue: even the campiest horror films—the good ones, anyhow—tend to engage those mechanics of storytelling that are calculated to inspire fear. The imagery employed in Cradle of Filth's work, and much of the black metal genre in general, may well achieve the level of the horrific and dreadful, but numerous stylistic and sociological factors would seem to work against its attainment of actual horror or dread, or even serious aspiration to it.

Metal is clearly capable of situating the personae of its speaking subjects firmly within the realm of fictional role-playing, as I have been at pains to show in the foregoing discussion, and the imagery and subject matter of much black metal can be traced to non-musical horror narratives. Yet many nearly ubiquitous traits of those narratives—the early establishment of a "normal" world into which horror makes incremental incursions, the archetypal "discovery" plot, a cast comprised of skeptics, "discoverers" (in Noël Carroll's nomenclature), victims, and survivors—find little or no analogy in the great bulk of this music.[8]

Perhaps most significant is the question of how successfully metal could ever achieve that element of prolonged, *for-God's-sake-don't-open-that-door* suspense on which much of the experience of horror in its mainstream forms depends. "[T]he relation between horror and suspense is contingent," Carroll observes, "but also unavoidably pervasive. Thus, in order to illuminate thoroughly the way horror stories function, one must show how horror and suspense can work together—albeit contingently—in concert" (Carroll, 1990: 129). Whether the "stories" of black metal function in this way at all is a question that must await further study, but it seems clear enough that this is not their primary goal (our experience of the quiet passage at the outset of Episode II, discussed above, may be steeped in the tense certainty that the song's prevailing musical ferocity will soon return, but the experience is hardly comparable to watching, say, an on-screen protagonist make her tentative way down the darkened upstairs hallway of an abandoned house toward the closed door of a bedroom in which a light has mysteriously been switched on). It is scarcely surprising that one searches the faces of the assembled crowd at a Cradle of Filth concert in vain for any sign of those responses—the hiding of the eyes (or ears), the involuntary grimace, motionless anticipation—we routinely observe in the audience of a successful horror film. Everything about the teaming, noisy, motion-saturated experience of this music in its typical public presentation militates against the accumulation of dread: a private affair by nature.

If there is hope for the ultimate acceptance of a song like "From the Cradle to Enslave" as a specimen of horror, it would almost certainly have to be framed in terms of habits in the consumption of horror in general that call into question the continued relevance of those narrative practices, perhaps even those psychological responses, that I have put forward as central to the genre. In the wake of *The Exorcist* (1973), Linda Badley has argued,

> [h]orror became a hysterical text or a theater of cruelty specializing in representations of the human anatomy *in extremis*—in disarray or deconstruction, in metamorphosis, invaded or engulfing, in sexual difference, monstrous otherness, or Dionysian ecstasy: the body fantastic (Badley, 1995: 26).

One telling moment in Bret Easton Ellis' 1985 *Less Than Zero*—an unblinking portrait of youth culture at its most jaded—displays an experience of cinematic horror in which the spectacle of cruelty is all that matters, the pursuit of localized, image-driven sensation overthrowing the traditional emotional *raison d'être* of the horror narrative:

> We drive to Westwood. The movie Kim and Blair want to see starts at ten
> and is about this group of young pretty sorority girls who get their throats
> slit and are thrown into a pool. I don't watch a lot of the movie, just the
> gory parts (Ellis, 1985: 97).

Documented ties on the part of male audiences (not female) between
a taste for graphic cinematic violence and a fondness for hardcore por-
nography further suggest that it is in brutish spectacle alone, rather than
tightly-wrought storytelling, that at least one segment of the modern
horror market seeks gratification (Zuckerman, 1996: 153).

Tellingly, the aesthetic experience Ellis describes—reduced to "just
the gory parts"—captures precisely the feeling of the music video for
"From the Cradle to Enslave," in which shots of the band performing
the song (in a church crawling with mutant dwarves and the occasional
quivering, vaguely neonatal latex monstrosity) are interlaced with brief
scenes of band members alternately doling out and receiving gruesome,
fatal injuries. It is no exaggeration to say that the video contains as much
graphic bloodletting as many contemporary slasher films, but disencum-
bered of all but the slightest trace of plot or character development.
Though the sort of violence depicted in this video has little to do with the
subject matter of the song itself, the video is certainly helpful in coming
to terms with the fundamentally non-narrative, image-governed conception of the craft of horror upon which the song's admission to the genre
may well depend. If the pursuit of genuine fear is no longer the issue,
an ominous atmosphere, a shadowy cast of gruesome monstrosities, a
sketchy protagonist, and a set of horrific impressions may suffice to make
the case.

Securing a place for themselves alongside the ranks of horror's literary and cinematic craftspeople is not, of course, a strategy guaranteed
to endear Cradle of Filth to all listeners in the black metal community.
In his online review of Cradle of Filth's retrospective 2001 collection,
Lovecraft & Witchhearts, metal fan Jeb Branin demurs: "Does anybody
really like this horror-movie-soundtrack metal…? Cradle of crap is more
like it" (http://www.inmusicwetrust.com/articles/50k04.html). If record
sales and concert receipts are any indication, the answer to Jeb's question would have to be, yes, people eat up this horror-movie-soundtrack
metal. And if fundamental tensions remain between the pulls of black
metal's purest ambitions and its cross-pollination with more mainstream
spheres of cultural production, Cradle of Filth have shown that this very
border territory, the dynamic moment of crossing over, can itself com-
prise a most stimulating creative canvas.

Notes

1.   On the panic heavy metal and related genres have prompted—explored in depth by Weinstein and Walser—see, too, Chastagner, 1999 and Wright, 2000.

2.   The band's major releases—album-length unless otherwise indicated—are *The Principle of Evil Made Flesh* (1994), *V Empire* or *Dark Faerytales in Phallustein* (EP, 1996), *Dusk and Her Embrace* (1996), *Cruelty and the Beast* (1998), *From the Cradle to Enslave* (EP, 1999), *Midian* (2000), *Bitter Suites to Succubi* (mini-LP, 2001), *Love-craft and Witch Hearts* (retrospective anthology, 2002), *Live Bait for the Dead* (2002), *Damnation and a Day* (2003), *Nymphetamine* (2004), and *Thornography* (2006).

3.   According to figures reported on Voote.com, Cradle of Filth in fact came in dead last in the voting, though the field was tight, with Cradle's 90 votes falling only 28 below the winner, Slipknot. (http://www.voote.com/jsp/WAppServerPage.jsp?TransID=RVOTES01&VoteID=18).

4.   Though related only tangentially to the particular formal issues at work here, Harris M. Berger lays a thoughtful groundwork for further study concerning the often subtle rhythmic logic of the multi-sectional heavy metal song, viewed through the lens of the drummer's experience (Berger, 1997: esp. 475–78).

5.   Without wishing to clutter these pages with technical jargon, a few further words of clarification will be helpful to readers with some conversance in matters of music theory. All of the chords that occur over the bass lines shown in Example 2 are "root position" chords; that is, where the bass plays a Bb, it is a Bb chord we hear in the guitars, not, say, a G-minor chord with a Bb in the bass. Naturally, the bulk of these chords are not complete major or minor triads, but heavy metal's characteristic "power chords," consisting only of the bass note shown and the pitch a perfect fifth above it (D and A, for example, or C# and G#).

6.   The "Golden Section" refers to that division by which the ratio of the smaller portion to the larger (e.g., the remainder of the song to its foregoing span) is identical to the ratio of the larger portion to the whole: around .618. It occurs just shy of the 4:05 mark in this case, in the middle of the final syllable of "everything."

7.   Suggesting that we must move outside of Walser's persistent fascination with the economy of "power" in understanding the semiotic function of Dani's scream here is not to imply that Walser is inattentive to the issues at play in this discussion. Quite the contrary. In his analysis of Judas Priest's "Electric Eye," for example, Walser teases out much the same sort of moral ambivalence I have explored in "From the Cradle to Enslave," observing that the song "semiotically calls up power and danger and offers identification with both sides: both the threat and the thrill of concentrated power" (Walser, 1993: 164). And the distinction I have sought to draw between hymn and fictional narrative, though not framed in this way, lies at the heart of Walser's brief account of Iron Maiden's "The Number of the Beast," whose chorus sounds like an affirmation of evil only if we ignore the narrative framework provided by the verses, in which the speaker plays the role of a dissenting victim (Walser, 1993: 152).

8.   Clearly horror exists in non-narrative forms as well, most distinctly in much of Edgar Allen Poe's poetry, and in the visual art tradition encompassing the work of Hieronymus Bosch, Francisco Goya, H. R. Geiger, and others. If our task here is

to locate a resonant reference point for black metal among the predominant horror genres of contemporary popular culture, however, these models seem of limited relevance at best (though a fuller study of this particular topic would, of course, involve coming to terms with Geiger's work in the realms of film set and creature design). Needless to say, the studious floridity of Dani Filth's lyrics—"From the Cradle to Enslave" employs 57 different, highly inventive, verbs, for instance, with only the most minimal repetition—communicates more directly with Poe's poetry or H. P. Lovecraft's flights of atmospheric scene-setting than Stephen King's linear prose.

Chapter 3

When Demons Come Calling:
Dealing with the Devil and Paradigms of Life in African American Music

Anthony B. Pinn

Finally, be strong in the Lord, and in the strength of his might.
Put on the whole armor of God, that you may be able to stand against the
wiles of the devil.
For we wrestle not against flesh and but against principalities,
against powers, against the rulers of the darkness of this world,
against spiritual wickedness in high places.
Ephesians 6:10–12 (KJV)

The imagery and assumed theo-existential truth of the above passage
has both explicitly and implicitly haunted and guided the ethical sensibilities of the dominant modalities of African American religion in the
United States—i.e., African American Christian churches—for centuries.
African American Christianity has drawn its vocabulary and grammar, its
imagery, symbolism, and posture toward the world from the rich stories
that make up the Hebrew Bible and the New Testament. Perspectives
on the complex nature and framework of human relationships are given
their weight and content in large part from the workings of situations outlined in scripture. In this regard, African American Christianity, as Ephesians 6:10–12 (above) would suggest, presents life struggles as tension
between physical forces and non-physical forces, between transcendent
realities and mundane presences intertwined within human history—
angelic and demonic personalities.

Theological imagery and doctrinal assertions, in various regions
of the United States, speak to this arrangement of synergy between
celestial and mundane forces. This is certainly the case within African
American evangelical circles, where this rhetoric and perception of the
workings of the world are most vividly expressed. The Church of God
in Christ, the fastest growing Christian denomination in African American communities, says the following concerning the reality of angels
and demons:

The Bible uses the term "angel" (a heavenly body) clearly and primarily to denote messengers or ambassadors of God with such scripture references as Revelations 4:5 [*sic*], which indicates their duty in heaven to praise God (Psalm 103:20), to do God's will (St. Matthew 18:10) and to behold his face. But since heaven must come down to earth, they also have a mission to earth. The Bible indicates that they accompanied God in the Creation, and also that they will accompany Christ in His return in Glory... Demons denote unclean or evil spirits; they are sometimes called devils or demonic beings. They are evil spirits, belonging to the unseen or spiritual realm, embodied in human beings. The Old Testament refers to the prince of demons, sometimes called Satan (Adversary) or Devil, as having power and wisdom, taking the habitation of other forms such as the serpent (Genesis 3:1). The New Testament speaks of the Devil as Tempter (St. Matthew 4:3) and it goes on to tell the works of Satan, The Devil, and Demons as combating righteousness and good in any form, proving to be an adversary to the saints. Their chief power is exercised to destroy the mission of Jesus Christ. It can well be said that the Christian Church believes in Demons, Satan, and Devils. We believe in their power and purpose. We believe they can be subdued and conquered as in the commandment to the believer by Jesus. "In my name they shall cast out Satan and the work of the Devil and to resist him and then he will flee (withdraw) from you" (St. Mark 16:17).[1]

Not all historical African American denominations provide such strong statements concerning the reality of unseen forces influencing human existence. Yet such commentary finds its way into African American Christianity in ways not confined to the formal doctrinal creeds and official theological postures of particular denominations. Paul Tillich's remark holds true in this case: Religion is the substance of culture; and culture is the language of religion. Regarding this, one is just as likely to find discussion of these invisible forces battling for influence in human history expressed in both oft-called "sacred" and "secular" songs as in formal theology.

Spirituals and the Worlds at War

Scholars such as John Lovell, Jr, have argued for the existence of spirituals long before the formation of independent African American churches in the nineteenth century, and it is through these haunting musical tunes that enslaved Africans articulated their rudimentary religious sensibilities and theological assumptions (see Lovell 1986). These songs speak of the slave's sense of a God present in the world, poised to bring about the redemption of the enslaved and the "righting" of the world. This God is understood to be loving, kind, just, and author of history understood as teleological in nature, both during the time of the biblical stories and the historical moment in which the slaves found themselves. In the words of one song: "Didn't my Lord deliver Daniel, deliver, Daniel, deliver Daniel? And why not everyone?" Or,

> God is a God!
> God don't never change!
> God is a God
> An' He always will be God (from Cone, 1972: 35).

God's plan for the fulfillment of human history, complete with its reframing of African American life, is accomplished through the perfect blend of divinity and humanity in the form of the Christ Event. Drawing from stories of the activities and attitudes of Christ, along with a deep sensitivity to Christ's humble family context, enslaved Africans embraced him and drew bold existential and ontological links between themselves and this representative of God on earth. They found in the material poverty surrounding his biblically rehearsed birth, and in the suffering that informed his *raison d'être*, epistemological links and similarities to themselves: Enslaved Africans faced hardship and undeserved pain and, more to the point, their plight would be rectified through the workings of God in human history.

> Children, we shall be free
> When the Lord shall appear.
> Give ease to the sick, give sight to the blind,
> Enable the cripple to walk;
> He'll raise the dead from under the earth,
> And give them permission to talk (from Cone, 1972: 35).

The uniqueness of Christ is the perfect balance between transcendent forces or realities and physical presence represented through the God/ man, Christ.

The absurdity of the slave system, with its Christian tendencies, gave rise to a cartography of struggle bringing into play a host of forces, only some of them physical but all of them deeply important and felt. The Christ Event confronts the evil found in the world guided by the work-ings of Satan and Satan's dominion. In the spirituals, enslaved Christians spoke of the battle between good and evil, and noted their souls and their existential condition as the prize and the battlefield respectively. In the words of one song:

> Kneel and pray, so the devil won't harm me
> Try my best for to serve the lord
> Kneel and pray, so the devil won't harm me
> Hallelujah[2]

Juxtaposed to the work of demonic forces, spirituals speak of the company of angels as a life-affirming and heaven-assuring event:

> O, I'm going to march with the tallest angel
> O, yes, march with the tallest angel
> O, yes, march with the tallest angel
> When my work is done[3]

Within the spirituals, proper human activity involves a push against demonic forces and an embrace of angelic forces—the assumption being the ultimate welfare of humanity is tied to the triumph of good over evil—the kingdom of God over Satan.

Blues and Deals with the Devil

In the blues such a distinction is not assumed. What is best for the individual (only limited attention is given to community) as outlined in the blues might entail a relationship with demonic forces over against the Christian God. Such a willingness to entertain demonic forces might suggest one rationale for calling the blues the "Devil's music" in that the music was conversant with Christian principles, grammar and vocabulary, but showed a willingness to entertain forces Christians fear and fight.

Some strains of the blues, perhaps to signify Christian assumptions within African American communities or as a genuine acknowledgment of a spiritual realm, speak to the workings of spiritual forces often presented in physical form.

> Devil's gonna git you,
> Devil's gonna git you,
> Oh, the devil's gonna git you,
> The way you're carryin' on.[4]

In this way, blues artists acknowledged the manner in which we move through the world accompanied and influenced by unseen forces:

> Black ghost, black ghost, please stay away from my door
> Black ghost, black ghost, will you please stay away from my door
> Yeah you know you worry po' Lightnin' so now, I just can't sleep no more.[5]

Whereas the boundaries between these forces and their effectiveness in human life are clear and based on the Christian faith for those singing the spirituals, for those motivated by the blues there is a more utilitarian approach—one that allows for flirtation with both angelic and demonic forces depending on which might offer the most efficient assistance. The blues lack the certainty of a teleological arrangement of history that gives the Christian comfort; instead, the blues are comfortable with paradox, or with a blending of opposites, manipulated and celebrated by the cleaver. Blues chronicler Robert Palmer captures this epistemological complexity when saying,

> Blues lyrics could be light, mocking, risqué, or could deal forthrightly with the most highly charged subject matter – intimate details of love, sex, and desire; a fascination with travel for its own sake that was rooted in the years of black captivity; the hypocrisies and foibles of preachers and other upstanding folks; the fantastic and often disturbing imagery of dreams; the practice and tools of magic and conjury; aggressive impulses that had to be severely repressed in everyday life; and in some blues, particularly the Delta Blues of Robert Johnson, an unabashed identification with the leader of the world's dark forces, the ultimate other (Palmer, 1982: 18).

The blues speak casually of life circumstances, the play and interaction of contrary forces—both visible and invisible—in ways of great discomfort to those singing the spirituals. There is, in the blues, no great fear of "hell," nor great yearning for "heaven" in that the former can't be any worse than the oppression they currently encountered. The latter takes a back seat to the significance and "feel" of life's earthbound pleasures and desires. The sense of commonality found in the blues is premised on the desire for advancement, for goods, for good feelings, for the good stuff of life. "Powers and principalities" offering excess to the riches of life, regardless of their nature or disposition, are approached. In most cases loyalty is first to the individual, based on the interests and desires of the individual, and codified by any force capable of making those desires real. Perhaps this understanding suggests one of the reasons for Pettie Wheatstraw's labeling as the "Devil's Son-in-Law and the High Sheriff from Hell" (in Palmer, 1982: 115).

I take no moral stance here, and I make no effort to judge the rhetoric and imagery of demonic forces in partnership or as foe. Rather, my concern is to suggest the rich and robust sense of operative forces pervading and influencing human existence found within the blues. I am aware of musicologist Jon Michael Spencer's critique of blues scholarship that uncritically assumes the blues to have evil intentions, a certain reading of blues as "devil music" in ways that simply reinforce stereotypical depictions of African Americans, and suggest a rather flat and reified notion of the nature and meaning of evil (see Spencer, 1993). I would agree with Spencer that the blues are not "evil" *per se*. That is to say, there is nothing about the blues suggesting it is intrinsically flawed; rather, the tension regarding the non-"godly" dimension of the blues seems an imposed paradoxical arrangement as opposed to being generated internally. In other words, the dilemma of commitments regarding blues and evil stems from a dominant Christian worldview projected onto the blues. Yet, even in saying this, I would not go so far as to say there is no interaction (if not in actuality at least in rhetoric) with forces considered evil by blues artists.

I want to suspend Spencer's assumptions concerning the normative state of Christianity as the religious orientation of African Americans, and thereby avoid his rather flat depiction of evil's function in American religion and life. Applying this to musical talent in African American communities, I argue while some gave thanks to God for their abilities—assuming God favored them with great talent as a gift—others spoke of a bargain with demonic forces as the source of their musical (and social) prowess. None represents this arrangement better than Robert Johnson.

Born in Mississippi, Robert Johnson is perhaps the blues artists most closely linked, as folktales would suggest, to demonic forces. The hardships of his early life—relocations, family disruptions—may have had something to do with his early interest in the blues, which was nurtured through the mentoring of Willie Brown, Charley Patton and Son House in Robinsonville, Mississippi. During these early years, legend has it, Johnson's musical ability was of limited appeal, pale in comparison to the other musicians making their way through the Delta. However, this changed after Johnson left the area for an uncertain period of time and returned with staggering musical abilities. Accounts by scholars suggest he worked under the tutelage of another musician, practicing his craft, and only returned when his abilities were at a high level.

For others, the account more explicitly involves demonic forces in the service of humans—for a price. By accounts provided by family members and others, Johnson's new abilities resulted from him selling his soul to the Devil in exchange for unparalleled talent. Some of his songs are pointed out as testimony to this exchange (Palmer, 1982: 111–31). While some artists give visual depictions of the demonic—often portrayed consistent with negative color symbolism as a large black figure—Johnson gave no such attention to the appearance of the demonic. Rather, his concern revolved simply around the ability of such forces to impinge upon human existence. Johnson recognizes the presence of such forces impinging on his life:

> I got to keep moving, I got to keep moving
> Blues falling down like hail, blues falling down like hail
> Mmm, blues falling down like hail, blues falling down like hail
> And the day keeps on remindin' me, there's a hellhound on my trail
> Hellhound on my trail,
> hellhound on my trail.[6]

Or, the connection between Johnson and the Devil as one of exchange is also present in shaded ways in the following lines:

> Early this mornin'
> >   when you knocked upon my door
> Early this mornin', ooh
> >   when you knocked upon my door
> And I said, "Hello, Satan,
> >   I believe it's time to go."[7]

Johnson alludes to the consequences of securing musical abilities from the Devil: One must surrender one's soul, one's self to forces beyond one's control. Hence, even this deal with invisible forces is only a temporary correction in that it is followed ultimately by damnation. And, much of the time prior to that is spent anticipating the inevitable, feeling the pursuit by "hell hounds." The alternative for Johnson appears to be movement, unpredictable and constant movement:

> I got ramblin', I got ramblin' on my mind.
> I got ramblin', I got ramblin' all on my mind.[8]

Had Johnson simply worked hard, under the guidance of formidable musicians, absorbing lessons without distraction, nor competition; or had he made a deal with evil forces? Even if the answer to the latter is "no," Johnson recognized the significance of such imagery for projecting a reputation as a "bad man," a formidable figure whose activities and music produced a deep gut reaction that both repelled and attracted listeners. Death for blues performers familiar with the world of diverse forces did not necessarily entail an end to all events. Rather it marked a transition, a movement to a new venue for activity; but one arranged in exchange for a liminal period of prowess. There is a sense of the tragic in this move in that life often remained difficult—marked by recognition, but not without its downside. They lived "hard" and died "hard."

In certain ways, even a deal with the Devil involved a signifying of such demonic forces in that at times bad men "ruled" hell through the maintenance of their self-centered and destructive ways. Or, in other cases, they joined the ranks of unseen forces and continued to move through human time and space—the "deal" with demonic forces and its aftermath both shrouded in mystery. Perhaps such awareness accounts for Robert Johnson's request for burial near the highway so that his evil spirit might continue to travel vis-à-vis the bus line. The need to hit the road, to traverse time and space, is not dampened by death:

You may bury my body, ooh
    down by the highway side
So my old evil spirit can catch a Greyhound bus and ride.[9]

Such deals with feared forces could only enhance his reputation in that Johnson understood lyrics alone (many of which he borrowed from other artists) could not cement his success and musical legacy. Rather, the personae of the artists, the overall ethos of *being* surrounding him needed to entail the wiles of the trickster and the dealings of the "bad man." In short, association, real or imagined, with demonic forces served the purpose.

Even this affiliation, this connection to the demonic, served as a modality of resistance to staid and reified notions of morality and ethics tied to what these blues men considered the hypocrisy of the Christian faith. In dealing with the Devil, they signified the claims of the Christian faith (its doctrine, theology—particularly its theodicies). These bluesmen instead embraced what Christianity condemned—erotic desires, material goods, and revenge. In this way, Johnson and other blues figures like him were involved in an inverted spiritual arrangement—whereby the needs and wants of the body were given priority over what Christians considered the proper welfare of the soul.

Despised black bodies sought assistance from despised "dark" forces. By so doing, it is possible artists sought to use metaphysical evil to battle the damage done by the socio-political and economic fall-out of racism as demonic force: Evil negates evil. Put another way, novelist James Baldwin in reflecting on his years as a young minister in a black evangelical church argued that, in his neighborhood, everyone belonged to someone: This was the nature of survival in a predator world. "Belong" provided a "space" and socio-cultural arrangements, the nurturing of talents and abilities. Early on, for Baldwin, "belong" meant the development of preaching ability that generated acceptance and appreciation. Musical artists seek commitment to a similar philosophy of relationship: They *belong* to something. For some, the proper modality of belonging was guided by the "rightness" of the Christian faith and its commitment to Christ. Yet, for others, the proper space for development of self and talent involved a relationship with demonic forces.

The Demonic and Rap Music

The bad man, the rebellious figure, continues his flirtation with demonic realities within the form of certain rappers. Such rap artists share many of the existential commitments and the moral sensibilities of blues performers like Johnson, and this includes a similar stance on synergy between demonic forces and rebellious humans.

While rap tends to avoid a direct appeal to demonic forces for the development of musical abilities and other markers of success in a troubled world, rap is not devoid of references to sensitivity to the presence and workings of demonic forces. Yet, rather than joining league with them actively, some rappers simply work in ways that seem influenced by the negative tendencies and character of the demonic, while others step through the world seeing the demonic lodged firmly around them. At the very least, some rap artists note an awareness of a delicate balance between life influenced by the divine and by the demonic, and press it into a macabre worldview. Such a tortured existence, one hanging between an absurd world and the workings of invisible forces impinging upon human existence, marks, for example, lyrics by Scarface.

Born Jordan Bradley on November 9, 1970, in Houston, Texas, Scarface made his early fame (or position as infamous) through the rap group "The Ghetto Boys," whose lyrics spoke without remorse of the "dark" side of ghetto existence. This group presented itself as predatory and determined to exercise its wants and desires without attention to moral and ethical consequences.

Since the early 1990s, Scarface has produced solo projects that continue along the same path of existential angst but with a glimpse here and there into the world of "powers and principalities" that influences but is not synonymous with the arrangements of human history.[10] As blues artists note the manner in which evil can follow "bad men," from birth, Scarface presents himself as dogged by the demonic even before he is able to consciously choose sides. He notes:

> I don't remember much about being born
> But I do remember this: I was conceived on February 10th
> Complications detected in my early months of ballin'
> Around my sonogram you could see the evil was swarmin'[11]

Furthermore, death is ever present and in some instances Scarface dissects the details of life's surrender to death: "you start your journey into outer space. You see yourself in the light but you're still feeling outta place."[12] Scarface, like so many other rappers, makes an appeal to relationship with the Divine as the last chance for humanity; but, he also recognizes the tensions between the forces of "good" pushing for this sort of relationship and the demonic that influences humans to behave in less than ethically robust ways. From his perspective, the existence of these two competing forces is real, oozing from every aspect of human existence in the 'hood. Death lurks around the corner, and the life of a "G" requires recognition of this and a willingness to accept the negatively serendipitous nature of such a life. Think in terms of the lyrics to "Make Your Peace" in which Scarface frames the demonic in terms of an alternate world invisible to human eyes, but nonetheless real:

> I had a dream and seen a double sun,
>> a different world was in the makin'
> The rule of this new world was Satan.[13]

Deals with demonic forces do not appear as commonplace in rap, although 2Pac's verse to "Smile," on Scarface's *Untouchable*, directly addresses this arrangement through which goods and prowess are secured:

> No fairy tales for this young black male
> Some see me stranded in this land of hell, jail, and crack sales
> Hustlin' and heart be a nigga culture
>> Or the repercussions while bustin' on backstabbin' vultures
> Sellin' my soul for material riches, fast cars and bitches
> Wishin' I live my life a legend, immortalized in pictures.[14]

In spite of the above, on the whole, rap artists do not generally suggest that one try to bargain with and out maneuver these demonic forces. On the other hand, one should simply recognize their presence and their impact on life in that such forces are everywhere, identifiable in the activities of neighbors and friends by the observant. In Scarface's words, "who the fuck is you gonna trust when your road dog is scheming? And every other corner, you're passin' a different demon..."[15] The world involves an absurd arrangement of forces that one cannot completely control, but that one can embrace or signify. It is this perspective that artists such as Scarface accept and articulate in their music, absorbing the paradox of life with a rather knowing way and with a somewhat defiant posture.

The difficulty of moving through a world haunted by such forces is not limited to Scarface and his existential angst and metaphysical uncertainties. Artists such as Snoop Dogg also wrestle with the various forces present in the world. Born October 20, 1971 in Long Beach, California, to Beverly Broadus and Vernall Varnado, Snoop Dogg's (aka Calvin Broadus) life was marked by the deep concern and religious orientation of his mother and the absence of his father. One of the few things given to him by his father, Snoop Dogg remarks, was a love for music. This love, combined with talent and skills "given by God", mark the emergence of a rap career. In short, he notes:

> In every rap I ever recorded, in the mad flow of every street-corner free-style I ever represented, there was only one thing I wanted to get across: the way it is. Not the way I might want it to be. Not the way I think *you* might want it to be. But the way it *really* is, on the streets of the 'hoods of America, where life is lived out one day at a time, up against it, with no guarantees… My raps describe what it's like to be a young black man in America today (Snoop Dogg, 1999: 2–3).

Snoop Dogg's rap shares with the blues a deep sensitivity to the nature and "flow" of life, the manner in which human relationships of all sorts shift and change in a variety of ways. He, like blues artists before him, recognizes the "dark" corners of life, noting both the promise and struggle associated with human existence. His is an existentially driven reality, but one that is also sensitive to the presence of realities uncontrolled by human intension. And the bad man is best equipped to maneuver through this troubled terrain. That is to say, "there was a whole new class of hero coming up—the pimp and the outlaw, the thug and the gangster—and if you wanted to stay alive on the streets of Long Beach or Watts or Compton or anywhere else where the American Dream was falling apart and fading away, you better get with their program. It was the only game in town" (Snoop Dogg, 1999: 41). Like the bad men of the century before him, Snoop Dogg is not troubled by this philosophy of connection; rather, he sees it as being a matter of fact and he embraces the paradox that is life: Stagger Lee reincarnated as a late twentieth-century gangbanger.

While the often ethically questionable nature of some of his lyrics might suggest a paradox, Snoop Dogg views his musical history as teleological in nature, a development framed and orchestrated by a God who has provided him with talent and opportunity. That is to say, "Just when you think you've got Him figured out, some blindside twist of fate makes you understand that you *can't* figure Him out. That's why He's God and you're whoever the hell you are. He calls the shots, makes the moves, and keeps it all in check" (Snoop Dogg, 1999: 149). He views his rap lyrics and music, as described above, as a matter of ministry, a way of transforming life and regenerating relationships. From his perspective all of life (and death) are controlled by forces unseen but felt: "…most of the time, most of us don't sit around thinking on how God can snap our string any time He gets mad or bored or needs another angel in heaven or another demon in hell. Most of the time, if we're honest, we don't give a thought o any of that metaphysical shit" (Snoop Dogg, 1999: 25–26).

Increased sensitivity to the fragile nature, the complex arrangements, of life came to Snoop Dogg, he recounts, when faced with the possibility of life behind bars without the possibility of parole. It was with the threat of freedom removed, of space reified and time controlled by others, that Snoop Dogg's interest in metaphysical questions and concerns was sharpened. He writes:

> My guess is, we all wonder about the time we've got set out for us on the planet and what we're going to do with it before the clock stops ticking and they put us in the ground… And that might be because, for those few, the reality of their life coming to a stone-cold stop is more than just some what-if trick their minds play on them. Every once in a while, a human being, no different from you or me, really does face down those odds, and when that happens, nothing is ever the same again (Snoop Dogg, 1999: 188).

Unlike Robert Johnson and numerous other blues performers, there is no hint of conjuration, of folk practices, at work in Snoop Dogg's tale; but the existence of "powers and principalities" seems just as felt, just as compelling. There's a rhetoric of responsibility and accountability in the autobiographical voice of Snoop Dogg that one does not find in blues artists like Robert Johnson; yet there is a paradox to life that resembles the depiction of life offered within so many blues tunes. Perhaps this paradox is even heightened in Snoop Dogg's story in that the battle between the demonic and the divine is made much more vivid.

On August 23, 1993 a man lay dead on the street, and Snoop Dogg and two others would be implicated in his murder. It is this tragic event, from which he was found innocent, that sparked his theological and existential reflection on and wrestling over deals with unseen forces as a framework for navigating the uncertainties of human (non) existence. As Robert Johnson hauntingly portrayed such a deal for talent in several blues tunes, Snoop graphically suggests a deal in exchange for continued life and prowess in "Murder Was the Case," a project spearheaded by Dr Dre (with Snoop Dogg as one of several receiving writer's credit for the title track). According to some, the title track was loosely "tied" to the murder charge Snoop Dogg faced at the time of its release. In his autobiography, however, Snoop Dogg is less than enthusiastic about that project, seeing it as potentially distracting from his solo project, *Doggy-style* ("Murder Was the Case" is also a track on *Doggystyle*).

While arguing the murder charge brought him closer to prayer and God, thereby recognizing the inability of humans to ultimately shape history and control visible and invisible forces, the lyrics suggest a world of forces at work. More important than an autobiographical authenticity to the lyrics—or the validity of seeing the piece as commentary on the trial—is the reflection on demonic vs. divine influence open to human use. Shot, one assumes, due to jealousy over his success, Snoop encounters the various forces marking the geography of human existence—all attempting to gain control of his soul:

> My body temperature falls
> I'm shakin and they breakin tryin to save the Dogg
> Pumpin on my chest and I'm screamin
> I stop breathin, damn I see demons
> Dear God, I wonder can ya save me...[16]

Based on Snoop Dogg's personal narrative of relationship to God, one would assume the deal struck in the track is with the Divine. However, the storyline is not so clear and the ethical system in large part leaves room to wonder. Is the voice he hears after praying that of God, or one of the demons he sees?

> I think it's too late for prayin, hold up
> A voice spoke to me and it slowly started sayin
> "Bring your lifestyle to me I'll make it better"
> How long will I live?
> "Eternal life and forever"
> And will I be the G that I was?
> "I'll make your life better than you can imagine or even dreamed of."[17]

The life Snoop secures as a result of the deal with the unnamed force entails the material goods and control that might make Robert Johnson proud. Yet it is one that does not mirror the more narrow and rigid moral and ethical outlooks generally associated with surrender to Christ, at least as typically presented by African American churches. The theological and ethical message is muddied in that the character's behavior results in a prison sentence. Is this punishment for not practicing more conservative Christian values, or is it simply the uncertain, perhaps double-crossing, arrangements of a deal with the Devil? Is it divine punishment, or the end of one's "run" through life—similar to Robert Johnson's deal with the Devil not preventing a painful death? Only Snoop knows; we are left to wonder with only a few certainties—one being the presence of both "good" and "evil" forces shaping and shifting the nature and substance of human existence.

A Not So Final Word...

A sensitivity to a world packed with both visible and invisible forces mark the lyrical content of African American forms of music such as the blues and rap. In both cases, the more ethically and morally aggressive artists flirt with such forces, signifying them and/or partnering with them based on a deep sense of individualized need and desire. The lyrical content offered by these artists, whether blues figures such as Robert Johnson or rappers such as Scarface and Snoop Dogg, suggest a theological articulation of life premised on the reality of the biblical notion of powers and principalities. While they might not approach such forces as did New Testament writers or as contemporary Christians might hope, they nonetheless move through the world sensitive to the host of forces and realities impinging on life, shaping and transforming it—all the while, in an ironic way, also enriching it. This is certainly one way to read Johnson's deal with the Devil, or Snoop Dogg's dream of an arrangement that provides wealth and power, while delaying death. In either case, there's a haunting and eerie narrative of the battle for the human soul, one firmly lodged in the lyrics of African American music.

Notes

1. http://www.ipfellowshipcogic.org/cogic_doctrine.html_
2. http://www.negrospirituals.com/news-song/all_i_do_the_chunrch_keep_a_grumbling.htm
3. "Members Don't Get Weary," http://www.negrospirituals.com/news-song/members_don_t_get_weary.htm
4. Bessie Smith, "Devil's Gonna Git You," http://www.geocities.com/Bourbon-Street/delta/2541/blbsmith.htm#devil
5. Lightnin' Hopkins, "Black Ghost Blues," http://www.geocities.com/Bourbon-Street/delta/2541/bllhopki.htm#black
6. Robert Johnson, "Hell Hound On My Trail," http://www.geocities.com/BourbonStreet/delta/2541/blrjohns.htm#Hellhound481
7. Robert Johnson, "Me and the Devil Blues," http://xroads.virginia.edu/~MUSIC/blues/matdb.html
8. Robert Johnson, "Ramblin' On My Mind," http://www.bluesforpeace.com/lyrics/rambling-mind.htm
9. Robert Johnson, "Me and the Devil Blues," http://xroads.virginia.edu/~MUSIC/BLUES/matdb.html
10. Whether or not Scarface converted to Islam does not negatively affect this analysis in that the lyrics to the referenced tracks do not clearly indicate an Islamic orientation vs. a Christianity orientation. To the contrary, the imagery and theological language embedded tends to shadow the Christian faith, and the awareness of demons and divine forces appears drawn from the Christian faith.
11. Scarface, "Last of a Dying Breed," *Last of a Dying Breed* (2000).
12. Scarface, "I Seen a Man Die," *The Diary* (2004).
13. Scarface, "Make Your Peace," *Balls and My Word* (2003).
14. 2Pac on Scarface, "Smile," *Untouchable* (1997).
15. Scarface, "Heaven," *The Fix* (2002).
16. Snoop Dogg, "Murder Was the Case," *Doggystyle* (1996).
17. Ibid.

Chapter 4

Dark Theology:
Dissident Commerce, Gothic Capitalism, and the Spirit of Rock and Roll

Charlie Blake

...the demonic is originally defined as irresponsibility... It belongs to a space in which there has not yet resounded the injunction to *respond*; a space in which one does not yet hear the call to explain oneself...
(Derrida, 1995: 3)

Did you ever wake up to find
A day that broke your mind
Destroyed your notions of circular time?
It's just that demon life that's got you in its sway.
It's just that demon life that's got you in its sway.
(Jagger & Richards, "Sway," 1971)

"Hello Satan," I believe it's time to go.
(Johnson, "Me and the Devil Blues," 1961)

Since its ascendancy in the early careers of Elvis Presley, Chuck Berry, and Little Richard, rock music in its various guises and through its end-lessly mutating genres and sub-genres has flirted consistently with an ambiguity essential to both its cultural power and its performativity in the market-place. On the one hand, it has frequently been driven, at least ostensibly, by an aesthetic of dissent from whatever dominant ideo-logical or cultural system is deemed to be in place. On the other hand, albeit with some notable exceptions, those involved in the generation and performance of music are invariably content to enjoy the fruit of their labors within the capitalist regime that enables their promotion and media deification. In this sense, deviance and defiance in Western popular music is generally diverted away from overtly political objec-tives and directed toward more ambivalent cultural targets. And in some cases—particularly within the genres of death metal, black metal, doom, and alternative country—the target has sometimes become explicitly religious, and indeed, theological. In other cases, however, what might be called the "Luciferean" or "Satanic" element in certain strands of

African American blues has combined with a closely related element in the European artistic and literary traditions conventionally associated with certain aspects of the Gothic, to generate a subterranean discourse of deviance and defiance that, once exposed to the light of rationality, not only decomposes into its constituent elements, but also reveals through its process of decomposition a *via negativa* through which the atheology of postmodern or late capitalism can begin to be mapped.

In referring to an atheology of late capitalism, what is being indicated here is a strategically perspectival understanding of its cultural matrix rather than its materiality *per se*, which I have here termed Gothic capitalism, and in which the image of the God of monotheism has not so much been destroyed or murdered as Nietzsche affirmed so lyrically, but has rather been shattered into myriad fragments, each of which still has the potential to reflect, refract, or distort some aspect of its omniscient and omnipotent aura, but in the form of abjection and desire rather than divinity. This image of capitalism and the accompanying shattered image of God can be understood as a conceptualization which draws, albeit indirectly, upon the "hauntology" and "spectropoeisis" of Jacques Derrida in his *Specters of Marx: The State of Debt, the Work of Mourning and the New International* and his *The Gift of Death*, as much as it does upon the ruminations of literary critics, art historians, horror aficionados and cultural or media theorists concerned with the various strands of "Gothicism" within musical subcultures and tribes. Derrida's belated encounter with Marx is useful here insofar is it generates a cluster of concepts (or, at least, pseudo-concepts) that illuminate momentarily the darker spaces of nineteenth-century capitalism's most potent critique and exorcism. In that flash of illumination, however, as Derrida teases out from the texts he seeks to unravel, it is not the clear and rational lines of the material infrastructure that is revealed by critique, but rather, the discarded or hastily concealed impedimenta of Gothic fantasy, from specters and demons to vampires and possessions, scattered like debris through the abandoned corridors of Marx's prose.

The value of Derrida's reading of Marx in *Specters of Marx* is that in highlighting the appearance and disappearance of phantasmal entities in Marx's writing, he is able to trace not only the ghosts that haunted Marx himself, but also those generated in his anatomization of nineteenth-century capitalism. In this sense, the critique gave birth to new specters, most notably those such as the fetishized commodities in that the famous spectralization of objects and things that Marx claimed as one of the central effects of the capitalist revolution. This is a spectralization that takes effect as the bourgeoisie sweeps its course through the century, radically altering social relations as much as those of production, distribution, and exchange. A movement in which, as Marx famously put it:

> All fixed, fast-frozen relations, with their train of ancient and venerable prejudices and opinions are swept away, all newly formed ones become antiquated before they can ossify. All that is solid melts into air, all that is holy is profaned, and man is at last compelled to face with sober senses, his real conditions of life and his relations with his kind (Marx and Engels, 2007: 16).

This vaporization of objects, identities, and relationships in the alembic of capitalism leaves Marx with a problem, however, in that the process of spectralization infects not only the objects and relations of deliquescent capitalism, but also the line of flight from that particular economic and social hell, in the form of the specter of communism which appears so dramatically in the opening sentence of *The Communist Manifesto*. For Derrida, Marx's obsession with the spectral and the phantasmal is indicative of a desire to divide social and economic goods into those that are material and those that simply aren't—in every sense. In other words, he seeks to rid his system of all that refuses to conform to his materialism, and in doing so, creates a haunted mansion whose ghosts refuse to be laid to rest, but instead, and in the best traditions of psychoanalysis, return to him and to us through repetition, abjection, and an aesthetic of violent demise. As one critic has astutely summarized:

> Derrida suggests Marx was obsessed with the figure of the ghost, and that he sought to exorcize it by ontologizing it, that is, by reducing that which haunts to the exclusive alternatives of being or non-being. In effect, he sought to complete a work of mourning that would eliminate spectrality by reducing alterity to the order of ontology (Cutrofello, 2005: 108).

Derrida, of course, refuses this absorption of alterity into ontology, and identifies the quasi-intermediate realm of hauntology as a zone in which we can learn to live with ghosts, rather than seeking to banish them from our shared, equal, and materialist communality. In this, he attempts to project a new kind of communism from his spectral reading of Marx that is always in some sense futural, to come, to be anticipated. However, this vision of communism is as inevitably haunted as any projected by Marx, for as Derrida notes through reference to Hamlet's ghost and the "time out of joint" in which the tragedy is enacted:

> ...everything begins by the apparition of a specter. More precisely by the *waiting* for this apparition...the thing ("this thing") will end up coming. The *revenant* is going to come. It won't be long (Derrida, 1994: 4).

The kind of communism envisaged here by Derrida bears comparison with the profligate and sacrificial general economy of the gift elaborated by the incendiary librarian and acephalic sociologist Georges Bataille, on whose work he once lavished some of his most intriguingly deconstructive devices, rather than the restricted economy which Marx inherited from his spectral mentor, Hegel (Derrida, 1978: 251–77). Indeed, the use of the term "atheology" in this essay also draws heavily upon the writings of Bataille, whose notion of the sacred in particular will be deployed below to indicate the ways in which Gothic capitalism and the transgressions of rock and roll might be said to coalesce. Similarly, the adjective "dark" in the "dark theology" of the title is not to be taken as merely a theatrical conceit, but may be understood as an indirect reference to the figure of the "dark precursor"—a curiously oblique conceptual persona who haunts the more shadowy spaces of some of Gilles Deleuze's most powerful critical philosophy, rearranging the past from the future and configuring the meeting point of the virtual and the real in ways that allow for the emergence of life and creativity amidst sweepings of a dead culture (Deleuze, 1994: 119–24). Accordingly, the underlying purpose of this discussion is to begin to sketch out, through reference to the acephalic explorations of the sacred in Bataille, the later meditations of Derrida on the phantasmal elements of capitalism, and more sporadically, the critical experimentation of Deleuze and Guattari, and how certain aspects of recent and contemporary musical culture might illuminate the past and future mutations of the capitalist imaginary. The focus of popular cultural concern here is specifically on those aspects of rock and roll and its progeny that deal with the darkest and most abject elements of the human condition and its design, including those elements that reach out to the supernatural and the occult for ontological anchorage or abandonment, which I describe here as symptoms of Gothic capitalism. Most especially it will be concerned with those aspects of popular music that might be described, with all appropriate reservations and qualifications in place, as demonic or diabolical.

The origins of rock and roll—the term here being used in its most general sense to denote a variety of musical genres deriving from a complex negotiation between a European-American tradition and an African-American spiritual-aesthetic imperative—are, it often seems, necessarily lost in the fogs of scholarly controversy that so often characterize investigations of popular culture in the twentieth century. Its conventionally rendered status as the wayward and unholy child of so-called "hillbilly" music, on the one hand, and "race" music, on the other, conceived at some point in the 1940s as the direct product of an industrial dispute over royalties and radio play (Brewster and Broughton, 2000: 28–29), while invaluable in terms of understanding its subsequent iconoclastic breach of ethnic and sexual proprieties in the 1950s and beyond, as often as not, and simultaneously, acts to veil its provenance rather than illuminate it. Indeed, the more one seeks to expose this provenance, the more one becomes aware of an encoded necessity in the form itself to conceal this provenance in layers of myth and misinformation, as though, in some sense, the essence of this most dynamic of streams of cultural innovation and confrontation can only be defined by the absence at the heart of its existence.

Nowhere is this more evident than in the debates surrounding the elusive and spectral figure of the so-called "King of the Delta Blues," Robert Johnson. Perceived historically and aesthetically by many influential rock musicians and scholars as the most important avatar of the darker side of rock and roll, as well as the instigator of some of its most plangent musical and lyrical phrasings, Johnson's pact with the Devil at the crossroads of highways 61 and 49 outside Clarksdale, Mississippi, as related by his fellow bluesman Son House, and then relayed as gossip and anecdote ever since, retains an enormous mythic power, whether or not his disciples and commentators regard the event itself as apocryphal, as most—though perhaps not all—undoubtedly do. Similarly, the interminable pursuit of Johnson's "true" identity, as initiated by the compulsive folk and blues collector and archivist Alan Lomax in the 1930s, has established him as a kind of semiotic deity, within whose kingdom of signs was initiated the hybridization of European and African American cultural traditions from which emerged, a generation after his death, the true spirit of rock and roll. It is, moreover, a process of aesthetic hybridization which is itself mirrored by the image of the crossroads (where two highways become one, or one becomes two), on which the pact was supposedly enacted.

Intriguingly, as image and icon and ritual space, crossroads appear to transcend specific cultural boundaries as sites of magical efficacy and dangerous phantasmal malingerings. That the Clarksdale crossroads conjoin three roads is as significant to the Yoruba traditions in which it is sacred to the *orisha* Esu-Legba, a limping old man who revels in chaotic conjunctions and bifurcations and spins messages (and, of course, opens gates) between worlds, as it is for various Indian traditions, and for the Graeco-Roman spiritology in which it is characterized as the *trivium*, sacred, and for very similar reasons, to Hecate, to Triformis, and to Artemis-Diana. On a more material level, as Craig Werner has argued, for a black southerner in the period in which the Delta blues was emerging from the plantation into the nascent highways and byways of American mass media, a decision taken at the crossroads could mean the difference between life and death, whether for existential or economic reasons, or more abruptly for many a potential victim, the successful evasion of a lynch mob (Werner, 2000: 65).

If the myth of the pact and its rich musical and lyrical progeny, both in Johnson's brief oeuvre—songs such as "Me and the Devil," "Hell Hound on my Trail," "Stones in my Passway"—as much as in those who have claimed him as their mentor, from Keith Richards, Eric Clapton and Jimmy Page to Bob Dylan, Glenn Danzig and Jack White, has been a constant source of nourishment to rock music since the release of *King of the Delta Blues Singers* in 1961, then the invisibility, the "becoming imperceptible" (Deleuze and Guattari, 1988: 232–309) of its apparent progenitor has been equally influential. From the beginning, the identity of Johnson was conjured up as an enigma by those who spoke of him. It begins with John Hammond, scion of the Vanderbilts and ardent socialist impresario of the "people's" music, who in 1938 heard some of Johnson's masters and put him on the bill of a programme of "American Negro Music" at Carnegie Hall, only to discover that he had died aged 27 shortly before the announcement in mysterious circumstances at another crossroads near the town of Greenwood, Mississippi.

The subsequent disappearance and reappearance of this romantic Gothic figure's semiotic ghost in the mass media is another absence as fortuitous for the myth of origin as the absence of any clear record of the most crucial events in and at the end of his life. As James Miller relates, the appearance of *King of the Delta Blues Singers* rode on the back of the folk boom and its attendant striving after musical authenticity in the late 1950s, but the album had no photograph of Johnson to share with listeners as there were no known photographs of Johnson in circulation. Instead, the album was graced with a painting of "an isolated, featureless black man hunched over a guitar" (Miller, 2000: 189). The liner notes describe the artist as "very little more than a name on ageing index cards, and a few dusty master records in the files of a phonographic company that no longer exists" and note that Johnson appeared and disappeared "in much the same fashion as a sheet of newspaper twisting and twirling down a dark and windy midnight street" (Miller, 2000: 189). With this arresting image, the promotional material surrounding the release of an album of songs that was to have a seismic effect on the rock music of the 1960s celebrates its foundational content through an image of the absence of the creator. It is an absence, moreover, that in the best tradition of negative theology, gestures far more effectively towards its ultimate signifying power and worldly authority than any mere positional definition would be capable of. For of the many things that might be said of rock and roll, one is certain. And that is that whatever its antecedal gestation in the human suffering and industrialized viciousness that characterize transatlantic slavery and forced migration, it has also been artistically and financially fruitful to subsequent generations of that hellish Diaspora in a way that would have been barely imaginable to its initiators. It is an unintended consequence that can be said to characterize certain key features of the transition from industrial to late capitalism—considered here as Gothic capitalism—in the latter half of the twentieth century and the early years of the twenty-first; a consequence that rimes perfectly with, and is perfectly encapsulated by, the transition from divinity to desire in the libidinal economy of popular music.

In the second volume of his planned three-volume study of human sovereignty and expenditure, *The Accursed Share*, Bataille reflected on the deeply embedded relationship between horror and desire that characterized, for him, so much about the human psyche and its extensions in economics, aesthetics, and politics in the twentieth century. He described this relation through the traditional device of assigning a classical figure to a complex—in this case Phaedra, the wife of Theseus who fell in love with her stepson Hippolytus. Hippolytus, it may be recalled, was mortified when his stepmother attempted to seduce him, and rejected her, whereupon Phaedra, horrified both by her own behaviour and her rejection at the hands of her stepson, committed suicide, writing a note to Theseus in which she accused Hippolytus of attempted rape. Theseus, in his grief and rage, implored the god of the sea, Poseidon, to avenge this perceived crime, which he did by sending out a supernatural bull-like creature from the waves as Hippolytus was riding by the seashore, which frightened the horses and caused Hippolytus' death from a fall. For Bataille, the Phaedra complex illustrated the way in which horror and desire are in an important sense constitutive of one another. He was concerned here with the way in which this mutuality gestures toward the realm of the sacred, which is possibly the most important category in his thought. He writes that:

> ...it is the combination of abhorrence and desire that gives the sacred world a paradoxical character, holding the one who considers it without cheating in a state of anxious fascination.

> What is sacred undoubtedly corresponds to the object of horror I have spoken of, a fetid, sticky object without boundaries, which teems with life, and yet is the sign of death. It is nature at the point where its effervescence closely joins life and death, where it is death gorging life with decomposed substance (Bataille, 1993: 253).

Bataille continues:

> It is hard to imagine that a human individual would not withdraw from such an object in disgust. But would he withdraw if he were not tempted? Would the object nauseate if it offered him nothing desirable?... So it was that Phaedra's love increased in proportion to the fear that arose from the possibility of a crime... Pure and simple danger frightens one away, while only the horror of prohibition keeps one in the anguish of temptation (Bataille, 1993: 253).

He then goes on to consider some examples of this tension between horror and desire, beginning with the image of the putrefying corpse, playing the characteristic tensions between prohibition and transgression that drive the engine of so much of his writing. But what is useful in this passage from the point of view of this discussion is the centrality of his vision of the sacred within horror and abjection, within transgression and annihilation, within ecstasy and sacrifice. It is a notion of the sacred which rimes very effectively with his associated notions of expenditure and general economy when applied, however indirectly, to what I have here described as the spirit of rock and roll and the dissident commerce that it enacts in the decaying semiotic cathedral of our twenty-first-century Gothic capitalism. Tellingly for the narcotically drenched, sexually polymorphous, cosmopolitan multimillionaire hobos who represent the best of our Western rock star tradition, in the words of one commentator, Bataille's notion of sacred is: "the forbidden element of society that exists at the margin where different realities meet" (Hollier, 1990: 128). Following the sociologist Emile Durkheim, Bataille held that the sacred and the profane designate a fundamental experiential dualism, in that these realms aren't mere oppositional metaphors like good and evil, but different orders of experience, relation and intimacy between the conscious subject and the phenomenal universe. The sacred is concerned with what he calls heterology, with ceremonial discontinuities, with excess, transgression and expenditure, with human sacrifice, eroticism and the excremental; while the profane is personified though the figure of God, who while co-extensive with and plausibly even the source of the sacred, remains as the signature of the profane. It is the signature inasmuch as it is God who guarantees those Apollonian or homological virtues that enable us to communicate at all—proportion, justice, measure, stability, the continuity of identity, and so forth—all of which can be obliterated in a moment by the Dionysian excesses and ecstatic annihilations of the sacred.

At the beginning of this discussion I referred to the *via negativa*, generally associated with the mysterious sixth-century figure known as the

Pseudo-Dionysius or Dionysius the Areopagite, who was drawn to the darkness and eroticism of the Christian God in a manner that was enormously influential and inevitably controversial within the various schools of mysticism that followed. As well as writing the *Celestial Hierarchy* which mapped out the ascending order of angels, thrones, intelligences and so forth, he was also responsible for the notion of apophatic theology—which is essentially the path through which the human soul resists the temptations of perception and intellect and comes to know God and even becomes deified through unknowing. The *via negativa* is the negative path which denies all but affect in the aspiration towards divinity. Along with the *via negativa*, I also mentioned the atheology at the heart of postmodern or late capitalism. Atheology is a term derived from Nietzsche's infamous and pronouncement of the death of God in *Thus Spake Zarathustra*. In this sense, it is the study of the absence of God and implications of that absence, as taken up by Bataille and others in the wake of Nietzsche's inflammatory affirmation of a world beyond God and nihilism. To an extent, it is simply about the consequences of superlunary nihilism for sublunary actors—and in that sense, it certainly aligns to certain strands of Gnosticism in which the creator God abandoned the universe on creating its womb to a demented demiurge, who, convinced that HE is the creator of the universe—and it is this demiurge who was subsequently worshipped by Jews, Christians and Moslems—creates material reality as prison for the shards of light aspiring to return to the plenum void of the Pleroma. This absent God, often translated as the "Stranger" or the "Alien" in collections of early Gnostic writings, may be a nothingness or a kind of plenum, or in the case of the kinds of gnostic theology that permeate so much rock music and contemporary popular culture—a shattered simulacrum, as I have suggested above, of the traditional Abrahamic deity, whose many shards each reflect a momentary trace of the sacred which, as Bataille elaborates, is often expressed or communicated through varieties of horror, transgression, eroticism, intoxication, excess, manic expenditure and the devil's share.

This at least is arguably the most authentic expression of the demonic rapture of the sacred. Obviously there are overtly Christian rock bands operating in the digitalized file-sharing economy of contemporary music. Indeed, and somewhat paradoxically, there are a number of Christian death, and even black, metal bands doing the circuit. And, of course, there are Islamic musicians and practicing Jews as well. Monotheism undoubtedly has its troubadours to this day. Nonetheless, it is notable how many musicians are dancing in the fragments of divinity and its inversion rather than worshiping at its traditional core: the faux Kabbalism of Berg and his acolytes (Jagger, Madonna), the auditing culture of Scientology, the Hollywood Satanism of the followers of Anton LaVey of the wonderfully kitsch Church of Satan and the arguably more committed Satanism of subsequent offshoots such as Michael Aquino's Temple of Set or Boyd Rice's Non projects—musique concrete combined with cheesy exotica and a taste for Barbie dolls. Or Nicholas Shreck of Radio Werewolf who trades in a version of Nazi Satanism that has parallels with the church-burning antics of Norwegian and Italian black metal cults, which do quite genuinely practice human sacrifice on occasions, and clearly view these rites as considerably more important than commercial success. Shreck and Rice, however, as well as claiming to be far more ironic than their fellow Satanists in Europe, are, of course, also friends and correspondents of the original poster boy of messianic Satanism, Charles Manson, whose virtual presence as a media phantom has long acted as the imprimatur of a certain decadent aesthetic in rock, metal and industrial genres, and thus of an invaluable promotional signifier for certain musicians in search of a brand signature more transgressive and dangerous than anyone else's. It was, after all, Trent Reznor of the chart-topping industrial combo Nine Inch Nails, and composer of "Hurt" so beautifully covered by Johnny Cash shortly before his death, who chose to live for a time in 10050 Cielo Drive, where Manson's acolytes murdered and defiled Roman Polanski's wife and guests in a Nazi-Satanic Blood Orgy that was, or so we gather, intended to catalyze a race war in Los Angeles. An address in which he also recorded not only his own multi-platinum disc *The Downward Spiral* but also the first commercially successful album by his then protégé Marilyn Manson, *Portrait of an American Family* (Baddeley, 1999).

These are, of course, just a selection of the figures in rock music who have plumbed dark theology for material for both their lives and art— from the satanic excesses of the Rolling Stones and the Crowleyite obsession of Jimmy Page of Led Zeppelin, through the early days of heavy metal in Black Sabbath and others, to the more recent and more strident pronouncements of Scandinavian musicians such as Count Grishnachk, Necrobutcher, Hellhammer or Euronymous. Indeed, any brief glance through a magazine devoted to the varieties of extreme metal (of which the best is probably *Terrorizer*), will provide eloquent testimony to the taste for transgression, desecration and blasphemy that many of these musicians nurture in and through the scenes that sustain them. Names such as Impaled Nazarene or Deicide or Rotting Christ or EyeHateGod are clearly directed as an affront to formal monotheism, if the advocates of monotheism can be bothered to look and listen. The abjection conjured up by band names such as Dying Fetus, Thus Defiled or Cephalic Discharge, or the melancholy violence permeating albums such as Infernaeon's *A Symphony of Sorrow*, Monstosity's *Spiritual Apocalypse*, or *Terrorize, Brutalize, Sodomize* by Vomitory, seem to indicate a need and a longing for the kind of transgression that Bataille associated with the sacred, and it is a transgression that the Gothic spaces of contemporary capitalism would seem to make allowance for. Thus while it is certainly often the case, as Keith Kahn-Harris has argued in a recent sociological survey of extreme metal scenes around the world, that there is a paradox at the heart of the genre, in that the same individual will be playing the most lyrically excessive and avant garde music, whilst simultaneously holding down a day job, and doing the sorts of quotidian things that most people do (Kahn-Harris, 2007), as Kahn-Harris also points out, there is an earthiness and authenticity to this paradox which clearly connects extreme metal to a collective sense of liminality that is ultimately revivifying to its participants, regardless of the death-soaked lyrics, grey and dismal worlds and impaled human skulls that litter the genre. Accordingly, while much of this transgression might be easily dismissed as little more than "showbiz" in a fairly characteristic grand Guignol mode of presentation, there are elements to the way in which rock and roll has appropriated certain religious, theological, blasphemous and heretical themes which are not just theatrical ways of marketing deviant and defiant identity to adolescents, but indicative of what might be termed— following Jerrold Hogle's influential definition of the Gothic as indicating a political unconscious beneath the psychological unconscious, which he has developed to some extent from Fredric Jameson's formulation from the 1970s—a symbolic encoding of the political unconscious bubbling under the stringencies and vicissitudes of capitalism as it has emerged from its industrial phase into whatever it is we are currently involved in (Hogle, 2002). In this formulation, there has been something rotten at the heart of capitalism as in its cultural effluvia since the beginning. We find reference to it, to this Gothic dissonance and decay, as we have seen, in the figure of Robert Johnson. Whether or not he genuinely encountered the devil or Esu or Papa Legba and exchanged his soul for the ability to play guitar like no other before him, we can never know. But the image and the imagery of his songs make that event far more important as a virtuality rather than as an actuality, in the sense deployed by Gilles Deleuze in *Difference and Repetition* (Deleuze, 1994: 207–14). We live in an age so used to the pixilated frenzy of MTV and computer games that it's easy to forget the pre-sensational concepts and percepts that configure rock music in its brief history. A history whose coordinates are wonderfully expressed by Greil Marcus in his classic study of rock and roll in *Mystery Train*, where in his essay on Robert Johnson he cites Scott Fitzgerald in *The Great Gatsby*, elegiacally evoking the wonder of an America in which the early settlers had felt

> compelled into an aesthetic contemplation he neither understood nor desired, face to face for the last time in history with something commensurate to his capacity for wonder (Marcus, 2000: 20–21).

Marcus goes on to praise Fitzgerald's capture of the wonder of America, and then goes on to make the point that this wonder also has a reverse side, and is one as central to the spirit of rock and roll as it is to those who carried the seed of that spirit into the second half of the twentieth century. Marcus' summary is eloquent, and I will quote it at length:

> To be American is to feel the promise as a birthright, and to feel alone and haunted when the promise fails. No failure in America, whether of love or money, is ever simple: it is always a kind of betrayal, of a mass of shadowy, shared hopes… Within that failure is a very different America; it is an America of desolation, desolate because it is felt to be out of place, and it is here that Robert Johnson looked for his images and found them (Marcus, 2000: 22).

That sense of desolation is curiously bound up with the imagery of expenditure, transgression, decay and eroticism in some of the most overtly commercial examples of popular music in the late twentieth and twenty-first centuries. The kitsch palaces and orgiastic excesses that we've come to associate with rock and hip-hop's most successful, when combined with the violence and horror and despair that frequently haunt their product, exemplify that desolation far more abruptly than the literary or cinematic arts because they are so often unapologetically juvenile and uninhibited. The unconscious of capitalism is not entirely buried here—its sores are weeping into the mediascape that constructs our daily reality.

Writing of Bataille's premonitions of post-industrial capitalism, Jean-Joseph Goux has noted that the mode of expenditure—determined by its solar profligacy and its demonic consumption—is closer to a theology of contemporary capitalism than it is a critique of the more utilitarian and productivist capitalism of Bataille's lifetime (1990). As an untimely thinker, Bataille indicates the ways in which the profane dimension of functionalist economics is but a small part of a more general economy of destruction and ecstasy in annihilation. This is that zone in which different realities met—the realm of the sacred, and in this broader sense of economics, one of the most terrifying conclusions that one can reach in thinking through the sacred and popular music is that our most authentically sacred contact with ontological transfiguration is probably far more likely to be effected by listening to glam metal trash like Motley Crü than to more sophisticated theologically driven artists such as Nick Cave. This is because aesthetic assimilation will always attempt to hobble the sacred, and return us to the profane level of utility in the end, even if it is just the utility of transient pleasure. Motley Crü in their recent re-incarnation and re-invention are the servants of Gothic capitalism in a way that a more sensitive and intelligent artist such as Nick Cave or Trent Reznor could never be. Gothic capitalism is a capitalism haunted by ghosts, demons and specters, by the entities which it has crushed to achieve its dreams of freedom and equilibrium. Gothic capitalism is a capitalism structured by an unbearable tension between an imagined past and a vertiginous future, by an impossible desire to find resolution between need and desire in a daylight that can never exist.

Part II
Film

Chapter 5

"Speak of the Devil":
The Portrayal of Satan in the Christ Film

William R. Telford

Introduction

The Nature and Aims of the Chapter

This chapter aims to examine the portrayal of Satan in the Christ film. The discussion is divided into two parts. Since Satan comes to us with a history, the first part sets the context for the subject by reviewing relevant aspects of the representation of the Devil in scripture, the Church Fathers, tradition and folklore, art, literature and film. The second part focuses on four biblical epics or Christ films that demonstrate, in particular, the various and interesting ways that filmmakers have treated this personification of evil (Cecil B. DeMille, *The King Of Kings*, 1927; George Stevens, *The Greatest Story Ever Told*, 1965; Martin Scorsese, *The Last Temptation Of Christ*, 1988; and Mel Gibson, *The Passion of the Christ*, 2004). Note will be taken not only of how Satan is portrayed, but also of the ways in which these portrayals relate to precursor texts and traditions, on the one hand, and to contemporary understandings of evil, on the other. The key emphases and approach employed in the chapter, therefore, are related to characterization, reception history, intertextuality, social context and ideology.

Approaching the Subject Critically

Films can be explored from a number of angles. They can be approached in respect of their form, style and other aesthetic qualities: camerawork, editing, sets and mis-en-scène, visual quality, lighting, soundtrack, music and so on. Films are also interesting for their social context and ideology. They reflect the culture in which they were produced, and the audiences for which they were made. One particular area of interest to me, as a biblical scholar, is intertextuality, film's use of sources and traditions and its treatment of such, especially in the Bible. Films, in other words, like narrative texts, can be approached with respect to their plot, set-tings, and characterization, as well as to their treatment of tradition. My focus in this chapter, therefore, will be on these aspects of the subject.

Speak of the Devil

Satan in Reception History

One cannot appreciate the depiction of Satan in any Christ film without taking into consideration a number of factors. Such factors include that film's relation to the genre, its aesthetic and other cinematic qualities, and the creativity of the filmmaker or a filmmaking process that involves, among others, the director, screenwriter and cinematographer. There is also another approach that can be taken, and that is to view the depic-tion of Satan in the Christ film through the lens of reception history. Satan comes to us with a history. His career begins rather haltingly in the Old Testament (or Hebrew Bible), develops in the intertestamental literature, and flourishes in the New Testament. His cosmic role is given theological substance by the Church Fathers, and his developing persona receives popular embellishment in culture and tradition. He comes to us having obtained visual representation in art, fictional transfiguration in literature, and cinematic incarnation in film. If that career were not already a distinguished one, he has enjoyed a resurgence of popularity in recent years (Clark, 2003: 35–39), for reasons that the conference on which this volume is based has creatively explored.

Satan in Scripture

Satan in the Old Testament (or Hebrew Bible)

As is well known, a "satan" in Hebrew means an "adversary" in a politi-cal or military sense, or an "accuser" or "prosecutor" in a legal sense (Breytenbach and Day, 1999: 726; Hiebert, 1987: 899). Rarely used in the Old Testament, the term "satan" refers in five contexts to human beings, and in three (post-exilic) contexts to celestial beings. Used with an article, "*the* Satan" first appears in the post-exilic book of Job (1–2), and thence in Zech. 3.1–2 where the two figures involved (both unrelated) are angels commissioned by God to accuse Job, in the first instance, and Joshua, the high priest, in the other. In 1 Chr. 21, "Satan" appears for the first time as a proper name, but here again the figure is a celestial being, with no identifiable personality, who, in this instance, tempts David to conduct a census (contrast 2 Sam. 24, where God *per contrarium* is held responsible for inciting David to do so) (Box and Macquarrie, 1965: 888). The name "Lucifer," the shining one (Isa. 14.12) is a reference to the king of Babylon, and the name "Beelzeboul" ("Lord of the flies/dunghill"?—the etymology is dubious) appears to refer to the god of Ekron (2 Kgs 1.2–3) (Bietenhard, Brown and Wright, 1976: 469). Nowhere in the Old Testament, then, is there the clear or unified notion of Satan as an independent being who is God's adversary *par excellence* (generally agreed by scholars, for example, Breytenbach and Day, 1999: 730; Elwell, 1988: 1907; Gaster, 1962: 224; Russell, 1992: 199), ,nor is there any account of his origin (McRay, 1986: 934).

Satan in the intertestamental literature

Fuelled by post-exilic oppression, Persian Zoroastrianism and Jewish apocalyptic, a dualistic tendency to account for the world as a battle between two opposing metaphysical forces becomes much more apparent in the intertestamental literature (1 Enoch, 2 Enoch, Jubilees, and the Testaments of the Twelve Patriarchs), where Satan emerges as a distinct personality (Box and Macquarrie, 1965: 888; Fuller, 1979: 341; Gaster, 1962: 225–26). Given other names such as Azazel (e.g., 1 En. 13.1), Beelzeboul (e.g., Testament of Solomon 6), Belial (e.g., 1QS 2.19) or Beliar (e.g., Jub. 1.20), "the devil" (Wisd. 2.24), "the evil one" (Testament of Job 43.5), Mastema (e.g., Jub. 10.8), Sammael (e.g., Martyrdom of Isaiah 1.8), Satanail (e.g., 2 En. 18.3), and Semyaz (e.g., 1 En. 6.3) (*gratia* Fuller for this helpful list; see also Massyngbaerde Ford, 1995: 1163), he is now chief among the demons. His origin is related to the "serpent" in the Garden of Eden (cf. 2 En. 31.3; Adam and Eve 14–16; Sot. 9b; Sanh. 29a), or to the Lucifer of Isa. 14.12–15 (cf. 1 En. 54.5–6), and their origin is traced to Gen. 6.1–4, the passage about the angelic "watchers" or "sons of God" who mated with the daughters of men (cf. 1 En. 54.6). Not everyone, of course, was prepared to accept that evil was thus to be attributed to the agency of an external, supernatural source, as Gaster (1962: 226) tellingly observes in citing the testimony of the writer of the Wisdom of Ben Sirach (Ecclesiasticus): "when an ungodly man curses Satan [*ton Satanan*] what he is really cursing is his own self" (21.27). Ancient writers, no less than modern filmmakers, therefore, evince alternative approaches to the experience of evil, rooting it in either metaphysical or psychological realities.

Satan in the New Testament

It is the New Testament that provides us, of course, with our most familiar view of God's supreme adversary, metaphysically conceived. The term "Satan" occurs some 36 times in the New Testament; its Greek equivalent, *diabolos* or "devil," some 37 times (Bietenhard, Brown and Wright, 1976: 469). Within the confines of these 27 writings, he is given such varied epithets as the enemy (Mt. 13.39), the evil one (1 Jn 2.13–14), the ruler or god of this world (Jn 12.31; 2 Cor. 4.4), the tempter (Mt. 14.3; 1 Thess. 3.5), the destroyer (1 Cor. 10.10), the father of lies and a murderer (Jn 8.44), the power of darkness (Lk. 22.53), the prince of the power of the air (Eph. 2.2), the adversary (1 Pet. 5.8), the deceiver (Rev. 12.9), the accuser (Rev. 12.10), the dragon (Rev. 12.3), and he is identi-fied with Beelzeboul (Mt. 12.24, 26–27), Belial (2 Cor. 6.15), Abaddon or Apollyon (Rev. 9.11) and the ancient serpent (Rev. 20.2) (Bietenhard, Brown and Wright, 1976: 469; Elwell, 1988: 1908; Fuller, 1979: 342; McRay, 1986: 934). In his efforts to seduce the unwary, he is described as prowling around like a roaring lion (1 Pet. 5.8) or transforming himself into an angel of light (2 Cor. 11.14), motifs, as we shall see, which have also been richly exploited by filmmakers. As prince of the demons (Mt. 9.34; 12.24), he is responsible for physical and moral evil, and the expul-sion of his minions, the evil spirits, by Jesus and his disciples heralds his own end (e.g., Lk 10.17–18; 11.20) (Box and Macquarrie, 1965: 889; Russell, 1992: 199). His ultimate fate, then, like that of the serpent (Gen. 3.15) is to be crushed under foot (Rom. 16.20). This, then, is the New Testament picture of him, and the key Gospel stories, on which our film-makers have also commonly drawn, are the temptation narratives (Mt. 4.1–11, Mk 1.12–13; Mt. 4.1–11; Lk. 4.1–13), the rebuke to Peter ('Get thee behind me, Satan!," Mk. 8.31–33; Mt. 16.21–23) and Satan's pos-session of Judas (Lk. 22.3; Jn 6.70; 13.2, 27).

Satan in Post-biblical Tradition (the Church Fathers, Tradition and Popular Folklore)

With the essential elements of the Satan figure having been adumbrated in this way in the New Testament, it was Church Fathers like Origen (c. 185–c. 254 CE) and Augustine (354–430 CE) who then went on to establish the classic elements, and these in turn were popularized by Gregory the Great (c. 540–604 CE) (Russell, 1992: 200). Tradition and popular folklore have also come to add a myriad other details, such as the association of the color black with Satan, his designation as "the Black (or Ethiopian) One" (Barn. 4.9; Acts of Andrew 22; Acts of Thomas 55; Paris Magical Papyri I.1238-39), and even, according to Jewish legend, as well as French and German folklore, his sartorial predilection for black silk (Gaster, 1962: 227–28). This chapter's title, "Speak of the Devil…," is a proverb at least as old as the seventeenth century: "Talk of the Devil, and he'll either come or send" (Opie and Tatum, 1993: 118).

Satan in Art, Literature, and Film

Art, too, drawing on Persian and Egyptian antecedents, and inspired, as we have noted, by New Testament texts such as the Revelation of John, gave him his beast-like appearance, later modifying these in favor of an essentially human shape, but with animal appendages (claws, tail, arms and legs entwined with snakes, etc.), as well as wings in reference to his heavenly origins. Mediaeval imagination conjured up other grotesqueries, and the classical satyr, too, a symbol of Paganism, contributed his horns and cloven hooves in the Renaissance period (Hall, 1996: 272).

Satan or Lucifer has also been a prominent character in the literary tradition, the influence of the Church Fathers extending into Old English literature in Anglo-Saxon poems such as *Genesis B, Christ and Satan* or the "harrowing of hell" narrative (Gaster, 1962: 227). A significant presence in Langland's *Piers Plowman*, the Devil figures also in the medieval mystery plays, such as those of York, Townely and Chester (Russell, 1992: 200). By turns comic or fearsome, literary treatments of the Devil tended to reflect the prevailing cultural and religious climate, the Protestant reformation, for example, contributing to an increase in fear of the Devil and the demonic. While eighteenth-century rationalism led to doubts about his existence, and humanism to a belief that evil was centered in humanity rather than in the supernatural (cf. Ben Sirach), political radicalism, inspired by the French revolution, tended to see Satan as a heroic rebel, with nineteenth-century Romanticism also taking up this theme (Russell, 1992: 201). Literary milestones along the way, marking the Devil's progress, included Marlowe's adaptation of the German Faust legend in *Doctor Faustus* (1588 or 1589), John Bunyan's *Pilgrim's Progress* (1678), and supremely, of course, John Milton's *Paradise Lost* (1667). The twentieth century has also produced some interesting and influential portrayals of Satan: C. S. Lewis, *The Screwtape Letters* (1942) or John Updike's *The Witches of Eastwick*, to name but two.

This last was made into a film, with Jack Nicholson as the Devil, and it constitutes one of a number of major examples of Satan's starring role in the cinema. Others include Yves Jacques' Richard Cardinal in *Jesus of Montreal* (Denys Arcand, 1989; see below), Robert de Niro's Max Cady in *Cape Fear* (Martin Scorsese, 1991) or Al Pacino's John Milton in *The Devil's Advocate* (Taylor Hackford, 1996). Elements in *The Devil's Advocate* conjure up the Faust legend, which has been taken up and developed in a number of other movies (cf., e.g., F. W. Murnau, *Faust,* 1926; D. W. Griffith, *The Sorrows of Satan*, 1927; William Dieterle, *All That Money Can Buy*, 1941; John Farrow, *Alias Nick Beal*, 1949; René Clair, *La Beauté du Diable*, 1950; George Abbott and Stanley Donen,

Damn Yankees, 1958; Stanley Donen, *Bedazzled*, 1967—remade by Harold Ramis in 2000—and Richard Burton and Nevill Coghill, *Doctor Faustus*, 1967), and horror films such as *Rosemary's Baby* (Roman Polanski, 1968), *The Omen* (Richard Donner, 1976) or *The Exorcist* (William Friedkin, 1993) have also brought us chilling manifestations of the evil one. Space doesn't permit me to say more about these now, but the reader should consult the filmography in the Appendix in which I have compiled a list of the films in which Satan has appeared (see also Walker, 1995: 182; Zwick, 1997: 75–76).

Satan in the Christ Film

This brings us, finally, to Satan in the Christ film. The following is a list of some of the major Christ films that have appeared in the last eighty years:

> *The King of Kings* (Cecil B. DeMille, 1927)
> *King of Kings* (Nicholas Ray, 1961)
> *The Gospel according to St. Matthew* (Pier Paolo Pasolini, 1964)
> *The Greatest Story ever Told* (George Stevens, 1965)
> *The Last Temptation of Christ* (Martin Scorsese, 1988)
> *Jesus of Montreal* (Denys Arcand, 1989)
> *The Miracle Maker* (S. Sokolov and D. Hayes, 1999)
> *The Passion of the Christ* (Mel Gibson, 2004)

I have omitted from the list Norman Jewison's *Jesus Christ Superstar* (1973), Franco Zefferelli's *Jesus of Nazareth* (1977) and Peter Sykes and John Kirsh's *Jesus* (1979) since Satan makes no substantial appearance in these films. I have included in the list Denys Arcand's *Jesus of Montreal* (1989), on the other hand. This is not strictly speaking a Christ film, which, on my definition, would be a biopic. It is an allegory, or perhaps a Christ-figure film, about actors who get drawn into a passion play and whose real-life experiences, especially that of the Jesus character, Daniel Colombe (Lothaire Bluteau), begin to reflect that of the Gospel story. Presenting the temptation scene in a contemporary setting, it offers one of the interesting depictions of Satan previously alluded to, that of the media entrepreneur or entertainment lawyer, Richard Cardinal (played by Yves Jacques), who, following the success of Daniel's play, invites the actor into his very high office overlooking the Montreal cityscape, and there promises him the world.

Of the other seven films listed, three can be reasonably easily dispensed with. In Nicholas Rays' *King of Kings* (1961), Satan's presence on screen is limited to a voice-over. The Devil is represented by a loud voice, which Jesus answers as if the unseen speaker were above him in the sky or middle distance. In S. Sokolov and D. Hayes' animated feature, *The Miracle Maker* (1999), resort is again made to a voice-over for the temptation in the wilderness, but the scene, which contains birds, is also framed with a shadowy silhouette of Satan at the beginning, and his brief appearance as a bearded man at the end. The Satan of Pier Paolo Pasolini's *The Gospel According to St Matthew* (1964) is likewise a bearded, bare-headed man, with dark hair, and voluminous black robes. Somewhat reminiscent of David Lean's single-take shot of Omar Sharif's lengthy approach to the well in *Lawrence of Arabia* (1962), but without the drama, Pasolini frames the temptation story by making him gradually approach Jesus from a distant horizon, and then depart after a scripted dialogue, in a similar fashion. The remaining four films present temptation accounts that are much more interesting, and it is sequences from these (shown at the conference) that I wish (briefly) to discuss. Each represents a different decade in the last ninety years, namely, the twenties, the sixties, the eighties and the new millennium.

The Portrayal of Satan in the Christ Film: Some Selected Sequences

The King of Kings (1927): Satan tempts Jesus in the Temple

A major classic, this was the first full-length, silent Hollywood epic on the life of Jesus, as seen from the perspective of Mary Magdalene. It presents Mary as a rich courtesan with Judas as her lover. Its many memorable moments include Mary's riding off in her chariot to rescue her Judas from the clutches of the carpenter of Nazareth (declaiming the immortal words "Harness my zebras—gift of the Nubian king!"), her subsequent exorcism by Jesus in a swirl of exiting demons, the moving giving of sight to a little blind girl, and dramatic crucifixion and resurrection scenes.

The film presents itself to us as if it were an illustrated Bible storybook. This is no accident since DeMille drew upon not only the religious art and paintings of the Renaissance, but also on the Bible illustrations of the Victorian period based upon it, in particular those of the painter James Tissot and the engraver Gustave Doré. A second element to note is the music. When the film was re-issued in 1931 with synchronized music and sound effects, DeMille made effective use of traditional Christian hymns played at strategic moments (in the temptation in the temple sequence, "By Cool Siloam's Shady Rill" can be recognized, for example, as well as excerpts from Handel's *Messiah*). A third feature is the intimate use of the camera, with medium, close-up and point of view shots which do much to humanize the biblical characters. The person chosen by DeMille to portray Jesus was the distinguished British actor H. B. Warner. Satan was played by Alan Brooks.

The sequence featuring Satan occurs just less than an hour into the film, after the cleansing of the Temple by Jesus. Jesus has received the adulation of the crowd, as well as of his eager followers. The crowd tries to crown him king, Judas himself producing a crown, but Jesus slips away from them. He is then found elsewhere on his own in the Temple court, when Satan appears in order to tempt him. The visual character-ization of both men is striking. Satan, one notes, is clean-shaven (as is Judas), dressed characteristically in black, in line (as we have seen) with legend and folklore, and bedecked with necklaces. Jesus, by contrast, is bearded (giving him a patriarchal air), and in white.

Where intertextuality is concerned, it is interesting to observe that the temptation takes place in the Temple precincts, and not, as in the Gospels, in the wilderness. The focus of the scene, too, is on the temp-tation (on Jesus' part) to seek worldly power, with the other Synoptic temptations being significantly omitted. Following the triumphalist music (the Hallelujah chorus from Handel's *Messiah*) that sets the tone for the scene, Satan cites only the third of Matthew's temptations, "Behold, the Kingdoms of the World—and the glory of them!" (Mt. 4.9; cf. Lk. 4.6, where it is the second temptation), and, when Jesus imagines himself as a Roman emperor (the ordinary crowd being turned into orderly legions of soldiers), adds "All this power will I give Thee—if Thou wilt fall down and worship me!" This imaginary episode, produced by special effects that would doubtless have impressed the audiences of the day, also raises the question whether Satan's materialization is to be read as a function of conflict within Jesus' own psyche.

One notes, in addition, the translocation by DeMille (or his screen-writer, Jeanie MacPherson) of Jn 6.14 ('When Jesus perceived that they would take Him by force, to make Him king—He withdrew, passing through the midst of them") from its connection to the wilderness feeding in the Johannine Gospel to its new and unique Temple setting (although Matthew's second temptation, Mt. 4.5–6, and Luke's third, Lk. 4.9–11, take place on the pinnacle of the Temple). In Jesus' reply to Satan, more-over ("Get thee behind me, Satan! It is written: 'Thou shalt worship the Lord, thy God—and Him only shalt thou serve'"), DeMille produces a characteristic conflation of two scriptural passages, the latter quotation (Deut. 6.13) from Mt. 4.10 (= Lk. 4.8), the former from Mk 8.33, words addressed to Peter in the confession at Caesarea Philippi. Another arresting element at the end of the sequence is the lamb, with all its sacrificial symbolism, a reminder that with Satan's departure, the lamb of God remains, and Jesus' salvific mission is soon to begin.

The Greatest Story Ever Told (George Stevens, 1965): Jesus meets the Dark Hermit

Perfectionism in pursuit of the perfect, George Stevens' film was the most expensive ever made. Though luminescent with its galaxy of stars, striking in respect of its settings (the film was made in Utah, Arizona and around the Colorado River), and memorable for sequences such as the raising of Lazarus as well as the crucifixion, this was, nevertheless, a commercial failure that set the Christ film back as far as Hollywood was concerned. The Swedish actor, Max von Sydow, played Jesus, and the British character actor, Donald Pleasence (known for his villains and eccentrics), Satan.

The sequence chosen for comment is again Jesus' temptation by Satan, this time located, in line with the Gospels, in the wilderness, and occurring just over half an hour into the film. The voice of John the Baptist (played by Charlton Heston) is heard over these wilderness scenes, the buttes and desert landscapes of Utah's Mesa country being shown to good effect. John's voice is heard in particular as the backdrop to Jesus' climb to the cave, an element that suggests to the viewer that we are hearing an internalization of Jesus' own debt to the Baptist's teaching and influence (and anticipating perhaps a similar inner-psychological reading of his encounter with Satan). The camera also concentrates on close-ups, focusing on John as he baptizes, on Jesus as he appears for baptism, and on both Jesus and Satan in the temptation section that follows. Further imposing vistas are seen when the preaching of John is heard at the beginning, and a grand choral climax (again from Handel's *Messiah*), with Jesus on top of a promontory, ends the sequence.

The episode under review presents us with Jesus' first encounter with Satan, the Dark Hermit, a figure who is to be, thereafter, a continuing presence throughout the film, greeting Jesus here in the cave at the summit of his climb, hailing him as "Son of David" as he enters Capernaum and comes to the aid of the woman taken in adultery, demanding his stoning after his own people reject him at Nazareth, sitting in the high priest's courtyard with Peter before his denial (and curiously voicing the words of Jn 3.16: "For God so loved the world that he gave his only begotten Son, that whoever believes in him should not perish but have everlasting life") and calling for his crucifixion in the trial before Pilate.

The characterization of Satan here is very interesting. Bald and middle-aged, he is dressed in a tattered, black (or dark grey) habit. Albeit with a slight air of menace, his advocacy of the easy life and its materialistic pleasures is made with geniality, naturalness, and a quiet reasonableness: "Long hard climb, wasn't it? Come on in, if you like. Some think the whole of life should be hard like that. An easy life is a sinful life. That's what they think. Not so. Life should be as easy as a man can make it." Jesus is made to respond to him (the voice of his own consciousness, perhaps), in a more formal, scripted way, however, citing the Hebrew Bible throughout in reply to his blandishments, and stiffly rejecting the force of his rationalism and secularism with a spirituality that characterizes the mystical, Byzantine Christ portrayed so powerfully by von Sydow (Telford, 1997: 135).

Set against a gigantic orange moon that enhances their effect (a feature that will reappear in Mel Gibson's *The Passion of the Christ* Gethsemane sequence), the traditional temptations of the Synoptic narratives are each presented to the viewer, though in a different order from that of Matthew and Luke (who, as we have already observed, themselves differ). The hermit first offers him food, which is the first temptation in both Synoptic accounts; then the world, which is the third Matthean/second Lukan temptation (cf. Mt. 4.8–10 = Lk. 4.5–8); then the temptation to throw himself down from the height (the second Matthean/third Lukan temptation, set in the temple; cf. Mt. 4.5–7 = Lk. 4.9–12); and finally, the temptation to turn stones into bread, which is again the first Matthean and Lukan temptation (cf. Mt. 4.3–4 = Lk. 4.3–4). While some have seen in the natural phenomena presented here (gigantic moon, desolate wilderness, striking vistas, high mountain, hermit's cave, etc.) the trial of Jesus as the "natural man" pursuing "the Emersonian ideal of self-reliance, so important not only to American literature and ideology but to the Western movie genre as well" (Stern, Jefford and Debona, 1999: 158–59), the inclusio in the temptation sequence formed by the motif of "food" and "bread" highlights, however, the emphasis on the nature of evil as submission to the seductive power of materialism.

Where ideology and social context is concerned, therefore, Bruce Babington and Peter Evans are right to comment: "At a time of growing counter-culture revulsion against materialist and consumerist excess, it seems logical, where conventionally devout audiences might equate the diabolical with pride and rebellion against the creator, that for more socially critical Christians and others the Devil should rather be identified with materialism and its consequences" (1993: 143). "The film is very much one with 1960s ideals of meditation and inner change as the responsibility of the individual," they declare, and "evil is portrayed through images of comfortable, middle-class conformism" (144).

The Last Temptation of Christ (Martin Scorsese, 1988): Jesus meets the Snake

Our next film to feature Satan in an innovative way is Martin Scorsese's *The Last Temptation of Christ* (1988). Based on Kazantzakis' novel about "the dual substance of Christ" and "the incessant, merciless battle between the spirit and the flesh," and directed by one of Hollywood's most distinguished filmmakers, this is one of the finest, most religious, and yet most controversial Christ films ever made. Filmed in Morocco, the movie presents a Jesus who struggles against his infatuation with Mary Magdalene, his childhood sweetheart, and, aided and abetted by Judas, makes a reluctant pursuit of his destiny to save the world. Willem Dafoe plays Jesus, Harvey Keitel, Judas, and Barbara Hershey, Mary Magdalene.

Having paid a visit to Mary Magdalene's brothel, and then a monastery (where he encounters Satan in the form of snakes), Jesus seeks out John the Baptist, and is baptized by him. There then follows (just less than an hour into the film) Jesus' principal encounter with Satan, in a series of three temptations that he experiences in the context of forty days and nights in the wilderness on John's instructions. The hallucinatory imagery is powerful, with Satan manifesting himself in the form of a snake (cf. Gen. 3), a lion (cf. 1 Pet. 5.8), and a column of fire (cf. Exod. 13.21–22). The tree of life (Gen. 2.9), and John the Baptist's axe (cf. Mt. 3.10 = Lk. 3.9) also make their appearance.

At the start of these temptations, Jesus sits, it is to be observed, in a self-made circle, reminiscent of the sacred circle as a protection against evil in Dennis Wheatley novels or the Celtic "caim," or "ritual of encompassment" which is deemed to provide spiritual protection from evil (de Waal, 1988: 159). Unlike Stevens' Christ (contrast *The Greatest Story Ever Told*), Jesus talks to himself (or to God) in ordinary instead of biblical language. The approach of the Devil in the form of a snake echoes the creation story (and his statement, "You're just like Adam" reinforces this) but the snake has the voice of Mary Magdalene (Barbara Hershey) and reflects the temptation to marriage, children, and domesticity that is Jesus' ultimate test in the film, the lesser course which beckons him away from his universal mission to die for the sins of the world.

In neither the Synoptic temptation narratives, nor in the Church Fathers is sexual temptation seen as a fitting and appropriate experience for the Son of God (Babington and Evans, 1993: 155). Here, then, we have a Satan for a post-sexual revolution generation that is not afraid to have its Saviour experience sexual desire. Although satanic temptation then goes on, as aforementioned, to take the form of a lion, a column of fire and the tree of life, it is interesting that Scorsese's devil here is a woman (see Babington and Evans, 1993: 165–66). The angel (of light) into whom Satan transforms himself later in the film is also a woman, albeit a pre-adolescent one, and here Scorsese deliberately altered his source novel, Nikos Kazantzakis' *The Last Temptation*, where the angel is a young man who turns himself into a negro slave. Where DeMille has used Jesus' satanic encounter in the Temple as a way of criticizing worldly notions of power, and Stevens has used the Dark Hermit as a means for expressing a critique of materialistic and hedonistic society, Scorsese uses Satan and the temptation narrative "as a vehicle for exploring Jesus' psyche" (Reinhartz, 2007: 188) and especially his feelings of sexual, emotional, and familial frustration.

The Passion of the Christ (Mel Gibson, 2004): Jesus and Satan in Gethsemane and Satan and his Demonic Child

Our final examples of portrayals of Satan in the Christ film come from Mel Gibson's recent *The Passion of the Christ* (2004), and I have selected for comment the opening scene in the Garden of Gethsemane, and the later vision of Satan and his (or her) demonic child, which comes approximately an hour into the film, when Jesus is being scourged by the Roman soldiers. Gibson's Satan is one of the most striking representations of recent years, and appears in a number of other places throughout the film, such as the tormenting of Judas, the observing of the passion and its participants (appearing among the Jewish crowds and the Jewish authorities, as well as the Roman soldiers) and howling in anguish at the moment of Jesus' death. Jesus is played by Jim Caviezel and Satan by a female actor, Rosalinda Celentano.

After a preface citing Isa. 53.5 ("But he was wounded for our transgressions, he was bruised for our iniquities; upon him was the chastisement that made us whole, and with his stripes we are healed"), this film opens with a full moon over Gethsemane (one already encountered in Stevens' *Greatest Story*, but here also reminiscent of horror movies). While the depiction of the Devil as a black-cowled, hermit-like figure is by now a familiar convention (cf. the Dark Hermit of Stevens' *The Greatest Story Ever Told*, but also Death in Ingmar Bergman's *The Seventh Seal*, 1957), the fact that Gibson's Satan is androgynous is a striking feature, albeit fitting for a generation for which evil cannot be seen to be gender-specific. In sharp contrast to Donald Pleasence's Satan, with her shaved eyebrows and unblinking stare, with her painted eyes, lips and (long-nailed) fingers, (s)he is erotically charged and "strangely beautiful or oddly alluring," appropriately, Gibson claimed, for "evil is alluring, attractive" (Powell, 2004: 73).

As this sequence commences, one also immediately notes the use of close-ups. Aramaic is the language spoken by the protagonists (with English subtitles), but Jesus, nevertheless, is depicted visually in classic (Aryan) style. The music is disorientating—jagged, intrusive, with drums, pipes and flutes—somewhat reminiscent of Peter Gabriel's world-music score for Scorsese's *The Last Temptation of Christ* (1988). Satan (death) has a live maggot in his/her nose, and a snake emerges from his/her black cloak, also reminding us of the snake in the wilderness in the previously discussed *The Last Temptation of Christ*. The maggot symbolizes death, and calls to mind the flies surrounding the dead donkey in the (later) scene of Judas' suicide after his encounter with the demonic children and its echoes of another of Satan's manifestations as Beelzeboul or "Lord of the flies." Here is a Satan associated not only with the decadent, but also with the horrific, the putrid, the obscene.

Here, too, we encounter an anguished or tortured Jesus (in contrast to Max von Sydow's mystical, controlled, and Byzantine Jesus in *The Greatest Story Ever Told*, or Willem Dafoe's weak, confused, and uncertain Jesus in *The Last Temptation of Christ*). Jesus crushes the snake's head with his foot, an action that powerfully conjures up, for the biblically literate, such passages as Gen. 3.14: "The Lord God said to the serpent, 'Because you have done this, cursed are you above all cattle, and above all wild animals; upon your belly you shall go, and dust you shall eat all the days of your life. I will put enmity between you and the woman, and between your seed and her seed; he shall bruise your head, *and you shall bruise his heel*'" (italics added); Rev. 12.9: "And the great dragon was thrown down, that ancient serpent, who is called the Devil and Satan, the deceiver of the whole world—he was thrown down to the earth, and his angels were thrown down with him"; and Rev. 20.2: "And he seized the dragon, that ancient serpent, who is the Devil and Satan, and bound him for a thousand years." In the words of one commentator: "With one strong, decisive movement, Jesus stomps the snake to death. The character of Jesus as mythic good guy is established with astonishing economy. The male is stronger than the female; the hero is stronger than evil. Jesus has come to kill sin" (Thistlethwaite, 2004: 130). With such a depiction, there is no room for the view that Satan (and hence evil) is an internalization of Jesus' own psyche. This is an objective view of Satan, inviting the viewer to share a metaphysical rather than a psychological understanding of the origin of evil.

Let me make a final, brief comment on the second sequence that I have referred to in this film, the much discussed scene involving Satan and the child (s)he holds while moving impassively through the scene of the Roman soldiers scourging Jesus. Throughout this lengthy scene, humanizing close-ups are shown of Mary, the mother of Jesus, and Mary Magdalene but, otherwise, the predominant emphasis is on the sadistic nature of the soldiers. "Satan," Adele Reinhartz points out, "moves in among the human characters that are her/his instruments of evil: the Roman soldiers and, even more obviously, the Jewish high priests and other Jewish authorities" (2007: 193). But what does the Satan and child image betoken in connection with the atrocity being enacted by the soldiers? In line with other elements of the film, is this the invocation of a horror film convention (cf. e.g. the satanic mother and child in *Rosemary's Baby*, 1968, or the dwarf figure in the red raincoat of Nicholas Roeg's *Don't Look Now*, 1973) or a literary one (cf. the dwarf figure pursuing Jesus in Nikos Kazantzakis' *The Last Temptation*), or even, as Price suggests (2005: 4), a liturgical one, a perverse invocation of the iconography of the early church (and in particular the Russian and Byzantine tradition) where Jesus himself is depicted as a diminutive adult?

Here, I believe (in line with others) that Gibson is giving us a perversion of the holy family, and especially the virgin and child, and a clue might be supplied by a similar scene in Gibson's *Braveheart* (1995), where, in the midst of a comparable torture scene, the tormented Wallace looks up to see two key figures in the crowd, his own dead wife, and the face of the child they never had. Running throughout his Christ film, Gibson presents us with a holy threesome who accompany the suffering Jesus (Mary, the mother of Jesus, Mary Magdalene, and the beloved disciple), and who, in seeking to bring him succour, represent, in a sense, the (holy) family, a familiar trope in Gibson movies (Christianson, Francis and Telford, 2005: 317–18). Here, with the Satan and child image, we have a diabolical family that acts as an evil counterpart to this holy threesome.

One can also see a related explanation for this curious image in a convention to be found in apocalyptic literature, namely, that evil parodies good, and God will be opposed by his diabolical equivalents until the end of time. Parody is a characteristic of the Book of Revelation, for example, the evil trinity of dragon, beast, and false prophet (Rev. 16.13) constituting a perverse parallel to God, Christ and Spirit, the beast that "was, and is not, and is to ascend" (Rev. 17.8) echoing the description of "the Lord God, who is and who was and who is to come" (Rev. 1.8). The Devil mimics God and, therefore, what we are encountering (with

Satan and his offspring) is the family theme again—only this is the diabolical equivalent of the holy family. It is Satan, the father/mother, with his demonic brood who hound Judas earlier in the film, and here in this sequence the androgynous figure carrying his/her grotesque, dwarf-like, fiendishly grinning and superannuated child through the Roman soldiers is evil's alternative "virgin and child" (see Reinhartz, 2007: 194 for a similar conclusion).

Conclusion

Satan's "biography" is a fascinating one, and reception history provides a rich and varied glimpse into the persona (or personae) that he, or more recently "(s)he," has developed in cultural transmission, whether in scripture, the Church, tradition and folklore, art, literature or film. Where filmmakers are concerned, such a cultural legacy has provided much grist for the satanic mill, and the four examples of Christ films, which we have briefly discussed, will hopefully have demonstrated, even to a limited extent, how diverse such portrayals are, the extent to which filmmakers have drawn on their precursor texts and traditions, how they have adapted them in line with the particular concerns and interests of their audiences, and what particular and current understandings of temptation and evil underlie their representations.

Appendix

Satan in Film

Alias Nick Beal (John Farrow, 1949) [Ray Milland]

All That Money Can Buy (William Dieterle, 1941) [with Walter Huston as Mr Scratch]

Angel on My Shoulder (Archie Mayo, 1946) [Claude Rains]

Bait (Hugo Haas, 1954) [Cedric Hardwick]

Bedazzled (Stanley Donen, 1967; remade by Harold Ramis, 2000) [Peter Cook]

Cabin in the Sky (Vincente Minnelli, 1943) [Rex Ingram]

Cape Fear (Martin Scorsese, 1991) [Max Cady]

Damn Yankees (George Abbott, Stanley Donen, 1958) [Ray Walston]

Doctor Faustus (Richard Burton, Nevill Coghill, 1967) [Andreas Teuber]

End of Days (Peter Hyams, 1999)

Faust (various versions, 1900, 1903, 1904, 1907, 1909, 1911, 1921, 1926) [Emil Jannings as Mephistopheles, 1926]

Heaven Can Wait (Ernst Lubitsch, 1943) [Laird Cregar]

Highway 61 (Bruce McDonald, 1991)

Jesus of Montreal (Denys Arcand, 1989) [Yves Jacques as Richard Cardinal]

Kill, Baby, Kill (Mario Bava, 1966)

La Beauté du Diable (René Clair, 1950) [Gérard Philipe]

La Voie Lactée (The Milky Way) (Luis Buñuel, 1969) [Pierre Clementi]

Leaves from Satan's Book (Carl Dreyer, 1919–21) [Helge Nissen]

Les Visiteurs du Soir (Marcel Carné, 1942) [Jules Berry]

Lost Souls (Janusz Kaminski, 2000)

Meet Mr Lucifer (Anthony Pelissier, 1953) [Stanley Holloway]

Rosemary's Baby (Roman Polanski, 1968)

Satan [or *The Dream of Humanity/Satana*] (Luigi Maggi, 1912)

Simon of the Desert (Luis Buñuel, 1965)

Tales From the Crypt (Freddie Francis, 1972) [Ralph Richardson]

The Devil in Love/L'Arcidiavolo (Ettore Scola, 1967) [Vittorio Gassman]

The Devil's Advocate (Taylor Hackford, 1996) [Al Pacino as John Milton]

The Devil's Eye (Ingmar Bergman, 1960) [Stig Järrel]

The Devil with Hitler (Gordon Douglas, 1942) [Alan Mowbray]

The Exorcist (William Friedkin, 1993)

The Greatest Story Ever Told (George Stevens, 1965) [Donald Pleasence]

The King of Kings (Cecil B. DeMille, 1927) [Allan Brooks]

The Last Temptation of Christ (Martin Scorsese, 1988) [Juliette Caton (Girl Angel) and Leo Marks (Voice of the Devil)]

The Omen (Richard Donner, 1976)

The Sorrows of Satan (D. W. Griffith, 1927) [Adolphe Menjou]

The Story of Mankind (Irwin Allen, 1957) [Vincent Price]

The Witches of Eastwick (George Miller, 1987) [Jack Nicholson]

The Undead (Roger Corman, 1956) [Richard Devon]

Toby Dammit (Federico Fellini, 1968)

Torture Garden (Freddie Francis, 1968) [Burgess Meredith]

Under the Sun of Satan (Sous le Soleil de Satan) (Maurice Pialat, 1987)

Witchcraft through the Ages (Benjamin Christensen, 1921) [Benjamin Christensen]

Chapter 6

Celluloid Vampires, Scientization, and the Decline of Religion

Titus Hjelm

Ever since the first silver screen adaptations in the early twentieth century, the vampire has been a recurrent villain—and sometimes the tragic hero—of feature films. Count Dracula, the archetypal vampire, has been the main character in over 200 movies since the genre-defining *Dracula* from 1931. This makes him second only to Sherlock Holmes in appearances on the big screen (Melton, 1999: xxviii). Few characters can claim similar persistent success as popular cultural icons. With the screen adaptations of *Bram Stoker's Dracula* (1992) and Anne Rice's *Interview with the Vampire* (1994), starring Tom Cruise and Brad Pitt, vampires hit the mainstream and have stayed there ever since. Hence, as a commercial venture, mainstream vampire films have been a considerable success. On the week of its release *Blade* (1998) went to number one at the box office, replacing Steven Spielberg's highly acclaimed *Saving Private Ryan* (Jordan, 1999: 15).

Concurrent with the mainstream success of vampire films and TV series (especially *Buffy the Vampire Slayer*), the last ten to fifteen years have witnessed a definite upsurge in the amount of scholarly interest in vampires, both mythological and fictional. Religious studies scholars and anthropologists have studied the vampire as a part of a wider "monster culture" which reflects the dark side of the world's cultures and religions (e.g. Beal, 2002; Gilmore, 2003). Literary scholars have a long history of studying the vampire as part of cultural history (e.g. Auerbach, 1995; Rickels, 1999; Mäyrä, 1999). Lately, in conjunction with an increased interest in the study of biblical influences on contemporary popular culture, biblical scholars and theologians have also been active in interpreting vampire fiction in the light of biblical texts (e.g. Kreitzer 1999; O'Donnell, 2000; Stone, 2001; Aichele, 2005b). Finally, scholars of popular culture have analyzed vampire fiction (both literary and filmed) from the perspective of cultural and social change (e.g. Jordan, 1999; Wilcox, 1999; Owen, 1999; Wyman and Dianisopoulos,

1999; Corbin and Campbell, 1999; Partridge, 2005: 230–38; Partridge, 2004a: 126–31).

Many of the more social scientifically oriented studies of vampire fiction have been eager to point out that the fascination with vampires is a sign of the times in the sense that "for those, particularly young people, who feel disenfranchised, disempowered, subject to the forces of a history in which they did not ask to be born, the vampire represents a fascinating icon of empowered self-interest" (Partridge, 2005: 232). While I have little disagreement with the above statement, the representation of the vampire in the new (and extremely popular) genre of horror/action film shows that the fascination with the vampire cannot be straightforwardly attributed to a "search for a spirituality" (Partridge, 2005: 232)—at least not in the sense claimed by Ramsland:

> Our fascination with vampires seems to be part of a deep disenchantment, or boredom, with science and rationalism—a feeling reflected in society's growing interest in mysticism, spirituality, and belief in the paranormal (Ramsland 1989, quoted in Partridge, 2005: 232).

In this essay my aim is to describe a change that has taken place in recent vampire films, one which questions Ramsland's thesis: a development in which religion and spirituality have been marginalized or completely written off in contemporary vampire movies. This "migration of the vampire soul" can be witnessed in the ways in which the films have replaced the mystical qualities attributed to the vampire—traditionally imbued with strong religious connotations—by a natural scientific worldview. I aim to demonstrate this change by comparing classic and contemporary film depictions of the nature of vampires, their motives, and the ways to destroy them.

As a source for the traditional, religious view of vampires, I am using classic Hammer Films vampire movies from the 1960s and 1970s, especially *Dracula has Risen from the Grave* (1968) and *Lust for a Vampire* (1970). The new genre of vampires has been most revealingly portrayed in the *Blade* trilogy (1998, 2002, 2004), *Underworld* (2003), and its sequel *Underworld Evolution* (2006). Although lacking in quantitative and chronological breadth, the choice of exemplary movies has been quite conscious. Firstly, early classics like *Nosferatu* (1922) and *Dracula* (1931), and some later treatments, especially *Bram Stoker's Dracula* (1992), have already engendered a wealth of analysis (e.g. Beal, 2002: 143–51; Roth, 1979; Corbin and Campbell, 1999; Wyman and Dianisopoulos, 1999; Fry and Craig, 2002) and there is little to add to that discussion. Secondly, I have omitted the whole discussion around *Buffy the Vampire Slayer*, the film (1992) and the subsequent series, both of which have spawned a whole field of "buffology" which deals first and foremost with the analysis of teenage experience as seen through the metaphorical lens of vampire slaying (Owen, 1999; Wilcox, 1999; South, 2003; Riess, 2004; Wilcox and Lavery, 2003). Although *Buffy* challenges many of the traditional religious concepts of vampire lore, the vampires remain a mystical creature, not really challenging what is traditionally thought of as "demonic" (cf. Partridge, 2004a: 131).

In addition to the analysis of the film content, I will situate the shift from religion to science and technology into a wider framework, discussing the interaction between popular culture, religion, and society. My argument is that views such as that of Ramsland quoted above are mistaken in suggesting that vampire fiction is popular because of its portrayal of vampires as mystical anti-heroes in a scientifically saturated age. The "scientization" and "genetization" of the celluloid vampire shows that science is not the antithesis of the fascination with the vampire. On the contrary, the contemporary film representations of the bloodsucker show a lingering fascination with questions of ultimate meaning—the answers are just found in science and technology, not in religion.

The Old and New Paradigm Celluloid Vampires

So, what do I mean by "the migration of the vampire soul"? For the purposes of comparison, I have devised a table that illustrates the differences between what I call the "old paradigm" and "new paradigm" celluloid vampires. I have chosen three characteristics that best highlight the nature of vampires as depicted in film and also provide the best ground for comparison between the two different paradigms (cf. Kane, 2006). The three characteristics are the origin, motivation, and nemesis of vampires.

Table 1: *The old and new paradigm celluloid vampires*

	Old Paradigm Celluloid Vampires	New Paradigm Celluloid Vampires
Origin	Demonic	Genetic
Motive	Malevolence Desire	Survival Power
Nemesis	Faith 'Mysticism'	Technology

First, portrayals of the origin of vampires reveal much about their nature, especially in relation to what is considered natural, unnatural, or supernatural. Second, vampires have been depicted as the embodiment of evil so often that their malevolent motivation is taken for granted most of the time. While this is indeed the case for the majority of the classic vampire films, the new paradigm celluloid vampires have expanded the view by depicting vampires as a part of a Darwinian struggle for survival and power, instead of a one-dimensional demonic "other." Third, the most explicit reference to the nature of vampires has been the method of their destruction. An examination of the "technologies of destruction" of the old and new paradigm vampires reveals a great deal about the changing picture of the celluloid vampire.

The Demonic and the Genetic: The Origin of the Vampire

How does one become a vampire? The folklore and the fictional depictions vary, but it is generally recognized that the bite of the vampire is contagious. There is variation about whether the victims are transformed into vampires before or after death (Melton, 1999: 504–508), but in fiction the bite is the almost universal mark of the vampire.

So far so good, but where does the first vampire come from? The old paradigm vampire films show a notable neglect of this question. Count Dracula is the undead prince of Transylvania, but his origin is rarely if ever explicitly discussed in the films (cf. "Origins of the Vampire" in Melton, 1999). A significant exception to this neglect of detail is Francis Ford Coppola's *Bram Stoker's Dracula* (1992). In the opening scene, the count finds his wife dead, having committed suicide after being wrongly informed by the count's enemies that he has fallen in battle. Desperate and enraged at the priests who deny salvation to the wife who took her own life, Dracula denies God and makes a pact with darkness. This is symbolically verified with Dracula plunging his sword into a crucifix, which immediately starts to bleed excessive amounts of blood that the grieving count drinks as a sign of a "blood-pact," heightening the supernatural feel of the scene.

Interestingly enough, one of the few direct references to the relationship between vampires and the Christian Devil is made in Roman Polanski's vampire satire *The Fearless Vampire Killers* (1967). At the beginning of the famous dance scene in which the unfortunate heroes are exposed as humans because they are the only ones who have reflections on the ballroom mirrors, count von Krolock, the leader of the vampires, addresses the party crowd by hailing Satan and thus implying a demonic origin. Although in other respects quite the opposite of Coppola's serious adaptation, Polanski's film is one of the few that explicitly take their cue from Stoker's short mention (in the words of the character Abraham van Helsing) that Dracula's origin can be traced back to him "having dealings with the Evil one" (Melton, 1999: 117–21).

The seven Dracula movies produced by Hammer Films and featuring Christopher Lee mostly follow Stoker's original portrayal of the vampire, but with new twists in each successive film. The notable feature of the series is that in every one Dracula is killed, but brought back to life by mystical means at the beginning of the next "episode." In some of the films the evil count is brought back to life accidentally, but in most of them, *Taste the Blood of Dracula* (1970) most explicitly, the resurrection is undertaken by a group of "cultists" or individuals seeking excitement or power. The resurrection scenes are portrayed as highly supernatural with count Dracula materializing out of the combination of dust and few drops of blood. Riding the wave of movies depicting satanic cults, such as *Rosemary's Baby* (1968) and *The Devil Rides Out* (1968) (also featuring Christopher Lee), vampire films adopted the idea of satanic rituals—only this time the devil summoned was count Dracula. Although his origin is still shrouded in mystery, the films leave little room for doubt that the count is a demonic, supernatural creature.

The general mystery surrounding the origin of vampires in the old paradigm is in stark contrast to the portrayals of the new paradigm celluloid vampires. In the newest vampire films the supernatural element is almost completely replaced (or at least marginalized) by a natural, genetic explanation of vampirism. Although some previous fictional accounts—notably Richard Matheson's novel *I Am Legend* (1954)—have represented vampirism as a form of disease, the new genre of vampire film, starting with *Blade* (1998), has had the most impact in etching the idea of vampirism as a genetic defect into popular consciousness.

Blade, who originally appeared as a character in Marvel Comics and is played by Wesley Snipes in the films, is a vampire hunter and a reluctant vampire himself, keeping the craving for blood at bay with a special serum. Although blood is a central element of all vampire movies, the Blade series gives it a whole new meaning. In the first film, the secret of vampirism is discovered when the heroine Dr Karen Jenson, who is introduced as a haematologist, examines a blood-sample and discusses her findings with Whistler, Blade's human companion and mentor:

Karen: It is simple. Why do vampires need to drink blood?

Whistler: Because their own blood cannot sustain haemoglobin.

Karen: Right. So it's a genetic defect, just like haemolytic anemia. That
                means we have to treat it with gene therapy. Rewrite the vic-
                tim's DNA with a retrovirus. They've been using it on sickle cell
                anemia (*Blade*, 1998).

To an average observer this doesn't mean much, but the dialogue's
strong rhetoric of medical expertise paves the way for the genetic explanation of the nature of vampires. While vampirism is shown to be a
"genetic defect" in the first film, the notion is crystallized in *Blade II*,
in a dialogue between Blade, Karel Kounen, a human "familiar" of the
vampires, and Overlord Eli Damaskinos, the leader of the vampires. The
dialogue also reveals the gist of the plot in *Blade II*: Blade's joining of
forces with his former enemies to combat a dangerous mutated strain
of vampire.

Damaskinos: As you may know, vampirism is an arbovirus, carried in the
                saliva of predators. In this case, vampires are the vector. In 72
                hours, it spreads through the human bloodstream, creating
                new parasitic organs.

Blade: Like cancer.

Damaskinos: Cancer with a purpose.

Kounen: Unfortunately, viruses evolve too. We've encountered a new
                one. We've dubbed it the "Reaper" strain. And like any good
                pathogen, it appears to have found a carrier (*Blade II*, 2002).

Perhaps the most powerful example of the triumph of science over
mysticism and religion comes later in the film with the autopsy of the
new breed of vampire. The caped villain of ages past is now lying on the
table, helpless in the face of the scalpel and the test tube. With this scene
the transition from prayer and wooden stakes to the *CSI*-type fascination
with details of anatomy is complete.

Another massively popular new paradigm vampire film, *Underworld*
(2003), follows the path set by *Blade*. In *Underworld*, however, humans
are largely helpless bystanders in a war between vampires and lycans
(i.e. werewolves). Introducing a whole new mythology, the origin of
both races is revealed in a dialogue between a captive werewolf "scientist" and Viktor, leader of the vampires. The lycan explains that they
are on the brink of discovering a weapon to help in the battle against
the vampires.

Lycan:	We've been searching for someone with a special trait. A direct descendant of Alexander Corvinus. Hungarian, a warlord, who came to power in the early seasons of the fifth century. Just in time to watch a plague ravage his village. He alone survived. Somehow, his body was able to change the disease, mould it to his benefit. He became the first true immortal. And years later, he fathered at least two children who inherited this same trait.
Viktor:	The sons of the Corvinus clan. One bitten by bat, one by wolf, one to walk the lonely road of mortality as a human. It's a ridiculous legend. Nothing!
Lycan:	That may be, but our species do have a common ancestor. A mutation of the original virus is directly linked to his bloodline. [...] We needed a pure source. Untainted. An exact duplicate of the original virus. Which, we learned, was hidden away in the genetic code of his human descendants and passed along in its latent form down through the ages all the way to Michael Corvin. For years, we tried to combine their bloodlines. And for years we failed. It was useless. Even at the cellular level, our species seemed destined to destroy each other. That is, until we found Michael. The Corvinus strain allows for a perfect union. A triple-celled platelet, which holds unspeakable power (*Underworld*, 2003).

As can be seen, there is some ambiguity regarding the completely natural explanation of vampires (and werewolves). According to the legend, vampires came into being as a result of a descendant bitten by a bat and werewolves have their genesis in an ancestor bitten by a wolf—a mythical sequence in an otherwise completely genetiziced discourse. Although dismissed as myth by Viktor, the narration of the captured werewolf given above is shown to be correct in the sequel, the aptly named *Underworld Evolution* (2006). Although the nature of the vampire as a genetiziced creature is introduced and emphasized in the portrayal of the motivations and killing methods (see below) of vampires, the original "myth of origin" does have a non-natural element in it. If the killing methods of vampires show a completely new type of celluloid monster, the origin stories leave some room for doubt in *Underworld*.

Similarly to *Underworld*, the shift from mystical to completely scientific explanation of the origin of vampires is treated with some ambiguity in the *Blade* trilogy. The trilogy starts with a confrontation between Blade, a scientized "cyborg" and a "cult" of evil vampires, who are, although sharing the same genetic makeup, juxtaposed against the scientific Blade as more mystical creatures, to the extent that their main objective is the resurrection of LaMagra, an "ancient blood-god" (see Jordan, 1999). In *Blade II* the theory of vampirism is completely geneticized, with not only the origins of vampires explained in unprecedented scientific rhetoric, but the whole storyline concentrating on a mutation in the vampire gene. However, in *Blade Trinity* the element of mysticism is brought back by introducing Dracula or Drake, the father of all vampires. Thus the genetic explanation of vampirism is combined with an origin myth, complete with an immortal (anti)hero. In one of the vampire hunters' words: "He was the first of his kind. The patriarch of *hominus nocturna*" (*Blade Trinity*, 2004).

Blood and Identity Politics: The Motives of the Vampire

The need to feed on blood is the governing trait of vampires, both in folklore and in the literary and cinematic renditions (Melton, 1999: 53–59; cf. Marberry, 2006). Echoing biblical verse (Deut. 12:23; Lev. 17:11), one of the most memorable lines from Bram Stoker's *Dracula* is the madman Renfield's crazed shout: "The blood is the life! The blood is the life!" Drawing from existing folklore and consequently influencing all later vampire fiction, Stoker immortalized perhaps the most systematic trait of fictional vampires.

For the old paradigm celluloid vampires the need to feed did not, however, manifest as a compulsive characteristic. For example, the films that follow Stoker's original story most loyally, notably *Count Dracula* (1970), starring Christopher Lee, and *Bram Stoker's Dracula* (1992), portray the count as a withered old man in the beginning sequence, which takes place at Dracula's castle in Transylvania. After feeding on the sailors and passengers of the *Demeter*, the ship that brings the count to England, he has gained his vitality and youth. Therefore, if feeding vitalizes the vampire, it could be that it is possible for it to go on for long periods of time without blood, as the depictions of the old Dracula suggest.

It has been noted that in the beginning of their cinematic career, vampires were portrayed quite straightforwardly as malignant creatures (Kane, 2006). In the early films, especially *Nosferatu* (1922) and *Dracula* (1931), the stars of the show had little resemblance to the guilt-ridden blood-drinkers in *Interview with the Vampire* (1994) or to the tragic lover of *Bram Stoker's Dracula* (1992). Later, largely thanks to Christopher Lee's memorable performances, the malevolence was combined with more open expressions of lust and desire (Kane, 2006). The important point is that in the old paradigm portrayals Dracula and other vampires drank blood and killed because they *wanted* to, not primarily because they *needed* to. Thus the vampire was first and foremost identified with evil and the chaos of the supernatural.

One of the most apparent novelties of the new paradigm movies is that—concurrent with the change of status in the depiction of origins—being a vampire is less about being evil and more about accepting one's own racial traits—notably "the thirst." Blade is in fact different from other vampires, not only because of his unique genetic makeup, but also because of his refusal to accept his nature. This theme is taken up several times in the three *Blade* movies, most notably in *Blade II*:

Blade: My name is Blade. I was born half human, half vampire. They call me "the daywalker." I have all their strengths, none of their weaknesses, except for the thirst. Twenty years ago I met a man who changed all that. Whistler. He taught me how to hold the thirst at bay (*Blade II*, 2002).

Later, after the unlikely alliance between Blade and the "normal" vampires against the mutated "Reaper" strain has been sealed, the issue of identity is brought up again in a dialogue between one of the vampires and Blade.

Nyssa: Why do you hate us so much?

Blade: It's fate. It's in my blood.

Nyssa: Well, it's in mine too. I'm a pureblood. I was born a vampire. You know the thirst better than any of us, shooting that serum of yours. The only difference between us is that I made peace with what I am a long time ago (*Blade II*, 2002).

The theme of survival comes up in not only individual life stories of vampires, but also in the survival of the entire vampire community. *Blade* is built on the tension between vampires that work in the shadows, trying to influence humanity with subtle manipulation, and the villain that seeks unlimited power. Those trying to maintain the balance survive by more conventional means, by owning blood banks, medical research facilities, and so on. The moral of the story is (from a vampire point of view) that "blending in" is the key to survival. Disrupting that are both power-hungry individuals (*Blade*) and the mutated vampires that cannot control their thirst, who act "like crack addicts" (*Blade II*). Even if there is some optimistic (again, from a vampire point of view) talk about a "vampire final solution" of enslaving all humanity in *Blade Trinity*, the quest for power eventually turns against the vampires.

As noted before, humanity has little role in *Underworld* and its sequel, *Underworld Evolution*. In fact, the films do not have a single scene with vampires feeding on humans. Nevertheless, blood does have a central role in the survival story of the vampires in the *Underworld* saga. Now, however, survival is not about surviving *per se*, but retaining racial purity.

"Racial hygiene" figures particularly prominently in the discourse of Viktor, the leader of the vampires. As a reaction to an origin myth narrated by a captive werewolf and to the possibility of combining vampire and werewolf genes (see above), Viktor's response leaves no room for doubt: "There can be no such union. And to speak of it is heresy" (*Underworld*, 2003). Later Lucian, leader of the werewolves, reveals the full magnitude of Viktor's contempt for racial blending: "We were slaves once. The daylight guardians of the vampires. I was born in servitude, yet I harboured them no ill will. Even took a vampire for my bride. It was forbidden, our union. Viktor feared a blending of the species. Feared it so much, he killed her. His own daughter, burnt alive for loving me. This is his war, Viktor's, and he's spent the last 600 years exterminating my species" (*Underworld*, 2003). Near the end of the film, Viktor's perspective is explained by him: "I loved my daughter! But the abomination growing in her womb was a betrayal of me and of the coven! I did what was necessary to protect the species…" (*Underworld*, 2003). Using geneticized rhetoric to justify their motivation, the new celluloid vampires differ considerably from the almost one-dimensionally malevolent old paradigm vampire. However, as always, there is a battle between good and evil. The difference is that now the evil can be found within the vampire community. Echoing real life, the "bad guys" are not always those completely "other," but individuals and groups within the community that hunger for blind domination or who are obsessed by racial purity based solely on prejudice.

The Crucifix and the UV Bullet: Destroying the Vampire

Perhaps nothing reveals more about the paradigm shift in vampire films than the changes in the portrayals of the destruction of the vampire. Vampire folklore is ripe with myriad ways of killing the undead and reflects the beliefs of the nature of the creature. Later fictional accounts have added some features that have since become the stock of vampire lore, most notably the aversion to sunlight (Melton, 1999: 192–96).

The demonic nature of the old paradigm vampire is apparent in the ways in which vampires are kept at bay and eventually destroyed in most films. The crucifix is the most obvious bane of vampires, but the methods of their destruction are also infused with mysticism and religious (Christian) symbolism. The stake through the heart would kill any living person, but for killing vampires it is the only method, bullets or any other conventional means having little or no effect on the supernatural creature (Melton, 1999: 79–80). In a striking combination of the cross and the stake, the final scene of *Dracula has Risen from the Grave* (1968) is a wonderful example of the role of religion and faith in the old paradigm films. Dracula approaches his castle with the seduced heroine, but needs to remove a large golden cross that blocks the entrance. At the castle they are confronted by the heroine's suitor and a renegade priest who has been enslaved earlier by the count. A fight ensues between Dracula and the hero, during which the cross falls from a cliff, pierces the ground below and stands upright. As might be expected, at the end of the hand-to-hand combat, both the hero and the villain fall from the edge of the cliff. The young hero grabs a vine and is saved from falling to his death, but Dracula plunges down to the bottom of the hill, only to be impaled by the shiny golden cross standing proud in the ground.

This, however, is not the end of the evil count. In a twist of the impaling myth, the recitation of the Lord's Prayer is needed to ensure that the vampire's demise is final. Because the hero, who earlier has professed to be a stout atheist, does not have the faith, the fallen priest recants and plays an instrumental part in Dracula's destruction by reciting the prayer (in Latin). This eventually kills the vampire and, in the process, the priest himself is drained of strength. After Dracula's body disappears in a familiar gust of wind, leaving behind only the black cape, the hero finds faith and as a closing gesture makes the sign of the cross, all the while his beloved looks upon him approvingly. Thus the importance of faith and religion is not only highlighted in the powerful symbolism of Dracula being impaled by a golden cross, but also in the two "conversion" experiences of, firstly, the wayward priest and then, secondly, the atheist hero.

Whereas atheism as a counterpoint to religion might have resonated with 1960s viewers in a way unimaginable earlier in the century, the juxtaposition of science and religion and the triumph of the latter in fighting the vampire has earlier precedents in vampire fiction. Timothy K. Beal wonderfully expresses this crossing of boundaries between "archaic" religion and modernity in his analysis of what he calls "rituals of resacralization" in Bram Stoker's original *Dracula*:

> The contamination introduced by Dracula, which fundamentally alters the state of Lucy and Mina, must be combated by the male heroes of the story with specific rituals that work to resacralize and reorient their

women and their world... One is the modern medical rite of blood transfusion, performed on Lucy, the ineffectiveness of which suggests the terrifying ineffectiveness of modern western medical science in the face of
this *unheimlich* outbreak of the primitive and non-western... The other
is the ritual slaying of the chaos monsters [with the classic implements: a
crucifix, garlic, communion wafers, and a wooden stake], first the undead
monster Lucy and finally the king of monsters Dracula. Unlike the modern
medical rites practiced initially on Lucy, these rites, which are identified
with primitive, non-western religion, prove effective (Beal, 2002: 134).

Even if we do not want to apply Beal's postcolonialist reading to
the depiction of Dracula in the later movie versions of Stoker's original
story, the bottom line remains the same: modern science, its fascinating achievements notwithstanding, is powerless against the onslaught
of the demonic vampire. In the Hammer series of vampire films, this is
perhaps most explicitly depicted in *Lust for a Vampire* (1970), the film
adaptation of Sheridan Le Fanu's early female vampire story *Carmilla*
(1872). In one of the scenes the father of a recently deceased board-
ing school student—the victim of the lead female vampire Carmilla—
discusses her daughter's strange death with a professor: "I can do
nothing," says Professor Herz. "We are talking about matters beyond
science, about the dark imaginings of man, about metaphysics, the
nature of good and evil. You don't need a doctor, you need..." (*Lust
for a Vampire*, 1970). Herz is then interrupted in mid-sentence by the
entrance of a Catholic bishop and his entourage. There can hardly be a
more obvious way of underlining the fact that, concerning the subject
of vampires, science is helpless. From this point on we enter the realm
of faith and religion.

Moving to the new paradigm, we find a completely different conception of the means of fighting vampires. As a logical extension of the fact
that vampires are a product of genetic mutation, modern technology is
harnessed in full force to combat the creatures. In fact, the new paradigm movies use metafiction to dispel the conventional understanding
of vampires (see Partridge, 2004a: 129–30). *Blade Trinity*, for example,
opens with a voice-over narration that takes a very explicit stance against
the old paradigm myths. The voice of Hannibal King, one of the vampire
hunters helping Blade, narrates: "In the movies Dracula always wears a
cape and some old English guy always manages to save the day at the last
minute with crosses and holy water. But everybody knows that movies
are full of shit" (*Blade Trinity*, 2004). Already in *Blade* (1998) the issue of
religion and vampires is taken up. Although some of the traditional ways
of destroying vampires remain, they have a new meaning as "biological
weapons" (cf. Partridge, 2004a: 131). Garlic, with its mystical properties

in the old paradigm movies, has become "allium sativum," the effects of which are explained in medical terms:

Karen:	So what do you use, then? Stakes? Crosses?
Whistler:	Crosses don't do squat. Some of the legends are true, though. Vampires are severely allergic to silver. Feed them garlic and they'll go into anaphylactic shock. [Brandishing a uv-light lamp] And of course there's always sunlight, ultra-violet rays. (*Blade*, 1998)

The common understanding that bullets do not have an effect on supernatural vampires is well put by Melton: "[I]f a vampire was hurt by the attack, the harm was very temporary, and the vampire quickly recovered to wreak vengeance upon those secularists who would put their faith in modern mechanical artifacts" (Melton, 1999: 80). This theme remains, but now some of the bullets are customized to affect vampires:

Kahn:	[Examining a bullet round containing blue liquid] I have to run a few tests. It's definitely an irradiated fluid of some sort.
Selene:	Ultraviolet ammunition.
Kahn:	Daylight harnessed as a weapon (*Underworld*, 2003).

The most dangerous nemesis of the new paradigm celluloid vampires is not, however, any of the individual weapons devised by the technological geniuses of the films. The true threat to vampires is the possibility of viral warfare, hinted at in *Blade*, but brought to full fruition in *Blade Trinity*. As in all the Blade films, and also in both installments of *Underworld*, one of the supporting characters is a scientist. In *Blade Trinity*, the virologist character explains the key to the destruction of vampires—this time for good:

Hannibal King:	So we kill a few hundred of them a year—big deal. There are thousands of them out there, maybe tens of thousands. We need a new tactic.
Blade:	Like what?
Sommerfield:	A biological weapon… For the last year, I've been working with synthesized DNA in order to create an artificial virus targeted specifically at vampires. We're calling it DayStar.
Hannibal King:	Think about it Blade. We could wipe them all out in one single move (*Blade Trinity*, 2004).

The dark imaginings of men, metaphysics, or the nature of good and evil play little if any role in the scienticized discourse pertaining to the destruction of the vampire. Although the old paradigm crucifix and the stake through the vampire's heart also represent "technologies of destruction" in some sense, at the end of the day it is faith that kills the demonic enemy. The ending scene of *Dracula has Risen from the Grave* quoted above is perhaps the most explicit example of the secondary nature of technology in the old paradigm films. In the new paradigm films technology has become a means in itself—a logical consequence of the overall scientization of the vampire.

The Migration of the Vampire Soul: "Immanentization" and the Continuing Enchantment

Throughout this chapter I have emphasized the difference between the old and new paradigm celluloid vampires. Whether we look at the depictions of the nature, the motivations, or the ways of destroying vampires, the role of mysticism and religion—Christianity in particular—has decreased to the point of being completely obsolete, only to be referred to as a metafictive "myth." This is what I have called "the migration of the vampire soul": the demystification and immanentization of the vampire figure in popular film. The Devil's spawn of the classic era of vampire films has become a freak of nature, a genetic defect. The remaining question is how to assess this change against the broader backdrop of religion and popular culture.

The question of de-spiritualization of the vampire film can be approached from two directions. One is from the *production* side, analyzing how and why the films possibly reflect contemporary culture. Perhaps more interesting, however, are the possibilities that the new paradigm vampire films open up on the *reception* side. That is, can the scienticized new paradigm vampire fiction offer raw material for meaning making in the contemporary world?

Speaking about contemporary vampire films as *zeitgeist* is tricky at best (see Roth, 1979; Phillips, 2005). Analyses of popular cultural artefacts can rarely straightforwardly explain *why* certain types of popular culture spring up at certain times. The interaction between producers and audiences is so complex that broad explanations as to why a particular character (the scienticized vampire, for example) becomes a trend tends to lack cogency, at least from a critical social-scientific perspective (cf. Boelderl and Mayr, 1995; Rickels, 1999). A few "mundane" interpretations can, however, be made.

First, a caveat: What I have presented here does not claim that religio-mystical vampires have disappeared from the screen altogether. On the contrary, most of the numerous non-mainstream films faithfully reproduce the classic image of the vampire. The number of small-scale vampire film productions is probably second only to zombie movies, which have always been popular among independent producers of horror cinema. If quantity is the measure, the supernatural and religious aspects of vampires continue to attract audiences and producers.

Second, although it seems that the new paradigm celluloid vampire has come to stay, this might be attributed as much to the change of genre in vampire films as to any change in the appeal of the vampire. The *Blade* trilogy and the two *Underworld* movies are first and foremost action films, not horror films in the sense that *Dracula* (1931) or the Hammer vampire productions were. Because action works at a completely different level to horror (see Carroll, 1990), the immanentization of vampires is a logical extension of the genre change. James Bond is not interested in the religious (or any, for that matter) sensibilities of his enemies. He is interested in how their threat could be removed. And so it is also with the new paradigm celluloid vampires.

Third, from a quite simple perspective, popular culture has undergone a significant pluralization which makes unequivocally Christian themes less appealing for wide audiences (Partridge, 2004a: 131). Studies have shown that "stories that explicitly embrace religious language and definitions are often rejected by persons who are not already members of those traditions" (Clark, 2003: 228). Moving the vampire away from the demonic and towards the scientific—a worldview ironically rejected only by the most hardcore fundamentalists of any religion—can be seen as an outcome of the sensitivity that a religiously and spiritually pluralistic culture engenders.

At the outset of this chapter, it was claimed that Ramsland (1989) was perhaps a little too eager to explain the vampire phenomenon as disenchantment with science and fascination with the spiritual. The analysis of contemporary vampire films shows that the traditional trappings of institutionalized religion do not carry much weight in the new paradigm films. From the reception point of view, however, this does not mean that the scienticized genre has become de-sacralized.

Recent years have witnessed the emergence of what could be dubbed the "functional" paradigm in the study of religion, media, and culture (Hjelm 2005). This approach focuses on the reception of media and popular culture, and the meaning making involved in the reception process. The approach is well illustrated in the distinction made between "religion online" and "online religion," now commonly used in the study of religion and media (Helland, 2000). Hoover and Park summarize the taxonomy as follows:

> Simply put, *religion online* is the self-conscious use of the online context by religion organizations or movements for purposes of publicity, education, outreach, proselytization, and so on. *Online religion*, by contrast, is the far more interesting issue of the online context becoming or being used as a locus of religious, spiritual (or other similar) practice (Hoover and Park, 2005: 248).

Popular cultural products can similarly be analyzed according to their explicit religious content on the one hand, and the "religious" or spiritual uses that they are put into on the other (Clark, 2003). Looking at the relationship between meaning making and the scientization of the new paradigm celluloid vampires, it can be readily seen that *Blade* and *Underworld* fall within the fold of the wide-ranging contemporary fascination with genetics. In a Bergerian sense, science has become the "symbolic universe" which orders most aspects of everyday life, thus supplanting obsolete religious explanations of the world (Berger, 1973: 34–37; Berger and Luckmann, 1967: 92–128). The chaos of the supernatural in the old paradigm films has become the chaos of science gone awry. However, this does not mean that scientization has made the figure of the vampire less awe-inspiring (see Douglas, 1982: 9). On the contrary, Stoker's ineffective blood transfusion has been supplanted by technological fetishism and scientists have become the high priests of the contemporary cinematic meaning-making experience. In this sense vampire films have come closer to science fiction and the utopian vistas that it provides for the construction of meaning.

That said, even if a world ruled by natural laws and harnessed by science and technology has become the new master narrative in vampire film, the moral side of the story remains. What differentiates the new paradigm from the old is that the answers to questions of "ultimate significance" (Luckmann, 1967) are no longer portrayed in readily recognizable forms. For example, from a human perspective, both the vampires and werewolves in *Underworld* are evil, yet the audience knows which side they are on as the story progresses. Also, although not embedded into a religious framework, Blade's mission to destroy all vampires can be seen as a highly spiritual quest—a quest of ultimate significance. If religious themes are marginal in the new celluloid paradigm vampires, there are still numerous possibilities to read spiritual meaning into the stories the movies tell.

The new paradigm celluloid vampire provides a new and perhaps a more tangible backdrop especially for the burgeoning vampire sub-culture (Keyworth, 2002; cf. Miller et al., 1999). Whereas pacts with the Devil might be somewhat passé in contemporary youth culture, the scienticized version of vampirism offers hope for many: being a vampire is not necessarily "evil" in the sense it used to be. The empowerment gained from being part of a subculture (Partridge, 2005: 232) does not automatically entail moral inferiority, even if the subcultural lifestyle tends to marginalize its members. And, last but not least, maybe one day the "arbovirus" will be found!

However, the fascination with the scientized celluloid vampire has analytical significance beyond the confines of a subculture. In their own way, the new paradigm celluloid vampires both reflect and construct the broader socio-cultural milieu. Although it is impossible to discern straightforward causal patterns in this interaction, the migration of the vampire soul in contemporary film can be seen as emblematic of moder-nity. The new paradigm movies push traditionally conceived institution-alized religion further into the margins, but provide new frameworks for meaning-making. Whether taken as entertainment, as metaphor, or as a serious building block of one's identity and spirituality, the demonic figure of the vampire continues to fascinate by drawing our attention to something beyond our everyday lives.

Chapter 7

A Man of Wealth and Taste:
The Strange Career of Hannibal Lecter

Brian Baker

In Thomas Harris' *Hannibal* (1999), the eponymous serial killer relocates to Florence. Having disposed of the librarian of the "fabled Capponi library," Lecter, posing as one "Dr Fell," proceeds to give a lecture on Dante and Judas Iscariot to the Studiolo, "the most renowned medieval and Renaissance scholars in the world" (Harris, 2000: 934), in order to secure his nomination for the now-vacated position. Lecter proceeds to give a slide show involving death by hanging of avaricious betrayers, of which Judas is the archetype and the policeman who pursues Lecter/Fell, *Commendatore* Pazzi, is the modern analogue. Pazzi is also a member of the audience for the lecture. Lecter/Fell proceeds to read (literally, in a flawless Tuscan "without accent") Canto XIII of Dante's *Inferno*, which narrates Dante and Virgil's encounter with the seventh circle of Hell, the violent. Dante comes across a wood in the Second Round, filled with trees full of "poisonous thorns" (Dante, 1961: 167). Dante hears voices but presumes they come from people hidden behind the trees; but when he reaches out his hand to unthinkingly pluck "a twig from a great thorn" (Dante, 1961: 169), the tree trunk itself cries out: "'Why dost thou tear me?'": "from the broken splinter came forth words and blood together" (Dante, 1961: 169). These are men turned into trees, men that had committed violence against themselves. This is the circle of Hell for the suicides.

The tree explains that he was once the Chancellor of Emperor Frederick II, and who was himself accused of treason, blinded, and cast into prison, where he committed suicide. His name is Piero delle Vigne, whose courteous language and reverence towards his former "master" (he also calls Frederick "Caesar" and "Augustus") indicates his undimmed faithfulness, and whose suffering arouses pity in both Virgil (who calls delle Vigne "wounded soul" [Dante, 1961: 169]) and Dante (who cannot question the tree further, "such pity fills my heart" [Dante, 1961: 171]). The tree, impelled to speak truth in Hell, reveals that "never did [he] break faith with [his] lord" (Dante, 1961: 171); but the true horror of his suffering is still to be revealed. When the suicide dies, Minos, the keeper of Hell, throws the soul down to the seventh circle, where it sprouts and grows into a "savage tree." Once it bears leaves, "the Harpies, feeding on its leaves, cause pain and for the pain an outlet" (Dante, 1961: 171). To return for a moment to *Hannibal*, this is the point in the lecture that Lecter/Fell begins to quote directly from Dante:

> *Surge in vermena e in pianta silvestre:*
> *L'Arpie, pascendo poi de la sui foglie,*
> *Fanno dolore, e al dolor fenestra* (Harris, 2000: 936).[1]

Lecter/Fell describes the scene in the *Inferno* thus: "he tells of dragging, with the other damned, his own dead body to hang upon a thorn tree" (Harris, 2000: 936). In fact, delle Vigne is describing what will happen on the day of judgment: he, like the other shades in Hell, will drag their own body to be hung on the very thorn tree that sprouts from where their soul fell, a kind of torture that echoes the crucifixion of Christ (the body hung up, the thorns). The lines of Dante that Lecter/Fell quotes are crucial, for they describe the leaves that grow and are eaten by Harpies, causing pain; the leaves grow again and are eaten again. Neither Lecter/Fell nor John D. Sinclair notice what seems to be a clear reference here to the suffering of Prometheus, the Titan of Greek mythology who attempted to amend the fault of his brother Epimetheus (who made Man but was so prodigal in assigning talents to other beings that nothing was left for Man; Prometheus was impelled to steal fire from the Gods and give it to humans to recompense them for lack of other abilities), and was punished by being chained to a rock while vultures pecked at his liver, which grew back as fast as it was consumed. Prometheus, in the hands of Romantic poets such as P. B. Shelley, becomes the figure of titanic suffering for rebellion against the (unjust) rule of the Gods; I will return to this shortly.

In the *Inferno*, delle Vigne is a pitiable figure, whose suffering stirs great sympathy in Dante and his guide. In *Hannibal*, Lecter/Fell paints a quite different picture. Lecter/Fell avers that " 'Dante recalls [...] the death of Judas in the death of Pier della Vigna for the same crimes of avarice and treachery' " (Harris, 2000: 937). Not so. Delle Vigne in fact offers precisely the reverse of the figure of Judas in his faithfulness. If he were as treacherous and avaricious as Lecter/Fell suggests, delle Vigne would be in a lower circle of Hell, much closer to Satan. Why, then, is Lecter/Fell so wrong? Is it that Harris himself misunderstands the import of Canto XIII, stressing the confluence of hanging, betrayal, and avarice to the detriment of Dante's actual text? If it is Lecter/Fell's mistake, wouldn't the "most renowned" scholars of the Studiolo notice? This is probably unresolvable, but I would like to suggest a possible solution: that Harris introduces the Promethean figure of delle Vigne purpose-fully to suggest a figure of titanic suffering, but through a quasi-academic sleight of hand, wishes to stress not the Promethean or satanic rebel-lion against God—a type that I will argue in this chapter is increasingly identified with Lecter himself—but the Judas-like properties of Lecter's antagonist in this section of the novel, *Commendatore* Pazzi. This typing of the hanged betrayer immediately foreshadows Pazzi's own death by hanging, engineered by Lecter, who, in the words of Katherine and Lee Horsley:

> [with] a flamboyance which goes beyond that of his previous excesses, […] crafts an elaborate replication of artistic depictions of the death of Pazzi's ancestor. Although Lecter's previous "punishments" invariably fit the crime, none so richly evokes the torments of Dante's *Inferno*. As a prelude to the murder, he impresses on his victim the appropriateness of this punishment, given that the Pazzis themselves, historically, are the embodiment of the greed and betrayal under the surface artifice and beauty.[2]

The greed and betrayal of Pazzi, when seen as analogous to that of Judas (and of Lecter/Fell's creative mis-reading of delle Vigne), almost serves to legitimize his murder. One can, however, trace the lineaments of an alternate reading of this scene, indicated by Lecter/Fell's significant reading of the *Inferno* section in which delle Vigne tells of the Harpies eating the leaves of the thorn trees. In this alternative reading, Pazzi is not Judas, but God's instrument, albeit an avaricious one; and Lecter not the betrayed, but God's adversary: Satan.

Before attending Lecter/Fell's lecture, Pazzi prays in the Pazzi chapel in Florence, "one of the glories of Renaissance architecture" (Harris 2000: 931). While Pazzi does not deceive himself about the rather venal nature of what he is about to do (or try to do), he says, "aloud to God,"

> "Thank you, Father, for allowing me to remove this monster, monster of monsters, from your Earth. Thank you on behalf of the souls We will spare of pain." Whether this was the magisterial "We" or a reference to the partnership of Pazzi and God is not clear, and there may not be a single answer (Harris, 2000: 931).

The text here seems to point to Pazzi's presumption in accounting himself God's appointed "partner," and its rationalization of self-seeking, avarice, and corruption, but his gesture to look up at the point of death, hoping "so much, that God could see" (Harris, 2000: 942), does suggest a deeply felt faith. The rhetoric of "monster," though, repeats that which is used to characterize Lecter from *Red Dragon* through to *Hannibal*, not only by characters within the narrative world of the texts, but also by the putative narrator of the novels, whose presence is particularly intrusive in *Hannibal*. Pazzi's use of it puts him on the side of the sane, if not the side of the angels. Lecter *is* a monster; in a sense, Pazzi is right to plan to dispose of him. However, as I have argued elsewhere, in the development of Harris' fictions involving Lecter, Hannibal "the cannibal" is increasingly situated at the center of the narrative, to the extent that we are given access to Lecter's interiority (see Baker, 2007). From a position of monstrous Other, Lecter increasingly becomes stabilized at the center of the narratives as the Self, offered for identification (and perhaps sympathy). Lecter is re-placed at the center of the narratives as a redefinition of his subjectivity, achieving a stability guaranteed by his contrast with the fractured, fluid masculinities of the serial killers Francis Dollarhyde (in *Red Dragon*) and Jame Gumb (in *The Silence of the Lambs*). As Sabrina Barton suggests, "In the economy of selves that the movie sets up, if one marginalized group is allowed to find a subjectivity that feels stable and authentic, another must take its place at the negative pole of performativity" (Barton, 2002: 315). As I shall argue in this essay, however, this re-alignment of Lecter with Self rather than Other does not conflict with his satanic characterization, but rather follows the Romantic readings of Milton's Satan but as the *hero* of *Paradise Lost* rather than as God's "evil" adversary.

I would like to stress here both the signs of the diabolic and the heroic in the characterization of Lecter. Part of the stabilization of Lecter's subjectivity is his alignment with the hero of what Peter A. Schock identifies as "Romantic Satanism," the Romantics' use of Milton's Satan as a symbol for heroic, transgressive rebellion, what Schock further calls "an idealized antagonist of an Omnipotence embodying the dominant political and religious values of an era" (Schock, 2003: 5). Schock writes:

> The presence of various forms of "Satanism" in Romantic writing has been widely acknowledged. [...] Peter Thorslev identifies the following speech as the *locus classicus* of the satanic stance in Romantic writing:
>
> > The mind is its own place, and in itself
> > Can make a heaven of hell, a hell of heaven.
> > What matter where, if I be still the same,
> > And what I should be, all but less than he
> > Whom thunder hath made greater? (*PL* I, ll.254–58)

> Satan's defiant assertion of autonomy, delivered on the burning plain
> of hell, was so broadly influential [that different types of adaptation of]
> Satanism have been extended to cover a range of Romantic attitudes or
> stances—typically individualism, rebellious or defiant self-assertion, and
> daemonic sublimity (Schock, 2003: 3–4).

For Romantic poets such as Shelley, the figures of Satan (derived from a reading of Milton's *Paradise Lost*) and Prometheus are in close proximity as heroically rebellious figures, as is noted by Mario Praz in *The Romantic Agony*, who writes: "Milton conferred upon the figure of Satan all the charm of an untamed rebel which already belonged to the Prometheus of Aeschylus" (Praz, 1954: 55). In his Preface to "Prometheus Unbound," Shelley writes:

> The only imaginary being resembling in any degree Prometheus, is Satan,
> and Prometheus is, in my judgement, a more poetical character than
> Satan because, in addition to courage and majesty and firm and patient
> opposition to omnipotent force, he is susceptible of being described as
> exempt from the taints of ambition, envy, revenge, and a desire for per-
> sonal aggrandisement, which in the Hero of *Paradise Lost*, interfere with
> the interest. [...] Prometheus is, as it were, the type of the highest perfec-
> tion of moral and intellectual nature, impelled by the purest and truest
> motives to the best and noblest ends (Shelley, 2000a: 734).

Milton's Satan is re-read by the Romantics not as a figure of evil, but as a heroic figure ("courage and majesty") who resists the totalizing power of the monotheistic God ("firm and patient opposition"). Satan becomes not only a figure for Romantic self-assertion, but also (punningly as Lucifer, the "Son of Light") a curious precursor of Enlightenment emphases on freedom—freedom from arbitrary power, freedom from tradition, freedom of speech, and particularly "freedom of moral man to make his own way in the world" (Gay, 1973: I.xii, 3; quoted in Day, 1996: 66). This idea of independence, freedom from tutelage, is vital to Immanuel Kant's characterization of the Enlightenment project (such as in his short essay "An Answer to the Question: What is Enlightenment?") and Aidan Day characterizes it as "humankind's 'resolution and courage' to use the understanding without the guidance of another" (Day, 1996: 65).

The autonomous Enlightenment and Romantic subject is self-presented in contradistinction to social, political/ideological, hegemonic forces. This, then, is somewhat ironic, as the very nature of this stable unitary subjectivity (inherited from the Enlightenment) recapitulates the hegemon One God (Blake's Urizen) that is rebelled against. The "tragic rebel" of Milton's Satan simply reflects the One God that is his antagonist. The Romantic Satan finds its analogue in what Mario Praz calls the "Byronic Fatal Man":

> Rebels in the grand manner, grandsons of Milton's Satan and the brothers of Schiller's Robber, begin to inhabit the picturesque, Gothicized backgrounds of the English "tales of terror" towards the end of the eighteenth century. [...] Certain qualities can be noticed here which were destined to recur insistently in the Fatal Men of the Romantics: mysterious (but conjectured to be exalted) origin, traces of burnt-out passions, suspicion of ghastly guilt, melancholy habits, pale face, unforgettable eyes (Praz, 1954: 59).

At the end of his chapter on "The Metamorphoses of Satan," Praz connects the Enlightenment libertine "the Divine Marquis" with the Romantic "Satanic Lord" Byron (Praz, 1954: 81). In these figures, love is implicated in cruelty and violence; desire with destruction; life with death. Here we shade into the Gothic, and Praz himself cites the figure of the vampire (sex/predation, love for/absorption of the Other) as a typical generic form of the *caractère maudit* of both Romantic love and its object of beauty. (Although Harris is careful to assert the cannibal as different from the vampire, the motif of predation and consumption is present in both.) In Ridley Scott's film of *Hannibal*, it is the "satanic" figure of the "mad, bad and dangerous to know" Lord Byron that mediates the characterization of Lecter. In flowing coat and broad-brimmed hat, he is every inch the Gothicized Romantic hero.

Hannibal Lecter is, I would like to suggest, a late avatar of Romantic Satanism, a figure of grand rebellion against a God who boundlessly outmatches Lecter's own appetite for consumption: *"Hannibal Lecter had not been bothered by any considerations of deity, other than to recognize how his own modest predations paled beside those of God, who is in irony matchless, and in wanton malice beyond measure"* (Harris, 2000: 994; Harris' italics). In fact, the ravenous God seemingly present here is much like a deficient demiurge that creates Earth and Man that can be found in the religious teachings of Zoroaster and Gnosticism, and is echoed in the rule of Urizen in the works of the Romantic mythographer-poet William Blake. Blake is, of course, himself indebted to Milton, and is an early example of "Romantic Satanism" to the extent that in *The Marriage of Heaven and Hell*, Blake famously writes that "the reason Milton wrote in fetters when he wrote of Angels & God, and at liberty when of Devils & Hell, is because he was a true poet and of the Devil's party without knowing it" (Blake, 1975: plates 5–6, p. xvii). Lecter's satanic rebellion takes the form of a denial of God: in *Hannibal Rising*, having found and buried the corpse of his sister, Lecter declares:

"Mischa, we take comfort knowing there is no God. That you are not
enslaved in a Heaven, made to kiss God's ass forever. What you have is
better than Paradise. You have blessed oblivion. I miss you every day"
(Harris, 2006: 222).

Traces of Milton can be found even in this denial of God's existence,
which at the same time calls up images of servitude (and the key word
"Paradise") that signify a satanic antagonism.

Lecter, faced with a world in which his sister is a victim of cannibalism,
a malign world, also adopts a satanic position of rebellion against the rule
of conventional morality, albeit a transgression relocated as revenge in
the most recent Lecter book, *Hannibal Rising*. Curiously, though, Lecter
does come to adopt a kind of code of ethics in the course of the novels.
This is proposed most pithily by Barney, the former nurse in the Baltimore State Hospital for the Criminally Insane that houses Lecter in *The
Silence of the Lambs*, who says to Clarice Starling in *Hannibal*: "He told
me once that, whenever it was 'feasible', he preferred to eat the rude.
'Free-range rude', he called them" (Harris, 2000: 831). This chimes with
Lecter's line to Clarice Starling on their first meeting (when she is sprayed
with "Multiple" Miggs' semen): "'Discourtesy is unspeakably ugly to
me'" (Harris, 2000: 413). Also, at the end of the film of *The Silence of
the Lambs*, after Lecter puts down the phone in his last conversation with
Clarice, during which he guarantees her ongoing safety from him, he is
seen slowly pursuing the oleaginous and undeniably "rude" Dr Frederick
Chilton, once Director of the Baltimore State Hospital, somewhere on a
street in South America, in order to "have him to dinner." In the course
of the novels, Lecter is increasingly seen to murder mainly those who
threaten him directly or anger him; there is method in his murderous or
monstrous "madness."

Lecter is, of course, a serial killer, one of the types of "evil" in contemporary popular culture. Richard Dyer, in his BFI Modern Classic
text on Fincher's *Seven*, notes that the "serial killer has become a widespread figure in films, novels, television series, true crime coverage
and even painting, poetry, opera and rock music," and that "they have
increasingly been seen to be expressive specifically of masculinity in
contemporary society" (Dyer, 1999: 37). I would like to reiterate here
not only that serial killer fictions signify the boundaries of rational discourse: the incommensurability of the Other to reason is the point at
which these texts point towards "evil," the monstrous, and the discourse of religion; but also that serial killer fictions signify the limit-
case of representations of normative subjectivity and gender roles in
contemporary Anglo-American popular culture. Serial killers are arche-

typal fragmented subjects, emblematic figures indicating the rupture of the unitary subject under the pressures of modernity, particularly in an American context. The serial killers are then non-human or even post-human figures, their fluid or ruptured subjectivities (Gumb is a "failed" transsexual, Dollarhyde obsessed with his own "Becoming") throwing into relief the unitary self of monotheism, Enlightenment rationality, and Romantic feeling.

Lecter increasingly comes to stand in the place of that unitary self, but it is bound up with evil and particularly with the satanic: he asks Clarice Starling, "Can you stand to say I'm evil? Am I evil, Officer Starling?" (Harris, 2000: 409). Richard Dyer, in his BFI Modern Classic book on David Fincher's *Seven*, argues as follows:

> The notion of evil, rather than sin, is a common way of dealing with serial killers, often in a context where all other explanations fall short. This is equally true of the coverage of famous cases and in fictions, as at the end of *Halloween* (1978) where the psychiatrist admits that there is no explanation for the remorseless killer Michael other than that he is evil incarnate. Somerset [in *Seven*] himself invokes the notion, when he says that, if, when they finally get the killer, he turns out to be "Satan himself," that would be satisfying. However, he goes on to say that the sad fact is "he's not the devil, he's just a man," not an embodiment of the otherness and exteriority of evil, but the common fact of sin (Dyer, 1999: 13–14).

It is interesting that Dyer makes a distinction between "sin" and "evil," suggesting the former is quotidian, while the other is transcendent or mythical. In *The Silence of the Lambs*, it is noteworthy that Lecter characterizes Buffalo Bill as sinful rather than evil, particularly considering his own implied self-definition (as evil):

> "What is the first and principal thing he does, what need does he serve by killing?"
> "Anger, resentment, sexual frus–"
> "No."
> "What, then?"
> "He covets" (Harris, 2000: 607).

Lecter's assumption of a Biblical discourse in characterizing the serial killer is significant, as is his shutting down of Starling's psychology-based (and perhaps rather pat) answer. It is also, in Dyer's terms, somewhat hierarchical: sin is everyday, while evil is uncommon. Lecter's satanic grandeur is contrasted with Jame Gumb/Buffalo Bill's rather ludicrous name, anonymity, and occupation as a seamstress. In Demme's film, Ted Levine's performance emphasizes the banality of Gumb, the absence of the quality that ultimately heroizes Lecter: taste.

Lecter is a particular type of serial killer, then, distinct from the fractured, unstable, transformative, or masked subjectivities of other fictions (and other serial killers within Harris' fictions). Others do not assume his grandeur, and neither are they surrounded by the signs of the satanic. For Lecter, these signs abound. In *Hannibal*, the policeman Praz engages a female thief, Romula, to "botch" a pickpocketing in order to get Lecter's fingerprints (Lecter would seize Romula's wrist, around which was a wide silver bracelet). Romula, clutching her baby as part of her "act" (an ironic inversion of Madonna and child), awaits Lecter's coming:

> At the moment of touching Dr Fell she looked into his face, felt sucked to the red centers of his eyes, felt the huge cold vacuum pull her heart against her ribs and her hand flew away from his face to cover the baby's face and she heard her voice say *"Perdonami, perdonami, signore,"* turning and fleeing as the doctor looked after her for a long moment (Harris, 2000: 896).

Back with Pazzi, Romula exclaims: " 'That is the Devil. [...] Shaitan, Son of the Morning. I've seen him now' " (Harris, 2000: 897). Later in *Hannibal*, after Lecter has effected his and Clarice Starling's escape from Mason Verger's demonic man-eating pigs, Tommasso, the Sardinian keeper of the pigs, characterizes Lecter as a kind of Lord of the Flies, having supernatural control over other demonic entities:

> "the pigs, you must know, the pigs help the *dottore*. They stand back from him, circle him. They kill my brother, kill Carlo, but they stand back from Dr. Lecter. I think they worship him" (Harris, 2000: 1165).

Perhaps the most important of the satanic signs is the name Lecter assumes in Florence, "Dr Fell." Clearly, there is a kind of atrocious punning at work: "fell" can be connected to hanging and the *Grand Guignol* fate of Pazzi, who, disembowelled, falls to his death (attached to a rope and noose, of course). "Fell," as used in the phrase "fell fiend," is also peculiarly apt for the Lecter "monster." However, the most insistent allusion seems to be with Lucifer, "Son of Morning," the "fallen" archangel of *Paradise Lost*. There, Milton several times in book I, notes Satan's eyes:

> his baleful eyes
> That witness'd huge affliction and dismay
> Mixt with obdurate pride and steadfast hate (Milton, 1966: I, ll.56–58);

and

> ...yet shone
> Above them all th' Archangel; but his face
> Deep scars of Thunder had intrencht, and care
> Sat on his faded cheek, but under brows

> Of dauntless courage, and considerate pride
> Waiting revenge. Cruel his eye, but cast
> Signs of remorse and passion to behold
> The fellows of his crime (Milton, 1966: I, ll.599–606).

Lecter's red or maroon eyes, so powerful that they suck in Romula's consciousness like a vacuum, or command the host of demonic pigs, express his Satanism. The pathos that attends Milton's Satan in his fallen state is not entirely absent from Lecter: he too, as *Hannibal* and *Hannibal Rising* reveal, has witnessed "huge affliction and dismay," and seems to feel "remorse and passion" for the memory of his lost sibling, Mischa. In fact, *Hannibal Rising*, which begins with the young Hannibal and his sister playing in the grounds of their home, Lecter Castle in Lithuania, before the arrival of invading German troops during 1941, perhaps suggests some kind of time "before the fall," a pre-diabolic consciousness lost when his sister is taken from him. *Hannibal Rising* narrates this "paradise lost," and ultimately the revenge Lecter wreaks upon those who killed and ate Mischa. Its title suggests perhaps a new, self-made Hannibal Lecter, ascending from his "fallen" state to become the aesthete-monster we find in the other books.

In *Paradise Lost*, Satan famously asserts what Peter Schock calls his "autogeny":

> ...Who saw
> When this Creation was? Remember'st thou
> They making, when thy Maker gave thee being?
> We know no time when we were not as now,
> Know none before us, self-begot, self-raised
> By our own quick'ning power (Milton 1966: VI, ll.856–61).

Schock suggests that "Romantic readers of Milton found the Manichean postulate of Satanic self-assertion compelling" (Schock, 2003: 37); "Romantic Satanism contains a reconception of Milton's fallen angel that is patently an image of apotheosis, an emblem of an aspiring, rebelling, rising human god who insists he is self-created" (Schock, 2003: 38). Self-begetting is, then, a form of freedom, not only from the forms and conventions of "civilized" behaviour, but also from the dominion of God's (deficient) Creation. When Lecter asserts "Nothing happened to me, Officer Starling. *I* happened" (Harris, 2000: 409), it is a declaration of an identity self-begotten, free from the taint of "influence." It is noteworthy, of course, that Lecter is also wrong about this, as Harris goes on to demonstrate with *Hannibal* and *Hannibal Rising*, which give ample evidence of an originary trauma that did "influence" Lecter and make him into Hannibal "the cannibal." Something did indeed happen. Perhaps this is another sleight of hand on Lecter's part, a disavowal of his own history of trauma, and a marker of his difference from, yet similarity to, the other serial killers, Francis Dollarhyde and Jame Gumb, whose subjectivities are not as seemingly fixed as Lecter's ("'*I* happened'"), but who also wish to transform themselves (to re-create the self or self-beget). The question that Clarice Starling puts to Lecter in *The Silence of the Lambs*, "'Are you strong enough to point that high-powered perception at yourself?'" (Harris, 2000: 411) remains unanswered in public; but Harris suggests at the very beginning of *Hannibal Rising* that "pleas and screaming fill some places on the grounds [of Lecter's internal "memory palace'] where Hannibal himself cannot go" (Harris, 2006: 1), suggesting Lecter's capacity for self-analysis is limited by the very trauma he disavows.

When Milton's Satan declares his self-begotten status, it is an assertion of radical freedom from the power of God (in the face of the facts of his terrible defeat) to shape subjectivity. Satan's declaration insists that he is *not* a subject at all, but a free individual who exists outside of the dominion of God; Hell becomes a perverse zone of "liberty." Satan's famous lines "The mind is its own place, and in itself/Can make a heaven of hell, a hell of heaven" (Milton, 1966: I, ll.254–55) are echoed by Blake's "London," wherein humanity suffers under the "mind forg'd manacles" that are constitutive of human subjectivity and human society. To escape the "mind forg'd manacles" is to assume freedom, to issue a declaration of independence, but even if "the mind is its own place," Satan and the other rebel angels are still cast into Hell. For Hannibal Lecter, the mind truly *is* its own place, his "memory palace" a place of escape when he is incarcerated. Lecter is aware of the deficiency of his internal freedom—"'Memory [he tells Starling] is what I have instead of a view'" (Harris, 2000: 406)—and longs for physical liberty, to have a "view" of the real Florence rather than a memory and a drawing on the wall. Satan's rhetoric of self-begetting as a radical form of liberty, and the insistence on the resources of the self's own mind, is undermined.

In working towards a conclusion, I will now return to the idea of Lecter's "strange career" that is proposed in my title. In one sense, the sequence of Harris' "Lecter novels" indicates a trajectory from outside to inside, from Other to Self. Throughout the novels, Lecter is labeled "the fiend" or "the monster," not only by the rational characters within it, but also by the narratorial voice. This characterization (as Other) is compromised by the reader's increasing access to Lecter's interiority, and indeed the increasing concreteness of the "memory palace" within Lecter (which is not even mentioned until *Hannibal*). Just as Lecter moves from monstrous Other to Romantic satanic hero, the reader is offered the opportunity to move inside Lecter's mind. Perhaps as a consequence or a corollary, the discourse of evil or radical unknowableness/Otherness gives way to psychology, just as Starling, Will Graham, Dollarhyde, and Gumb are explained by the very psychology Lecter explicitly derides. Harris' novels continually point to the limits of rational discourse, and gesture towards the discourse of religion ("monster," "evil," "sin") to signify that which lies outside the explicatory powers of science, medicine, or reasoned understanding, but are ultimately conservative in their ultimate recourse to psychology to *explain* Lecter, to make his otherness more explicable (and thereby less troubling).

Lecter's career is not only from outside to inside, but is also inside to outside: from confinement to freedom. In *Red Dragon* and the beginning of *The Silence of the Lambs*, Lecter is imprisoned in his small cell, visited by Will Graham and Clarice Starling. He then effects his escape, and by the end of Harris' *The Silence of the Lambs* he is recovering from facial plastic surgery, drinking an "excellent Batard-Montrachet" (Harris, 2000: 741) and writing a note to Starling assuring her "I have no plans to call on you [...] the world being more interesting with you in it. Be sure you extend me the same courtesy" (Harris, 2000: 641). In the film, as I have stated above, he speaks rather more immediately to Starling on the telephone, after which he leisurely pursues Dr Chilton down a South American street. By the end of both texts, then, Lecter is "at large," physically free, and *Hannibal* narrates his efforts to maintain that freedom. The perverse ending of that novel, with Hannibal and Clarice the oddest of odd couples established in romantic happiness somewhere in Buenos Aires, the last image of the pair "dancing on the terrace" (Harris, 2000: 1220), signifies a freedom not only from the cell but from the past: "for many months now, he has not seen Mischa in his dreams" (Harris, 2000: 1220). Trauma is undone; paradise is regained. Perhaps the word one should use here to characterize Lecter's ultimate state of being is "unbound." For the satanic/Promethean Romantic hero, as I have argued in this essay that Lecter ultimately becomes, destruction is often the end, but at the end of *Hannibal* (which is, in terms of narrative chronology, the end of the sequence: *Hannibal Rising* returns to Lecter's youth) Harris follows P. B. Shelley rather than Blake, Milton, or Byron. The end of Shelley's "Prometheus Unbound" offers a kind of cosmic redemption for the suffering Titan, his release an affirmation:

> Neither to change, nor falter nor repent:
> This like thy glory, Titan! is to be
> Good, great and joyous, beautiful and free;
> This alone is Life, Joy, Empire and Victory (Shelley, 2000b: Act 4, ll.575–79; p. 762).

The ending of *Hannibal* is not revolutionary, but its implications—
that Lecter is "released" into a quasi-normative heterosexual romantic
relationship with an equally happy Clarice—do set the self-delusory
"freedom" of Milton's Satan on its head. For Hannibal and Clarice,
their interpenetrating and mutually enveloping minds truly can "make a
heaven of hell, a hell of heaven."

Notes

1.   It should be noted that the original Italian given in the Oxford edition of
Dante I have used, translated with notes by John D. Sinclair, is slightly different. It
runs:

> *Surge in vermena ed in pianta silvestre:*
> *L'Arpie, pascendo poi delle sui foglie,*
> *Fanno dolore, ed al dolor fenestra (Inferno XIII, 100–103; p. 170).*

The variation in spelling also extends to the name of the suicide: where Sinclair has
Piero delle Vigne, Harris has Pier della Vigna. I have followed Sinclair's spelling here.

2.   Katharine and Lee Horsley, "Learning Italian: Serial Killers Abroad in the Novels
of Highsmith and Harris," unpublished paper. I would like to thank Lee Horsley for
allowing me to see a manuscript version of this work before publication.

Chapter 8

Demons of the New Polytheism

George Aichele

> [I]t is a peculiarity of demons to operate in the intervals between the gods' fields of action, as it is to leap over the barriers or the enclosures, thereby confounding the boundaries between properties (Deleuze, 1994: 37).

> In an age of unbelief… just why monotheism should be an advance on polytheism is not immediately apparent (Miles, 1996: 110).

Gods of the Bible

Near the end of his book, *God: A Biography*, Jack Miles offers a polytheistic reading of the Jewish scriptures. Throughout his book, Miles argues that if the Tanakh is read as a biography of God, then it presents the one, lonely God as a being who suffers from a severe psychological disorder, a self in which several distinguishable personalities struggle for dominance, without lasting success. Miles concludes:

> The extent to which the Tanakh is a character-dominated classic may appear to better advantage if we imagine how its action might unfold if the several personalities fused in the character of the Lord God were broken loose as separate characters. When the Lord God's character is parcelled out in this way, what results is a story that immediately begins to assume the familiar contours of a more "ordinary" myth (1996: 398).

What results in Miles' account is a story in which six different finite gods or *daimones*, both male and female, play greater or lesser roles (1996: 398–401). Miles does not suggest that anyone has ever actually read the Bible in this way, or that anyone should. He presents this reading as a thought experiment, a limit-reading that illuminates his understanding of the Bible's story of a deeply disturbed singular God by its contrast to the conventional monotheistic ways in which the Bible is actually read by Jews and Christians, and the problems that accompany those conventional ways of reading.

As Regina Schwartz notes, the Bible as a canon authorizes and indeed requires monotheism, obscuring the contrary claims of some of its component texts (1997: 9).[1] Perhaps this is because, as John Docker claims,

"Monotheism...introduced the notion of canonization, of certain texts as canonical and others as heresy" (2001: 162). In other words, monotheism and the concept of a single, authoritative biblical canon reinforce one another. In contrast, Docker says, polytheism is anti-canonical (2001: 168). Dare we go even further and speculate that a monotheistic impulse itself was one important factor motivating the Torah's canonizers in post-exilic Judaism, and that this impulse appeared again with the imperial success of early Christianity and the consequent desire to produce a universal scripture—something on the order of one God, one text, one people?

Miles' reading of the Tanakh suggests that the concept of One God does not simply emerge as the henotheistic victor of an ancient cultural struggle for faith, culminating during or after the Babylonian exile when the other deities are transformed into illusions and the *monos theos* that will dominate the modern world alone remains. At numerous points throughout his book, Miles suggests that polytheism lurks just beneath the surface of the Jewish sequence of texts, which he reads as a continuous narrative.[2] He notes that "While consciously emulating [God's] virtues, the West has unconsciously assimilated the anxiety-producing tension between his unity and his multiplicity" (1996: 6), and he claims that "the emergence of monotheism from polytheism can be recovered for literature as the story of a single God struggling with himself" (1996: 21). I argue in this essay that as modernism disintegrates in the world today, the biblical canon's synthesis of many gods into one begins to unravel—that is, not only God but the Bible becomes schizophrenic— and the many *daimones* appear once more, albeit transfigured into more contemporary forms.

The polytheism within the Bible appears in other ways as well. The multiplicity within the biblical deity himself is perhaps most explicit in the scriptures' plural euphemism, "Elohim," a term which the Jewish Publication Society sometimes translates as "divine beings."[3] The more specific and evidently singular Yahweh frequently hides behind Elohim in the biblical texts. Polytheism also underlies the henotheism implied in the Bible's recurring metaphor for the covenant as a marriage. A promise of marital fidelity is unnecessary if only one potential marriage partner exists in the entire universe. It is only because there are numerous quite real deities out there to whom Israel might pledge its faith that the covenant is significant. The marriage trauma described in explicit allegory in the Book of Hosea and the connubial delights detailed in the Song of Solomon, which have traditionally been understood by both Jews and Christians to refer to the covenant, both connote the commitment between one deity among many and his chosen partner, whether the wedded couple be understood as God and Israel or as Christ and the Church.

This latter, Christian allegory of the Song also appears in less allegorical but more bizarre language in the Book of Revelation, where the Lamb in that surreal marriage narrative is only one of several conceivable spouses for the Bride. Among Revelation's god-like beings are the "one like a son of man," the "woman clothed in the sun," and the whore of Babylon, as well as numerous other monsters and beasts. The "spectacle" of John's Revelation also correlates well to the sensory appeal of polytheism. Considered in this light, the vivid apocalyptic warfare narrated in that book, or in its Old Testament cousin, the Book of Daniel, suggests mythic struggle between various gods in a cosmos where no One God clearly rules. As Catherine Keller says of the singing monsters of Revelation 4, "If divine awareness disseminates through their irreducible difference, their eyes belong neither properly to themselves nor to God. Eyes, stars, gems twinkle in a Morse code illegible within logocentric eschatology, signalling a future in which we humanoids sing along" (Keller, 2001: 277).[4]

Indeed, Philip Davies argues that the biblical God (Elyon or Most High) dies in Daniel 7, for "on either side of chapter 7 lie two dispensations, the 'before' and 'after,' the rule of the old bearded and white-haired Elyon, and the rule of the new humanoid being" (1995: 130). Even Daniel's name for the old God, echoing Gen. 14:18–20, 22, hints at polytheism, for Elyon or "most high" implies other, lesser gods. Thus the peaceful meeting between Abram and Melchizedek in Genesis 14 reads less as two monotheists who recognize that they have different names for the same One God than it does as two polytheists who can afford to be tolerant, since their respective pantheons have room for unknown gods.

What remains after Elyon's death in the Book of Daniel is a chaotic world, not unlike our present-day world with its many demons. As Davies says:

> Monarchy is dead, and the universe is run by warring beings, whether humans on earth or gods in human form in heaven. The cosmos has lost its ruler, and history has consequently lost its author and its meaning. This is what moderns might call the "death of God" (1995: 133).

Indeed, that is precisely what Friedrich Nietzsche does call it in the famous "madman" parable (section #125) of *The Gay Science*. Nietzsche's madman claims that human responsibility for God's death ("*we have killed him*—you and I. All of us are his murderers" [1974: 181, his emphasis]) requires that human beings themselves become gods. "Is not the greatness of this deed too great for us? Must we ourselves not become gods simply to appear worthy of it?" (1974: 181).

Miles' discussion of the Book of Daniel also suggests a similar conclusion. Miles describes Daniel's story as the "second ending" of God's biography— i.e., of his life. According to him, in Daniel the God of the Bible withdraws into silence and "seems to have abdicated in favor of Gabriel and Michael, the counselor and the warrior prince… If there is a heavenly 'prince of Persia' and a 'prince of Greece', presumably there are other princes as well" (1996: 370). On this reading the biblical angels and their apocalyptic opponents, so pronounced in both Daniel and Revelation, are not so much superhuman creations of God as they are lesser, or perhaps simply younger and more lively, deities. Or else they are divinized human beings. From the Nietzschean point of view there is little difference. For polytheism, the distinction between the divine and anything not divine (including the human) is less sharply drawn than it is for monotheism.

This same ambiguity appears elsewhere in the Bible as well. The "sons of God" (that is, Elohim) in Gen. 6:2 have traditionally been understood as rebellious angels, but they might just as well be godlike human kings. The "angel" with whom Jacob wrestles in Gen. 32:22–32 is variously identified in that text as a "man" and as "God" (again, Elohim). The angel Gabriel, as he addresses the eventual mother of Christ, is nearly indistinguishable in Lk. 1:26–38 from the Holy Spirit, but he also behaves like a human rapist (Aichele, 2005a). As Timothy Beal says, "The parts add up to more than any comprehensible whole" (2002: 75). Here we have important precursors to the contemporary polytheistic fictions discussed below.[5]

For as long as biblical monotheism has been with us, we have known that the idea of the One God was deeply flawed. The logical force of the problem of evil, perhaps made clearest in David Hume's *Dialogues Concerning Natural Religion*, is implicit already in Jeremiah's complaint, "Why does the way of the wicked prosper?" (12:1), and explicit in the eloquence of Job's innocent sufferer. A good, omnipotent, omniscient God and the world that we live in are incompatible. The Satan of Job's chapters 1–2 is little more than an expression of a perverse side of the One God, someone who does his divine dirty work for him. If God is morally good, then only some power equal and opposed to that of God can adequately account for the reality of evil.

In other words, God does not really answer Job in chapters 38–41, because a satisfactory answer would require more than one god, or no god at all. As Miles says, "[for polytheism] there is always…another god to whom, at will, the incompatible may be transferred. It is not so for the devotee of the [monotheistic] Lord God. Everything redounds to the Lord God's credit. Everything also redounds to his blame" (1996: 407–408). Conversely, "What polytheism would allow to be externally directed anger against a rival deity, monotheism…must turn into the Lord God's inwardly directed regret" (Miles, 1996: 33). Polytheism features numerous finite deities or supernatural powers and thus obviates the classical problem of evil. Evil results not from a monodaimonistic Satan, the alter ego of the monotheistic God and the sole ruler of Hell, but from conflicts between the many *daimones* or finite gods.

The monotheistic ideology of most biblical scholarship rejects the thought that Satan is another god.[6] The Bible's "demons," especially those of the New Testament gospels, are understood to fit somehow within the monotheistic canonical frame, as angels or spirits, creations of the One God who have somehow gone bad. Within that frame they have become minions of Beelzebul or Satan,[7] who is himself no more than a renegade angel. The canonical intertext counters any thought that its demons, or Satan, might be gods. Unlike the *daimones* of the Pagan Hellenistic world, which were superhuman powers indifferent to human values and who thus might be either beneficial or harmful to human beings, the *daimonia* of the Bible are always harmful, but ultimately they will be damned by the One God. Perhaps this is why the richly significant, classical *daimōn* was demoted to the merely nasty biblical *daimonion*.[8] Yet despite the canonical pressure, as "Mot," Satan is one of the multiple gods in Miles' story, and Satan has always functioned in the Christian imagination more as a second, strangely attractive god than merely as a rebel angel.

The philosophical problem of evil is not the only difficulty within monotheism. Schwartz associates the emergence of biblical monotheism with the needs of community identity, especially in a situation of scarcity. "Scarcity is encoded in the Bible as a principle of Oneness (one land, one people, one nation) and in monotheistic thinking (one Deity), it becomes a demand of exclusive allegiance that threatens with the violence of exclusion" (1997: xi). According to Schwartz, this exclusivity culminates in modern nationalism, imperialism, and totalitarianism— that is, the universalization of "the kingdom of God." In the contemporary world, where dwindling supplies of oil are contested by imperialistic powers closely associated with two competing forms of monotheism, each of them explicitly invoking holy war, the relation of monotheism to both scarcity and exclusivity seems indisputable.

Citing the work of Jan Assmann, Docker claims that "the monotheistic presumption of true and false religion" is a "murderous distinction… [that rejects] everything as Paganism that went before and which is outside itself" (2001: 162). Docker argues that monotheism is inherently intolerant. In contrast to monotheism, says Bart Ehrman,

> Basic tolerance was one of the central aspects of ancient Greco-Roman [polytheistic] religion. Unlike some forms of Christianity that eventually arose in its midst, the empire's other religions were altogether forbearing of one another… There was no reason that everyone should worship the same gods any more than everyone should have the same friends. All the gods deserved to be worshiped in ways appropriate to them… There was no sense of exclusivity in Greco-Roman religions, no sense that my gods are real and yours are false, that you must convert to my gods or be punished (2004: 30–31).[9]

This is not to say that polytheism is a cure for everything that ails us today. In any case, there is surely no way that we can revive the Hellenistic polytheism that Ehrman describes. However, perhaps recent interest in forms of polytheism, both in popular culture and in postmodern thought, derives from recognition that we dare not continue any longer in the illogical, intolerant way of monotheism.

Post-canonical Gods

Polytheism figures significantly in contemporary popular culture. It is perhaps most evident in texts of fantasy and science fiction, and the fact that these genres have advanced in recent decades from marginal to mainstream status in our culture is also important in this regard. These texts imagine multiple superhuman powers in a wide variety of ways, from the more traditionally-conceived demons and finite gods of Robert E. Howard's "Conan" stories to the massively powerful, artificially-intelligent entities set loose on the Internet in William Gibson's cyberpunk novel, *Neuromancer* (as well as its numerous sequels and imitators). Included are texts such as Neil Gaiman's novel, *American Gods*, in which various familiar deities from non-Christian religions emigrate to the USA, where they are confronted by strange new gods of American high-tech consumer capitalism, and James Morrow's "Godhead trilogy" (*Towing Jehovah*, *Blameless in Abaddon*, and *The Eternal Footman*), in which various angels, demons, and other metaphysical entities (including several separated parts of God's exploded corpse) infest the world after the Christian God dies. Indeed, Morrow's God's multiple personalities (1996: 380) are reminiscent of the psychotic God who appears in Miles' reading of the Tanakh. In addition, numerous science-fiction stories from authors such as Arthur C.

Clarke and Iain M. Banks explore Nietzsche's madman's prediction that humans will evolve into godlike beings.

In contrast, no high god appears in J. R. R. Tolkien's immensely popular Middle Earth stories, written shortly after Howard's Conan stories, unless the One Ring ("to rule them all, and in the darkness bind them") is a god. Of course, that would be an evil god! There is no mention in *The Lord of the Rings* of Ilúvatar or Eru, who is identified in *The Silmarillion* as the "Father of All." Nevertheless, Tolkien's Middle Earth is filled with the supernatural in many forms, including numerous *daimones* ranging from Tom Bombadil and Galadriel to Sauron and Shelob, among others. Tolkien's essay, "On Fairy-Stories" (1966: 33–99), makes it clear that for him the world of Faërie is pervaded throughout with the supernatural. Indeed, his Middle Earth stories culminate in the catastrophic disintegration of this supernaturally-saturated world, a deterritorialization to be followed by a new, reterritorialized human world from which the gods have departed.

These stories of the fantastic include not only novels but also TV shows, films, video games, and comic books, ranging from stories of popular superheroes such as Superman—and indeed, superhuman aliens are especially well-suited to function as the *daimones* of a science-obsessed age, much as fairies and ghosts did for the mentality of an earlier period—to Gaiman's sophisticated *Sandman* series. Whether fairies or extraterrestrial beings, these superhuman entities, like the ancient Hellenistic *daimones*, are largely indifferent to the needs or concerns of human beings; they only help or harm humanity when that happens to suit their own, inscrutable interests (Ehrman, 2004: 25). To be sure, Superman himself is a partial exception to that generalization, but his many super-opponents are not. In the following I consider somewhat further two of these stories.

In the narrative world of *Buffy the Vampire Slayer*, both the TV series and the movie that preceded it,[10] vampires, demons, and other creatures of supernatural evil are quite numerous. According to Buffy's story, these evil powers are older than the human species and stronger than most human beings. Vampire slayers, young human women endowed with special "demon powers" that enable them to fight the evil forces, have protected weak humanity since the beginnings of civilization. Buffy Summers, the story's principal character, is the latest in this long succession of vampire slayers. In the TV series, she lives in a typical middle-class California suburb, which just happens to be a "hell mouth" or portal between the human world and multiple realms of supernatural evil. In the movie, Buffy fights alone, as per the slayer tradition, but in the TV show she acquires allies, who are for the most part human beings, but several of whom are demons.

Much of the considerable irony and humor of the Buffy stories derives from tensions created by the sudden insertion of supernatural and often richly symbolical entities into a world that is otherwise quite banal. For example, at one point Buffy holds up her pager and says, "if the apocalypse comes, beep me!" Crosses appear in nearly every episode, but the cross is never anything but a weapon to be used against vampires—that is, it has no other meaning to Buffy or her friends. Buffy herself wears a small silver cross on a chain around her neck, but she explicitly denies that it has any Christian significance. The exception to this occurs when Buffy's Jewish friend, Willow Rosenberg, balks at using a cross to ward off vampires. Once Willow sees the practical effectiveness of the cross against vampires, and its lack of theological significance to other characters, she drops her objection.

Buffy's world contains many gods, demons, hells, and heavens. However, no high god is ever mentioned, no El Elyon, much less the universal, monotheistic God. The supernatural beings of Buffy's stories are all quite finite and thoroughly physical, even the "First Evil," Buffy's greatest opponent, who evidently must take physical form in order to fight her. Another divine opponent is the goddess Glory, who like the First Evil can change her shape, but who must always have some sort of physical embodiment. Glory is not particularly evil but rather is completely self-absorbed and indifferent to humanity. Numerous other gods and god-like beings appear in other episodes of *Buffy the Vampire Slayer* and its spin-off series, *Angel*, and while each one of them is despatched in its turn, there are always more to come. The story's characters even comment on the seemingly endless supply of supernatural beings.

Although most of the supernatural beings that Buffy encounters are evil, it is clear that not all of them are. Two major characters in the series are good vampires, Angel and Spike, and other benevolent demons appear from time to time. In the cosmos of Buffy, vampires are "normally" undead humans who have been possessed by malevolent demons, and thus both Angel and Spike are noteworthy exceptions— perhaps especially Spike, who has become good as a direct result of his love for Buffy.

My second example is China Miéville's urban fantasy novel, *King Rat*, in which the traditional tale of the Pied Piper of Hamelin is retold from the rats' standpoint.[11] According to Miéville's version of the story, the Piper is not simply the folk-tale Ratcatcher who saves the townsfolk of Hamelin from a plague of rats, and who then takes the town's children away with him when the citizens renege on their agreement to pay him. Instead of the traditional story, or in addition to it, the Pied Piper of *King Rat* is a supernaturally evil being ("a dangerous god" [Miéville, 1998: 151]) who is able to lure and catch whatever living creatures he wants with seductive flute music. Hearing his music, the creatures enter a trance state in which they dance themselves to death.

Standing opposed to the Ratcatcher is the King of the Rats, along with his allies, Anansi and Loplop, respectively the lords of the spiders and birds. Mention is also made of the leaders of various other species— including "Mr. Bub, the Lord of the Flies" (Miéville, 1998: 134, alluding to 2 Kgs 1:2–3)—but these characters do not appear in the story. These entities are finite deities transplanted from various fairy tales and nursery rhymes into the modern urban world.[12] Like his supernatural colleagues, the rat king is not just another one of his species. He is formed more like a man than a rat, but he is not a human being, and he displays distinctly rat-like characteristics and abilities.

However, King Rat possesses strength and powers beyond those of any natural rat or human. He is the rat God. He is also a physical being, a "monster" (Miéville, 1998: 37), which as Beal notes is one who "personifies otherness...within the well-established and accepted order of things" (2002: 4).[13] King Rat and his supernatural allies have not temporarily "assumed" anthropomorphic bodies, to be discarded later, as in ancient stories about divine incarnations and avatars. They are not materializations of beings who are "really" non-physical. Instead, like the gods and demons of Buffy's world, the Piper and the rat king and the other animal deities in *King Rat* are all splendidly physical, fully embodied, and disturbingly human, beings. *King Rat* describes a world in which numerous gods exist, and in which the logocentric separability of the physical and the spiritual is no longer thinkable.

Although he is very old ("I was here when London was born" [Miéville, 1998: 125]), King Rat is also evidently mortal. He too was subject to the Piper's musical enchantment on that fateful day in Hamelin (1998: 127–31), but he was able to free himself at the last moment, just in time to watch hundreds of his rat subjects dance themselves to death under the influence of the enchanting flute music. It seems that there is nothing that he can do about the situation, for the Piper's power to overwhelm even the king's rat sensibilities is absolute. Finally, the rat king realizes that the Piper can play only one tune at a time, and since each species requires its own, distinct tune of enchantment, this means that he can overcome only one species at a time. King Rat forcibly rapes a human woman, and the resulting child possesses both human nature and rat nature. This child is a miraculous hybrid of two genetic strands: a rat-man, both fully man and fully rat. He will be able to defeat the Piper, for if the Piper plays a rat-seducing tune, then the rat-man's human nature will be impervious to it, and if the Piper plays a human-seducing tune, his rat nature will be unaffected (Miéville, 1998: 134, 146). He is a material messiah, a mortal and permanently embodied god-man in a world that no longer comprehends non-physical, transcendent spirit. *King Rat* suggests that only a christological hybrid could successfully avoid an evil god's traps and counter his powers over both divine and human beings. The birth of this messiah does not result from divine grace or benevolence, but from a god's own struggle to survive.

Docker suggests that the One God of monotheism must be a non-corporeal spirit, eternal and present everywhere, but the many gods and demons of polytheism are always physical and quite local (2001: 158–59, 163). The One God is necessarily transcendent, limitless, and thus image-less, but the many gods are sensual, both because of their finitude and because of their materiality. The multiple gods and demons of these recent, popular stories are *not* non-material spirits and they are *not* universal: they have finite, physical bodies, and they are local, confined within space/time.[14] These gods are closer to humanity than we might like to believe. They are often mortal, and indeed, Conan and Buffy each kill several of them. By the end of *King Rat*, Anansi is dead and Loplop is quite mad. Even Morrow's Jehovah, his gigantic, dead, white, male body (complete with navel and uncircumcised penis) floating in the Atlantic Ocean, must be merely one god among many.[15] He too is a finite god, both in the extent of his body and in his manifest mortality.

Chaosmos and Schizophrenia

These numerous instances from recent fantasy and science-fiction stories do not prove anything, much less present a single, coherent statement of polytheistic belief, but they serve nevertheless as so many symptoms of a new polytheism. The monocentric, monopolizing, monotheizing grand narratives of modernism are no longer in control, and those stories are now being replaced by a multitude of inconsistent and sometimes incompatible little narratives, interacting with one another in what Jean-François Lyotard calls a "paralogy" (1984: 60), a paradoxical discourse with unpredictable outcomes. Polytheistic language has resurfaced also in recent theological and philosophical discourse, as postmodern understandings of difference have led to the thought of a non-unitary or multiple "universe" or "reality." The postmodern world is one of fragmented realities and plural discourses, and because of that it is not truly "one world" at all. It is, as Gilles Deleuze says, quoting James Joyce, "chaosmos": simultaneously chaos and cosmos (1994: 57, 128, 299). This world is both many and one, and it has no underlying or transcendental singleness to it.

This is one reason why the Christian canon no longer functions as authoritative. For modernist monotheism, the Bible's authority could be either defended or challenged in the name of fundamentalist dogma or historical science, but for postmodernism, "the Bible" no longer operates as a canonical entity. Its status as the universal Word of the One God becomes untenable, or in other words, the divine psychosis that Miles describes becomes so excessive that God disintegrates, much as in Morrow's trilogy. The One God whose coherent Word the Bible had been becomes many, and as a result it becomes possible to read biblical texts polytheistically, as Miles does. The various texts traditionally bound within the canonical testaments acquire new identities as they sink or float in intertextual currents beyond the control of any theological orthodoxy.

Logocentric belief in a coherent "biblical theology," an underlying, integrative, and dynamically translatable message of the Bible as a whole—that is, a "spirit" attached to but distinct from the "flesh" of the written text (as in 2 Cor. 3:3, 6)—can no longer be maintained. The individual relations between the biblical texts become problematic: the New Testament writings no longer justify or explain those of the Old Testament, and it becomes possible to read the four canonical gospels not as four versions of a single story but rather as four stories of four distinct Jesuses—in other words, to understand the Jesus of each gospel as a different ideological simulacrum or virtual being,[16] and not as a variant representation of a single historical or theological model. The canon no longer controls the meaning of its constituent texts, and postmodern readings of biblical texts (including many of the stories mentioned above, such as those of Miéville, Howard, and Morrow) place the scriptures in playful juxtaposition with a wide variety of non-biblical texts. The formerly-canonical stories, poems, and sayings are re-contextualized and take on remarkably different, polysemic, and fluid meanings. The biblical texts become postmodern texts, written for and about posthuman beings.[17]

In the terminology of Deleuze and his sometime co-author, Félix Guattari,[18] monotheism is "paranoid" and polytheism is "schizophrenic." Schizophrenia and paranoia are the disruption and concentration of identity, respectively. In schizophrenia, the personal self is "dismantled" (Deleuze and Guattari, 1988: 151), and the ego disintegrates into a "little group" (1983: 362). Thus self-identity is not merely personal but also communal: "There is no primacy of the individual; there is instead an indissolubility of a singular Abstract and a collective Concrete" (1988: 100). For Deleuze the individual is not the unitary atom of the Cartesian self but rather a contingent synthesis of "singularities" and "intensities" that mediates between the virtual and the actual (1994: 253–54).

In other words, the Deleuzean individual is a rhizome, a fluid and complex network of connections, with no fixed center and no clearly defined boundary. In the rhizome, as in schizophrenia, the logical opposition between one and many is deconstructed. The rhizome is a multiplicity, fractured by virtuality. "A rhizome may be broken, shattered at a given spot, but it will start up again on one of its old lines, or on new lines… Every rhizome contains lines of segmentarity according to which it is stratified, territorialized, organized, signified, attributed, etc., as well as lines of deterritorialization down which it constantly flees" (Deleuze and Guattari, 1988: 9). Like every rhizome, the individual is particular and transitory. It too is a simulacrum, a divergence of series (Deleuze, 1994: 69)—or to use a term that Deleuze does not use, the individual is essentially intertextual, a node in a network of differences.

What sort of deity is conceivable in a world that is "chaosmos" and for a self that is fractured, multiple, and "larval" (Deleuze, 1994: 78)? Deleuze describes a world and a self beyond the death of the One God, in which difference precedes identity (1994: 54)—that is, in which identity is always a totalizing and totalitarian construct. It is not surprising that the texts of Deleuze are peppered with polytheistic language, and although this language should probably not be taken terribly seriously, it is not innocent, either. In a universe in which difference precedes identity, in which semiosis flows without limit, in which there is no single, fixed center but only impermanent constellations of singularities, whatever supernatural or at least superhuman powers and authorities appear must be both multiple and fluid.

In contrast to schizophrenia, paranoia restricts the "nomadic" flows of desire. Paranoia favors instead a centralized, imperial, or "sedentary" organization characterized by hierarchical ("arborescent") reterritorializations. In paranoia, the schizophrenic flows and fracturings are inverted, and both self and world are organized. The paranoid condition favors that which is universal and monotheistic, and although neither Docker nor Schwartz uses the term "paranoia," each of them suggests that monotheism is deeply paranoid. As Christopher Frilingos says of the Book of Revelation: "A religious disposition was born: Christians believed that the vast resources of the Roman Empire had been mobilized against them…, that the entire world hated them" (2004: 117–18). Although the paranoia that produces monotheism arises in response to human institutions and events, it ultimately takes the form of the One God who sees and knows all, who is everywhere and yet invisible, who demands perfect obedience and who judges without appeal.

The unlimited flow of semiosis in schizophrenia is countered by what Deleuze and Guattari call the "despotism" of paranoia, which attempts to master the sign and its possible meanings. Paranoia seeks to stop the polytheistic flow of semiosis through definitive (canonical) interpretation of signs which culminates in a "full body," a Final Signified (Deleuze and Guattari, 1983: 281) which is the One God. Thus every "signifying regime" tends toward monotheistic paranoia. As a result, any meaningful exchange of messages belongs to the condition of paranoia, just as the theological claim that the Bible conveys a clear, coherent message that can be dynamically translated contributes to the monotheistic pressures exerted by the biblical canon. Nevertheless, although any signifying regime is inevitably paranoid and despotic, it also opens up (as its "dark precursor") the possibility of a schizophrenic "postsignifying regime" (Deleuze and Guattari, 1988: 119). This is the space of what Deleuze, following Nietzsche (and Klossowski), calls the "Antichrist" (1990: 296–97), where "What we encounter are the demons, the sign-bearers: powers of the leap, the interval, the intensive and the instant; powers which only cover difference with more difference" (1994: 145). The demons, the sign-bearers, subvert monotheistic paranoia and open the possibility of unlimited semiosis.

The postsignifying regime echoes Lyotard's description of the postmodern as "that which, *in the modern*, puts forward the unpresentable in presentation itself" (1984: 81, his emphasis). Modernist thought reterritorializes reality into systematic totality; it seeks the universal, the Absolute of the grand narrative. It is thus either monotheistic or atheistic—that is, it is "biunivocal," to use Deleuze and Guattari's term, for it produces the exclusive choice of One God or no god. No other options. Yet modernist atheism is also monocentric; it is simply monotheism without God, mono-atheism. We still end up with the Final Signified, the full body. In contrast, the postmodern paralogy of little narratives is polycentric; these stories narrate a plurality of finite gods. Postmodern thought deterritorializes the human totality; it localizes and contextualizes. It is always provisional.

Modernist thought understands semiosis to be limited, the single meaning of each text "owned" either by its actual author or by an ideal reader. If multiple readings are allowed, they are eventually reclaimed by some more imperial, ecumenical unity, a grand synthesis of oppositions. In contrast, the postmodern brings a renewal of allegory—not the classical, hierarchical allegory of eternal Truth floating above the textual surface, but a midrashic allegory of surfaces that play endlessly upon one another, of polysemic juxtaposition and rhizomatic intertextuality. It is in this sense that postmodernism is polytheistic, and not in any traditional, premodern sense.

For Deleuze and Guattari, the postsignifying regime appears in the signifying regime's failure to signify adequately or completely, and the schizophrenic, rhizomatic flow of desire undermines the totalitarian, paranoid organization. However, the "lines of segmentarity" that are essential to defining the rhizome are also the means of its own reterritorialization, its transformation into its other, the re-creation of identity. Thus paranoia continually reterritorializes the schizophrenic "body without organs," even as schizophrenia deterritorializes the paranoid full body. There is a continual tension, an ebb and flow, between paranoia and schizophrenia (Deleuze and Guattari, 1983: 36–37).

Likewise, there is no simple binary opposition between polytheism and monotheism—at least, not in the postmodern world. They are not biunivocal. Instead, they stand in paradoxical, deconstructive tension with one another. As Docker says, speaking of Spinoza (one of Deleuze's heroes), "Such notions could permit recognition…of continuities between polytheism and monotheism, a fruitful tension, a wealth of paradoxicality," and finally, "practices and modes of cosmopolitanism and translatability" (2001: 163). Nevertheless, the mere existence of this fruitful tension counts heavily against classical monotheism: the one is not prior to the many. Instead, the *daimones* of the new polytheism are, as Beal says, "part[s] of a divinity that is deeply divided within itself about the future viability of the cosmos and of life as humankind knows it. Religion, in this context, is not simply cosmic, … [r]ather it is a locus for negotiating between the cosmic and the chaotic, which are, paradoxically, both interdependent and mutually exclusive" (2002: 22). Beal is speaking in this quote about the Ugaritic Baal-Anat Cycle, but his comment applies quite well to Miles' polytheistic reading of the Jewish scriptures, and it also nicely describes Deleuze's "chaosmos."

The New Polytheism

The new polytheism requires new understandings of the various religions. They can no longer be viewed (as in modernist liberalism) as many paths to the same goal, nor (as in modernist fundamentalism) as only one true path in the midst of many false paths. Instead, the religions offer various paths to various different goals, and in some cases, they may be so different that the "path/goal" metaphor does not work at all. For the new polytheism, Yahweh is not identical to Allah, and neither of them is God the Father or any other Person of the Christian Holy Trinity (or the Trinity itself). Nor are they various aspects or emanations of some One "God beyond god." The ancient Christian heretic, Marcion, was right about one thing: the god of gentile Christianity is not the god of Judaism. Postmodern inter-religious respect and dialogue (or rather, paralogy, as Lyotard says) begins with appreciation of real differences between the gods, instead of imperializing allegations of their oneness or sameness. Kevin Schilbrack argues that this new understanding will require a concept of "ontological pluralism" (2004: 3). Schilbrack claims that a truly "nonconvergent" pluralism in religion must treat reality as non-simple or "multifaceted" (2004: 9), and although Schilbrack does not cite Deleuze, Deleuze's approach would lend itself well to nonconvergent pluralism.

Perhaps I should stress once again that this new polytheism will not be a return to the old polytheism(s). Arising from recognition of the non-unity or non-identity of the real, postmodern polytheism is more fluid and anonymous than traditional polytheism. As Gaiman's novel, *American Gods,* makes clear, the plausible deities of our electronic culture are not likely to be identical to the old premodern ones. Like everything else in the postmodern world, the gods of the new polytheism are virtual beings, that is, simulacra or narrative constructs. They are "reality effects" (Barthes, 1986: 141–48), the semiotic products of divergent series. No single pantheon can contain the gods of the new polytheism, for there is no deep unity to their system. They cannot belong to a single family of gods, for the "family of man" itself disintegrates upon the emergence of posthuman beings.

As Gaiman's novel also makes clear, gods do not die, and they are not born, without struggle and suffering. Perhaps instead of simply disappearing, the ancient gods, angels, and demons have been transformed, or even now they are metamorphosing into something different, even as we too are changing, becoming posthuman beings, cyborgs, hybrids, humanoids. The Christian God, newly resurrected following his death as the One God of modernity, takes his place alongside numerous other deities, including Yahweh and Allah, each of them also resurrected, equally actual and equally virtual, each of them different. The Christian God is no longer the One God understood by modernist theism, and he is not the God of premodern Christianity either. He can no longer claim to be omnipotent or universal; instead, like all the other gods, he is distinct, finite, and physical. In a time and a culture for which Neoplatonism makes no more sense than does the flat earth or the geocentric cosmos, the Christian God is no longer thinkable as three-in-one. Yet perhaps even the Holy Trinity can survive now in some more limited, polytheistic form. Maybe in this postmodern form they too can survive the death of the One God.

Notes

1. See also Sanders, 1984: 43–44, 51.
2. See, e.g., Miles, 1996: 92–95, 140, and 332. It is instructive to note the biblical books that Miles omits from his biographical sequence, and to ponder how their inclusion might have disturbed the continuity of his reading. The omitted books are Jeremiah, Ezekiel, and most of the Minor Prophets. However, Miles makes reference to each of these omitted books in his discussions of other writings, with the exceptions of the minor prophets Joel, Amos, Obadiah, Jonah, Micah, Nahum, and Habakkuk.
3. For example, Gen. 6:2 and 32:29, 31, discussed further below.
4. See also Beal, 2002: 71–82, Frilingos, 2004, and Docker, 2001: 159–60. Deleuze describes Revelation as "the book of Zombies" (1978: 8).
5. The recent renewal of interest in angels ranges from kitsch knick-knacks and calendars to serious films and TV drama such as *Wings of Desire* (dir. Wenders, 1987) and *Angels in America* (dir. Nichols, 2003).
6. See, e.g., Kuemmerlin-McLean, 1997.
7. See Mark 3:22–26 par. However, if the "house" of the demons is indeed divided against itself, then Jesus' saying in this text takes on new meaning.
8. The polyvalence of the *daimones* is evident in the many descriptions that appear in Foerster, 2000: underlying animism, consuming power, the divine in humans, ghosts, magical beings. These demons are not always bad: the Greek word for happiness, *eudaimonia*, suggests "possession" by a good demon.
9. See also Ehrman, 2004: 443, Nietzsche, 1974: 191–92, and Docker, 2001: 163. In contrast, the Hellenistic philosophers, like the Christians, were more exclusive (Ehrman, 2004: 35).
10. The TV series picks up where the movie ends, forming a more or less continuous narrative. Theological aspects of the Buffy stories are discussed further in Aichele, 2005b.
11. This story is discussed further in relation to the Christmas story of the Gospel of Luke, in Aichele, 2005a.
12. Something quite similar appears in Gaiman's novel, *Anansi Boys*, the sequel to *American Gods*.
13. Cf. Deleuze, 1994: 29, 275.
14. See Kliever, 1979.
15. For a contrary view, see Walsh, 2000: 49–55.
16. See further, Aichele forthcoming. "The simulacrum is not a degraded copy. It harbors a positive power which denies *the original and the copy, the model and the*

reproduction... The simulacrum functions in such a way that a certain resemblance is necessarily thrown back onto its basic series and a certain identity projected on the forced movement" (Deleuze, 1990: 262, 265, his emphases).

17. See Aichele, 2006.

18. I will not distinguish here between Deleuze's solo writings and his joint writings with Guattari.

Chapter 9

Scriptural Dimensions of Evil:
Biblical Text as Timepiece, Talisman, and Tattoo

Larry J. Kreitzer

Within this study I would like to explore the importance of one particular biblical text upon the way in which evil has been portrayed, particularly within the cinema. The text concerned is the Book of Revelation, perhaps the most influential text of all in terms of the range of the weird and wonderful imagery it has inspired within art in general, and within cinema in particular. I propose to do this by concentrating on three separate, but interlocking, sub-themes: these I have entitled *Timepiece, Talisman* and *Tattoo*.

By *Timepiece* I have in mind the importance that is placed upon establishing a correct chronology in interpretations of Revelation. In this respect the biblical text is important in that it enables us to establish the divine timetable of history. It is crucial for interpreters to be able to discern the signs of the times, to know where they are within the overall plan of history. There has always been a great deal of interest in constructing elaborate chronological charts, matching biblical clues with people, places, and events, in order to plot out our place in the divine timetable. Most often the establishment of the timetable includes some sort of identification of the personified evil "beast" of Revelation 13–17.[1] Perhaps the obvious place to start in demonstrating this is with the German artist Albrecht Dürer from Nürnberg. Dürer had an astonishingly varied career as a painter and graphic artist, but the series of 17 woodcuts that he executed depicting *The Apocalypse* in 1498 is arguably his most influential work. Hauntingly memorable is the depiction of the seven-headed beast of Revelation, together with the Whore of Babylon who rides upon it, based on Revelation 17:3 (Figure 1).

Figure 1: "The Whore of Babylon and the Seven-Headed Beast" from Albrecht Dürer's *The Apocalypse* (1498)

The seven heads of the beast can be clearly seen here, as can the seductive beauty of the woman, who holds a chalice from which she drinks the blood of the saints. The date of Dürer's *Apocalypse* series is very significant, for it came at a point when apocalyptic fervour and expectation was reaching fever pitch. Many in Dürer's day believed that the year 1500 would be the time when Jesus Christ would come back to earth to inaugurate the millennium. Special significance was attached to the year. It was not unusual to have key years like this so identified. Similar expectations were fastened upon the years 500 and 1000, for example. But what gave Dürer's *Apocalypse* cycle added significance was the fact that it was closely followed by the rise of Lutheranism and the subsequent Protestant-Catholic split within the western church, a split which was often viewed as a fulfilment of prophecies about the end of the world. Dürer himself was quite favourably disposed to the Lutheran cause and the artistic imaginations he helped create were quickly called into service by both sides.

For example, there is a Lutheran cartoon which appeared in c. 1530 which was aimed at showing the corruption of the Roman Catholic church. The church was depicted by the seven-headed monster consisting of the pope, cardinals, bishops, and priests. The sign on a cross at the centre of the scene reads, when translated, "for money, a sack full of indulgences"; and a Dürer-like beast is seen emerging from the chest of indulgences at the bottom. The text at the bottom concludes with an allusion to Revelation 13:3: "The beast had received a mortal wound, signifying that Doctor Martin has struck the papacy a deadly blow. May God grant that it will soon be overthrown. *Amen!*" Interestingly, the identification of the Catholic church with the Beast of the Apocalypse is one of the most persistent themes over the years, and it is one that continues in film interpretations of the Book of Revelation, as I shall demonstrate below. Catholics soon retaliated with their own artistic versions of the seven-headed beast of the Apocalypse. One notable example shows a depiction of Martin Luther, whose seven heads proclaim him to be a hypocrite, a fanatic, and the incarnation of Barabbas, the betrayer of Christ.

Since the Reformation every generation, and virtually every denomination within Christendom, has attempted to give an artistic face to the beast of the Book of Revelation. A good example from England is the broadsheet published by William Peake in 1643 during the height of the English Civil War. The broadsheet is in both Dutch and English; it depicts the Pope riding the seven-headed Beast of the Apocalypse, i.e., the Catholic church.[2] Peake's broadsheet is an intriguing example of how seventeenth-century thinkers, writers, and artists employed the imagery of the Book of Revelation to offer political interpretations of their day, and in so doing presented their audiences with what was in effect the cinema of their own day. In short, the *Timepiece* motif is significant for interpreters of the Book of Revelation, because knowing *where* we are in time enables us to know who is who within the apocalyptic drama that is unfolding—who is on God's side and who is pitched against him.

By *Talisman* I mean the way in which interpretations of Revelation often contain an element whereby the faithful believers are protected from the evils of the day. The use of such elements of protection, or talismans, has a well-established history in literature. In 1997 I wrote an article entitled "The Scandal of the Cross," which sought to explore how the crucifix serves as a protection, a talisman, against vampires in *Dracula* films (Kreitzer 1997: 181–219). I would like to suggest here that films based on the Book of Revelation have a similar dynamic, although it is generally less specifically identified or defined as a crucifix; what functions as a Revelation talisman differs from film to film. Sometimes the talisman is a particular amulet or charm which contains magical properties, or an ancient relic or artefact with hidden spiritual powers. Sometimes the talisman is a bit of knowledge, the correct understanding of a piece of scripture, a more accurate translation of a cryptic text. The important point is that the talisman functions as a supernatural mechanism of protection, a vehicle of assurance.

By *Tattoo* I mean the way in which people are frequently identified as agents or instruments of satanic forces, particularly the way in which interpretations of Revelation address the curious passages in chapters 13–14 and the infamous "mark of the beast" discussed within them. Speculation focuses on the number 666, which becomes a cipher for the personification of evil, the Antichrist, as well as the ways in which the followers of the beast are said to receive his mark upon their hands and their foreheads (Rev. 13:16–17; 14:9). This corporeal identification, or satanic tattooing, if you will, sometimes takes a literal, sometimes a symbolic form. Occasionally, it is *encorporation*, in the most literal, physical sense where evil forces inhabit, or take over completely, the body of a human host.

These three sub-themes, *Timepiece*, *Talisman*, and *Tattoo*, are mixed in a number of creative ways within films which rely on apocalyptic imagery from the Book of Revelation for their story-line. I would like to suggest that the combination of the three elements means that such "*Revelation* films" can be distinguished from two other film sub-genres which also are frequent vehicles for the portrayal of evil on screen: the *Vampire* film (such as *Dracula* and *Interview with the Vampire*) and the *Possession* films (such as *The Exorcist* or *Stigmata*). To demonstrate the *Revelation* film genre, I shall concentrate on five films in particular, which cover four decades: *The Omen* (1976); *The Seventh Seal* (1988);

The Prophecy (1995); *End of Days* (1999); *Revelation* (2001). A host of other films could also be used, but these will serve to illustrate my purposes.

1. Richard Donner's *The Omen* (1976)

I turn first to one of the most influential occult-horror films which uses the Book of Revelation as a textual starting point, namely Richard Donner's *The Omen* (1976). The screenplay for the film was written by David Seltzer, who also produced a spin-off novelization for Signet Books in 1976 which was the best-selling paperback in the USA for a brief spell. The basic plot of this film seems almost tame to our ears nowadays,[3] but it rode a wave of popular interest in apocalyptic matters in the 1970s and the film was phenomenally successful. It cost $2.8 million to make and made over $60 million in 1976 alone. It was nominated for two Oscars, and won the Oscar for "Best Music, Original Score," which included Jerry Goldsmith's haunting *Ave Satani*, a remarkable re-working of a traditional *Requiem Mass*.

The story-line of *The Omen* concerns the American ambassador to the United Kingdom, Richard Thorn (played by Gregory Peck), who finds that his adopted son Damien is in fact the Antichrist, the Son of Satan (he had been substituted for the Thorns' own biological son who died at birth). Ambassador Thorn and his wife Kathy (played by Lee Remick) frantically try and protect their son, not realizing that they are up against a host of demonic forces about which they know little.

Much of the underlying apocalyptic imagery of the film is based on the Book of Revelation, drawing heavily upon popular interpretations of the book such as Hal Lindsey's *The Late Great Planet Earth* (1970). Thus, Father Brennan, a disaffected priest, whose room has pages from the Bible covering all the walls and windows, offers to Ambassador Thorn a poem containing an amalgamation of images drawn from such trendy readings of the Book of Revelation. There is one important scene in which Father Brennan arranges to meet Ambassador Thorn and explain to him what is going to happen to him and his family. In particular, he warns Thorn that their demonic son Damien will not permit his mother, Ambassador Thorn's wife Kathy, to have any other children who might rival his position in the world (somehow Father Brennan is aware that she will soon become pregnant again). Note the following exchange between Father Brennan and Ambassador Thorn, which was arranged by the priest in order to tell the Ambassador of the danger facing his wife:

Ambassador Thorn: Get on with it. Say what you have to say.

Father Brennan: When the Jews return to Zion, and a comet rips the sky, and the Holy Roman Empire rises, you and I must die. From the eternal sea he rises, creating armies on either shore, turning man against his brother, till man exists no more. The Book of Revelations predicted it all...

Ambassador Thorn: [*interrupting*] I am not here to listen to a sermon.

Father Brennan: It is by means of a human personality, entirely in his possession, that Satan will wage his last formidable offence.

Ambassador Thorn: You said that my wife was...

Father Brennan: [*interrupting*] Go to the town of Megiddo in the old city of Jezreel. There see the old man Bugenhagen. He alone can describe how the child must die.

Ambassador Thorn: [*interrupting*] Look here!

Father Brennan: He who will not be saved by the Lamb will be torn by the Beast.

Father Brennan's prophecy about the apocalyptic timetable is key for the overall plot, and it is repeated later at several points within the film. Yet one feature within this declaration by Father Brennan is worth high-lighting, for it has a very intriguing history in its own right. This concerns the fate of the Jews, the idea that somehow the destiny of the Jewish nation is an important trigger in the apocalyptic timetable; as Father Brennan ominously put it, "when the Jews return to Zion." This motif has a special role within English history, and in particular within the highly-charged millennial speculations of the seventeenth century. Indeed, it is almost impossible to understand the history of the interpretation of the Book of Revelation in the English-speaking world without going back to the seventeenth-century context, so determinative was it. How, and why, is this so?

Much credit for this lies with an enigmatic figure named Joseph Mede (1586–1638), a Cambridge biblical scholar and Hebraist who is widely regarded as "the father of English millenarianism." Mede was one of Milton's teachers in Cambridge and there is some evidence that he influenced his views on such matters (Matar, 1987: 109–124). Mede first published his ideas in a Latin book entitled *Clavis Apocalyptica* in 1627; it was translated into English and published posthumously in 1643.[4] The most important idea in Mede's work was that the millennial reign of Christ was taken to be a literal 1000 years, and that it was a *future* event. Mede's literalism over the meaning of the millennium of Revelation 20 helped set in motion an interpretative force which has continued unabated to this day, and Donner's film *The Omen* is one of the more influential cinematic examples of it.

One of the most memorable features of the film involves what I have been describing as satanic tattooing. The idea of the number 666, the "mark of the beast" mentioned in Rev. 13:18, also figures prominently within the film. The 666 emblem is even given as an on-screen graphic at the end of the film, and it was widely used in publicity photos and posters which promoted *The Omen*. Indeed, Damien is said at one point to be born on the sixth day of the sixth month at six in the morning, just to hammer the point home. In addition, Father Brennan has a birthmark on the inside of his left thigh which resembles the letters 666; Father Spilletto, the priest responsible for arranging the adoption of the demonic Damien to Ambassador Thorn, has 666 written on the floor of his monastic cell. Most significantly, Damien is shown to have a birthmark under his hair—this satanic tattooing comes in the form of a triangulated 666.

The Omen went on to inspire three sequels which followed the career of the Antichrist, Damien Thorn, including his rise to political power (he succeeds his father as US ambassador to the UK). The film has continued to capture the imagination of a movie-going audience. In 2001 a documentary was released on the phenomenon of *The Omen* film cycle. It was entitled *The Omen Legacy* and alleged to follow the true story behind the Damien Thorn character.

More significant was the release in 2006 of an updated version of *The Omen* directed by John Moore. The film was specifically timed for a mid-summer release, associating the apocalyptic imagery of the number of the Beast (666) with a release date of 6 June 2006 (sixth day of the sixth month of the sixth year of the new century); advertising posters of the film highlighted this date shamelessly. If anything the number 666 is given even more prominence in this updated version of *The Omen*, and there are many pointed references to it, most notably in the appearance of a triangual 666 in the scalp of the satanic Damien which is even more elaborate than was seen in the first film. The film also features an opening sequence which sees the Pope of the Roman Catholic Church presiding over a conclave of Vatican officials as they receive a report which asserts that the dreaded Armageddon is about to arrive. Interestingly passages from Revelation 8 are specifically read out (in Italian), and juxtaposed with contemporary images of various disasters, which are purported to be fulfilments of the biblical prophecies. These images include the attack on the Twin Towers in New York in September 2001, the *Columbia* shuttle disaster of February 2003, the South-Asian tsunami in December 2004, and the hurricane Katrina disaster in August 2005.

In any event, reviewers were generally quite critical of the film, viewing it as a rather slavish remake of the original. Adam Smith's review for *Empire* magazine perceptively comments on how *The Omen* (2006) *might* have made its message even more relevant to the contemporary political situation:

> The overwhelming impression is of a lost opportunity, given that the current American administration's sinister attempts to infect politics with religion provide a contemporary backdrop even more fertile for this Mephistopholean melodrama than the post-Vietnam paranoia that boosted the original movie, though the final shot, of Damien holding the hand of the President—the back of whose head bears a passing resemblance to George Bush's—at least demonstrates that Moore and co. noticed the possibilities.[5]

2. Carl Schultz's *The Seventh Sign* (1988)

Carl Schultz's *The Seventh Sign* (1988) is, as its title suggests, overtly based on imagery taken from the Book of Revelation. The publicity blurb tells it all:

> Time is running out. Revelation is at hand. Rivers are running red with blood, a desert is found shrouded in ice and the moon has turned to blood. Six signs of the Apocalypse have come to pass. Now only one woman can stop THE SEVENTH SIGN.

The film presents us with a mysterious Christ-like figure named David Bannon, who travels around the world breaking seals on prophetic documents and causing natural disasters to strike. David is in effect the embodiment of Jesus Christ returned, and he is serving as an instrument of divine judgment upon the earth. Father Lucci, a Vatican investigator, is sent to investigate the various portents, and he dismisses them all as natural events. Meanwhile, in New York a pregnant woman named Abby Quinn is eventually convinced that these events are somehow tied to the impending birth of her son. A clash of good and evil ensues with Abby Quinn caught in the middle and forced ultimately to decide whether she is willing to sacrifice herself for the safe birth of her child.

There is an interesting scene in which Abby Quinn encounters Father Lucci and learns from him the full significance of what is happening around her, including a supernatural hail storm from which he rescues her. The language and imagery of Revelation 6–8 undergirds the story-line. The following exchange between them takes place, with the duplicitous Father Lucci trying to determine how much Abby has learned from her Jewish friend Avi about her role in the apocalyptic timetable that is unravelling:

Father Lucci: Please, I need to know everything he's told you if I am to help.

Abby Quinn: He said if I can stop a sign the chain will be broken.

Father Lucci: Avi told you?

Abby Quinn: Yes, and God would grant the world a second chance.

Father Lucci: Has he told you which sign to stop?

Abby Quinn: No, that's what I am trying to figure out.

Father Lucci: No, It's imposs… I don't think a sign can be stopped.

Abby Quinn: He wouldn't have told me if there weren't a way. That's why I have to know what the other signs are. You said you knew them.

Father Lucci: They're no secret, Mrs Quinn. God has no secrets. The signs are contained in what the Bible calls the seven seals. The first four have already begun. The four horsemen of the Apocalypse; their signs are almost over. The fifth seal tells of the death of the last martyr…

Abby Quinn: [*interrupting*] The deaths could be stopped!

Father Lucci: Whose? Where?

Abby Quinn: What about the sixth?

Father Lucci: It begins with the sun turning to darkness. Then the earth will quake, and a star shall fall from the sky. And when the Lamb opened the seventh seal there was silence in heaven. The silence of the Guf[6]—empty. The stillbirth of a soul-less child. *You* are the seventh seal.

Abby Quinn: I am not going to let my baby die. One of the signs has to be stopped.

Father Lucci: How, Mrs Quinn? Do you know how?

Abby Quinn: With hope.

Interestingly the *Tattoo* sub-theme does not come through in this film as any special physical marking of Abby Quinn, as such—she does not bear a special "mark of the beast," or any satanic birthmarks, on her body. However, the fact that she is pregnant is in itself a sign, or at least it is the thing that identifies her as "the seventh seal." Abby Quinn's pregnancy identifies her as an object of supernatural agency, and ultimately her willingness to surrender her life for the safe birth of her child means that she becomes an instrument of divine deliverance for the world at large. *Why* and *how* her death satisfies the sacrificial desires of heavenly powers is left unexplained. This is a real oddity in the film's story-line, particularly since it is ostensibly the thing that drives the plot. There is a suggestion within the film that Abby and Father Lucci met earlier in a previous life and that her willing self-sacrifice for the life of her child is a re-enactment of a previous confrontation between them centuries before. However, this prior relationship is not clearly set out within the film and is communicated primarily through brief flashback scenes which last only a few seconds. In any event, in the opinion of Conrad E. Ostwalt Jr, the essential theme of *The Seventh Sign* is the "renewal of the world, yet the avoidance of the apocalyptic cataclysm" (Ostwalt, 1995: 59).

3. Gregory Wilden's *The Prophecy* (1995)

Gregory Wilden's *The Prophecy* (1995) offers a rather unusual slant on the battle of good and evil, one which concentrates on it as a heavenly battle. The story involves a priest who loses his faith and becomes a policeman, Thomas Daggett, and then finds himself involved in the struggle between good and bad angels who are in rebellion against God.

Much of the biblical imagery contained within the film is dependent upon the Book of Revelation and the mythology surrounding the fall of Lucifer as channelled through Milton's *Paradise Lost* (1667). A good example occurs in the opening scenes, as the faithful angel Simon explains the war in heaven in which he is engaged.

There is an interesting scene in which Thomas Daggett attends the autopsy of one of the fallen angels. An old Bible is found on the angel, whose name is Uziel; he is revealed to be one of Gabriel's lieutenants. The exchange between Daggett and the medical examiner is as follows:

Joseph: We found this in the lining of his coat.

Daggett: It's an old Bible.

Joseph: Yeah, hand-written. Beautiful, really. *[He turns to the frontispiece of the Bible and points to an symbol inscribed there.]* See this symbol? It matches a scar on his neck, exactly the same. *[The camera gives a close-up of the symbol on Uriel's neck.]* It's attractive, huh?

Daggett: Anything else?

Joseph: The velvet book-marker.

Daggett: *[Turning to the book-marker in the Bible.]* Cute.

Joseph: Why is that?

Daggett: Twenty-third chapter of Saint John's Revelations.

Joseph: And…?

Daggett: There is no twenty-third chapter.

Joseph: Well, maybe this is the teacher's edition.

Daggett goes on to translate a section of "the twenty-third chapter of St John's Revelations," searching for meaning in the Latin text of the illuminated manuscript:

> "And there were angels who could not accept the lifting of man above them, and like Lucifer rebelled against the armies of the loyal archangel Michael. And there rose a second war in heaven."

Later on in the film it is determined that the Bible is from the second century, and Daggett translates more from the additional chapter:

> "And there shall be a dark soul, and this soul will lead other dark souls and so become their inheritor. This soul will not rest in an angel, but a man, and he shall be a warrior."

This is a good example of how the text functions as a *Talisman* within the film, particularly as the additional chapter from the Book of Revelation provides a new perspective on the apocalyptic battle that is raging in the world. With the special insight granted through the text, Daggett is afforded a measure of protection in the face of the struggle between good and evil.

The Prophecy went on to inspire a further two sequels in fifteen years, each with the mesmerizing portrayal of the rebellious angel Gabriel by Christopher Walken. Both of the sequels continue the creative re-working of the Book of Revelation set out in the original. The sequels further illustrate how influential the biblical work has been for Hollywood's continuing fascination with the horror film genre.

4. Peter Hyams' *End of Days* (1999)

Peter Hyams' occult thriller *End of Days* (1999) is an excellent example of a film which portrays an apocalyptic timetable in operation, what I have been calling the *Timepiece* sub-theme. The film was released toward the end of 1999 and attempts to cash in on the millennial fever attending the arrival of the year 2000.[7]

The story-line is a mixture of contemporary plausibility and far-fetched occultic fantasy. A child born in 1979 is destined to be the bride of Satan twenty years later in New York City on the eve of the new millennium. Satan roams the streets of the city in search of his intended, who is named Christine York. He does this so that he can impregnate her before the new millennium arrives and thereby be released from his thousand-year-long imprisonment in the abyss. At the same time renegade Catholic priests, the Knights of the Holy See, are attempting to kill her as well. It is up to an atheistic security guard named Jericho Cane (played by Arnold Schwarzennegger) to find her, protect her from both sides, and save the day. Cane must rediscover his own faith and face up to the pain of losing his wife and daughter who died tragically some time before. He is assisted in this by a sympathetic priest named Father Kovak (played by Rod Steiger), who is one of the few people aware of what is really happening.

There is one crucial scene in which all three of the sub-themes I have identified as significant (*Timepiece*, *Talisman* and *Tattoo*) come into focus. The scene begins with Joshua Cane and Christine York going to the church which Father Kovak uses as his base of operations. The sub-theme of a *Talisman*, or protective device, comes through in the form of Father Kovak's secret knowledge of what is taking place. Father Kovak's translation programme of a Polish peasant's speaking prophecies from the Book of Revelation in a foreign tongue (it happens to be Akkadian) figures prominently as a means of interpretative insight for him. The chronological timetable, the *Timepiece* sub-theme, is similarly significant, with the apocalyptic events timed to take place on millennial eve, as it were. The *Tattoo* element is also brought out, as it becomes clear that Christine York bears the mark of Lucifer on her arm. The scene contains the following exchange between the central characters, concluding with a humorous slap at the impossible nature of apocalyptic timetables as the Joshua Cane character sarcastically responds to Father Kovac's explanations:

Kovak: Do you know anything about the number of the beast? The Revelation of Saint John from his dream?

York: 666?

Kovak: The number of the beast is not 666. Often in dreams numbers appear upside down and backward. [*Kovak writes the numbers 666 on a piece of paper and holds the page up to York, inverting it in the process to make his point.*] So 666 becomes 999, like in 1999, the year of his return.

York: What does that have to do with me?

Kovak: [*He opens a large Latin tome and reads from the title, pointing to some strange symbols on the title page*] Regressus Diaboli—The return of Satan. Does any of this look familiar to you?

York: [*She notices one of the emblems on the page and nods. She then rolls up the sleeve of her left arm and reveals a tattoo of the same emblem.*]

Kovak: She's been chosen. He's in her blood. The Holy Church has been searching for you since the day you were born.

York: Chosen for what?

Kovak: Every thousand years, on the eve of the millennium, the dark angel comes and takes a body and then he walks the earth looking for a woman who will bear his child. It all has to happen in the unholy hour before midnight on New Year's Eve. He consummates your flesh with his human body, and he unlocks the gate of hell. And everything as we know it ceases to exist.

Cane: [*Sarcastically*] So the Prince of Darkness wants to conquer the earth. But he has to wait until the hour before midnight of New Year's Eve? Is this Eastern Time?

5. Stuart Urban's *Revelation* (2001)

Stuart Urban's low-budget occult thriller *Revelation* (2001) is probably the best example of a Revelation film which uses the *Talisman* sub-theme within it. An almost unbelievably implausible story-line is presented here, beginning with the interests of a multi-billionaire Magnus Martel (played by Terence Stamp). Being a multi-millionaire is no longer enough—billions are now required to rule the world.

The story concerns a cryptographer named Jacob (played by James D'Arcy) and a feminist alchemist named Mira (played by Natasha Wightman) who go on the trail of an artefact called the Loculus. They encounter a host of other evil forces also in search of it, including the Knights Templar and the Central Intelligence Agency (CIA). So you get both the Roman Catholic Church and the CIA implicated as demonic agencies within this film. A number of specific references to the Book of Revelation are made, including the fact that John was exiled to Patmos and wrote the book there (Rev. 1:9). Not surprisingly, the Loculus is hidden in a church on the remote island. The description of Jesus as the Alpha and the Omega (Rev. 1:8 and 22:13) appears at several points, including a historical flashback scene in which Isaac Newton, "the great Alchemist of his age," tries to decipher the significance of the Loculus.

There is an important scene in which Jacob (who happens to be the billionaire's son) and Mira and her colleague Ray Connolly discover the Loculus in Patmos. The Loculus is determined by them to contain artefacts from the crucifixion of Jesus Christ, including the nails which were used to hold him to the cross. The trio figure out that the nails contain Jesus Christ's blood, and then the mystery of the Loculus becomes clear to us. A conspiracy hatched by a group of Vatican cardinals, led by the Grand Master, is to use the blood to extract Christ's DNA, which will then be used to resurrect him in the form of a cloned baby. At one level this means that Christ's cloning/resurrection is proclaimed by the corrupt church officials as the Second Coming of Christ. This is a novel twist in the way that Christ's Second Coming is generally thought to herald the end of the world, to say the least. The film certainly relies heavily upon the Book of Revelation in its bizarre plot, mixing it with a liberal amount of conspiratorial plotting by Vatican officials, and freely injecting the latest scientific technologies (cloning techniques, gene replacement therapies, etc.) in the process. As the promotional blurb on the DVD box explains:

> As the world unwittingly draws ever closer to the brink of a new and ter-
> rifying age, the stage is set for a showdown between the forces of 21st
> science and religion [sic] and an ancient evil that has cursed history.

Some Concluding Observations

This concludes our playful exploration into some of the ways that the Book of Revelation has been used in some films over the years. Interpreting the text as offering itself as a *Timepiece* by which to trace divine history, as a *Talisman* through which God's people can be preserved and protected, and by giving us the image of a *Tattoo* as a means whereby the good and evil can be appropriately identified, has, hopefully, provided us with a useful platform for discussion. I would like to suggest that the three-fold pattern could usefully be used to assess a number of other films, many of which turn to the Book of Revelation as a scriptural starting point. Interestingly, for about the past ten years or so I have been engaged in compiling a database of how scripture is used within cinema. Every time I watch a film I keep a list of what biblical texts are used within it, and how they are used. To my surprise, my rough calculations (of about 3,000 films) suggest that about *one out of every three* films either cites a biblical text, or has a direct allusion to one. The most common texts cited are those associated with funeral services (Psalm 23, Ecclesiastes, Job 1:21), or weddings ("Let no man put asunder..."). At the same time, it is worth noting that the Book of Revelation is also a major player in terms of the cinematic scriptural citation game. About *ninety* films of the 1,000 I have catalogued thus far make reference to the Book of Revelation within their story-line, most generally in such a way that highlights the apocalyptic dimensions discussed here, notably the beast of Revelation 13 and 17, and the Four Horsemen of chapter 6. Curiously, the christological element of the Book of Revelation seems to be rather downplayed by film-makers. Angels and demons abound, and any number of secondary beings serve as divine agents, but the depiction of a Christ-figure coming to judge the living and the dead and inaugurate a new created order is difficult to find in the cinematic world. Perhaps Stuart Urban's *Revelation* (2001) is the exception that proves the rule here, for the Christ-figure that is presented in this film is a genetically-engineered clone, which effectively means we have to start at the beginning again.

I wish that I could offer an easy and fool-proof pattern of how these three elements (*Timepiece, Talisman* and *Tattoo*) fit together within the various cinematic interpretations of the Book of Revelation. Could it be that one element gives way to another, depending on the social and political circumstances of the day? Or perhaps the prevailing religious expectations of a given time period and place, such as existed in the United States in the aftermath of the Arab-Israeli Six Day War in 1973, offer some key interpretative markers that allow us to map where we are in the cinematic world? Alas, the fact is that Revelation films are much more complex than we give them credit for and they defy simplistic or reductionistic analyses, although I think it would be fair to say that the millennium theme (the arrival of the year 2000) was a major factor in re-igniting interest in the relevance of the Book of Revelation for today's world. It is difficult to predict where Revelation films will go in the future, but it seems clear that the political complexities of the twenty-first-century world will play a major role.

In this regard, a brief concluding word needs to be mentioned about the so-called *Left Behind* phenomenon in the United States. This is an immensely popular series of books, the first of which was the 1995 bestseller by Tim LaHaye and Jerry B. Jenkins. To date the series of books has grown to an even dozen. It has also inspired a series of three films, based on the first three novels in the series, even drawing an actor of the stature of the Oscar-winning Lou Gossett Junior into the project. The third of these films, *Left Behind: World at War*, was released in late 2005. It blends together political interpretations of the fight against good and evil, appealing to key biblical texts in the process.[8] The appeal to an American, post-9/11 audience no doubt accounts for some of the success of the *Left Behind* series, but the phenomenon is so complex and multi-faceted that it warrants specialist study of its own. Sadly, that must remain the task for another day.

Notes

1. Kovacs and Rowland (2004: 147–59 and 177–89) contains a brief discussion.
2. See Bindman, 1999: 233, for a discussion of this point.

3. Prompting Harry Medved to include it within his *The Fifty Worst Films of All Time* (1978: 170–75).

4. Mede, 1643. The English translation was done by "Richard More of Linley in the County of Salop, Esquire, One of the Burgesses in this present Convention of Parliament." Mede's influence is discussed in Murrin, 1984: 125–46. The wider historical context of the period at the time is discussed in Capp, 1984: 93–124.

5. In an online review for *Empire* magazine (see http://www.empireonline.com/reviews/).

6. Elsewhere in the film, the "Guf" is described as "the Hall of Souls," where human souls wait until they are born.

7. For more on this see Cohen, 1999: 1615–28.

8. Bendle, 2005: 1–14.

Part III
Literature

Chapter 10

James Hogg and the Demonology of Scottish Writing

Crawford Gribben

James Hogg's *Private Memoirs and Confessions of a Justified Sinner* (1824) is a novel whose complex religious contexts have often baffled readers. The novel satirizes an extreme—and totally unrepresentative—form of Scottish Calvinism. Those critics who have been interested in situating the novel within this theological and cultural background have too often adopted a myopic reading that limits the influence of Scottish Calvinism to broadly soteriological themes: predestination, election, justification and antinomianism. By contrast, this essay argues that Hogg's debt to Scottish Calvinism went much further than these soteriological categories, for Scottish Calvinism also provided Hogg with the staple elements of his novel's demonology. A fascination with demons was typical of standard descriptions of Scotland's "worlds of wonder" in the late seventeenth and eighteenth centuries, and the demon that haunts the *Justified Sinner* emerges from and visibly reflects these earlier traditions of the Presbyterian occult. But this essay also argues that Scottish writers' interest in demonology is not inextricably linked to its background in the popular culture of early modern Calvinism. From the late nineteenth century to the present day, Scottish writers have continued to invoke themes from this earlier demonology to describe overt evil in the modern secular world.

Scottish Calvinism and the *Justified Sinner*

One of the most important themes in recent Hogg criticism has been the emphasis that the *Justified Sinner* is not simply a satire of the traditional faith of the Scottish Presbyterian churches (see, for a summary of this criticism, Gribben, 2004). This older line of argument dominated criticism of the novel for several decades after its rediscovery in the mid-twentieth century. These accounts of the novel's theological background varied in their sensitivity to Presbyterian orthodoxy, but Hogg criticism, within the wider literature of Scottish studies, has for many years been too ready to associate the faith of the Presbyterian churches with all manner of social and psychological evils. Marshall Walker's excellent survey of *Scottish Literature Since 1707* (1996) typifies this tradition in its description of the *Justified Sinner* as "one of the most penetrating and original novels in the Scottish tradition for its insight into the perversion of the Scottish psyche by Calvinism" (Walker, 1996: 13). Other scholars have echoed Walker's rejection of the value of Presbyterian orthodoxy with less of his sensitivity to its positive social contribution.

No one who reads Hogg's novel could doubt that Scottish Calvinism makes a crucial contribution to its themes and concerns. The novel presents a "found fragment" of spiritual autobiography within a larger editorial framework. The anonymous editor-character introduces and then comments upon a document found in the grave of an early eighteenth-century suicide, Robert Wringhim. Wringhim's memoir presents a strange tale that appears to emerge from a small and isolated antinomian sect, a sect that adheres to a militant and politically extreme form of Presbyterianism in the period immediately before the end of Scottish independence and the passing of the Act of Union (1707).

The memoir appears to recount a narrative of conversion. One morning, Wrighim's "revered father," the leader of the antinomian sect, "arose from his seat, and...embraced me, and welcomed me into the community of the just upon earth." This meant, the clergyman explained,

> that I was now a justified person, adopted among the number of God's children—my name [was] written in the Lamb's book of life, and...no bypast transgression, nor any future act of my own, or of other men, could be instrumental in altering the decree. "All the powers of darkness," added he, "shall never be able to pluck you again out of your Redeemer's hand" (Hogg, 2002: 79).

But that assurance was soon to be tested. Overcome by joy, Wringhim "bounded away into the fields and the woods, to pour out my spirit in prayer before the Almighty for his kindness to me." As he "wended his way," he encountered

> a young man of a mysterious appearance... I could not well avoid him... I felt a sort of invisible power that drew me towards him, something like the force of enchantment, which I could not resist...our eyes met, and I can never describe the strange sensations that thrilled through my whole frame at that impressive moment; a moment to me fraught with the most tremendous consequences; the beginning of a series of adventures which has puzzled myself, and will puzzle the world when I am no more in it (Hogg, 2002: 80).

The erotically-charged language is startling in the text—and all the more so when Wringhim discovers the stranger to be his second self: "The clothes were the same to the smallest item. The form was the same; the apparent age; the colour of the hair; the eyes; and, as far as recollection could serve me from viewing my own features in a glass, the features too were the very same" (Hogg, 2002: 80). Mistaking his new acquaintance for a Russian prince in humble disguise, Wringhim embarks on a relationship that is underpinned by both parties' commitment to an antinomian theology of predestination. That theology leads to a series of crimes against others—exploitation, rape, murder, and fratricide—and ultimately, as Wringhim increasingly suspects his new friend of diabolical purpose and ability, to his own lonely suicide.

But readers of the novel, approaching the memoir within the interpretive guidelines offered by the editor-character's framework, are prevented access to the final meaning of these events. The novel refuses to explain whether the mysterious stranger is merely a projection of Wringhim's imagination, as the editor-character suggests, or whether he is actually an incarnation of Satan, as Wringhim himself comes to believe. The editor-character admits to his confusion. The memoir, he claims, may be an allegory or a religious parable "showing the dreadful danger of self-righteousness. I do not know" (Hogg, 2002: 165). He is quite open about his ignorance:

> With regard to the work itself, I dare not venture a judgement, for I do not understand it. I believe that no person, man or woman, will ever peruse it with the same attention that I have done, and yet I confess that I do not comprehend the writer's drift. It is certainly impossible that these scenes could ever have occurred… I account all the rest dreaming or madness… in this day, and with the present generation, it will not go down, that a man should be daily tempted by the devil, in the semblance of a fellow-creature; and at length be lured to self-destruction, in the hopes that this same fiend and tormentor was to suffer and fall along with him… In short, we must either conceive him not only the greatest fool, but the greatest wretch, on whom was ever stamped the form of humanity; or, that he was a religious maniac, who wrote and wrote about a deluded creature, till he arrived at that height of madness, that he believed himself the very object whom he had been all along describing (Hogg, 2002: 174–75).

But a third reading of the novel is also possible. It is also possible that Wringhim's account was actually purporting to be an accurate narration of an encounter with the Devil. The editor-character's moderate dismissal of the tale reflects deep ignorance of the religious culture from which the memoir emerges—for, in the literature of radical Presbyterians, with which Hogg was certainly familiar, appearances of the Devil were far from uncommon. Wringhim, like his author, is certainly aware of this literary genre. Along with the Bible and the metrical psalms, the novel represents him reading the Covenanter hagiography, *A Cloud of Witnesses for the Royal Prerogative of Jesus Christ* (1778). In the genre of Covenanter hagiography that *A Cloud of Witnesses* typifies, Scottish Presbyterians had already reported the possibility that afflicted believers "should be daily tempted by the devil, in the semblance of a fellow-creature" (Hogg, 2002: 174–75).

Presbyterian Demonology and the *Justified Sinner*

The Devil was no stranger to early modern Scotland. In fact, as Hogg and other nineteenth-century writers reconstructed the religious history of sixteenth- and seventeenth-century Scotland, it was often to the occult possibilities of radical Presbyterianism that they turned. The doppelgänger theme, which Hogg exploits so skilfully, emerges repeatedly throughout these texts.

While the doppelgänger theme has a wider European context, it certainly has a distinctive Scottish origin. The orthodox Calvinism of the Scottish churches maintained, for example, that the divided self described in Rom. 7:15–25 and Gal. 5:16–17 represented a paradigm of authentic Christian experience. In other words, conversion—the individual's faith in Jesus Christ and repentance from sin—did not do away with the influence of the old sinful nature. Sin continued to affect the believer's psyche, always frustrating his best attempts to do good. In practice, therefore, the Christian life afforded no final escape from psychological or spiritual warfare, and evil influences in the believer's life were institutionalized as a normal component of godliness. There was always an interior "other," beset by evil, waging war against the good.

But that "other" was apparently sometimes externalized. The literature of radical Presbyterianism contains a number of volumes of anecdotes whose primary purpose was to demonstrate God's vindication of the truth and his opposition to his enemies. These providentialist narratives also featured accounts of the unusual. The most famous and influential of these volumes was Robert Fleming's *The Fulfilling of the Scripture, or, A Discovery of the Accomplishment of God's Holy Word in his Providential Works* (n.p., 1669). Fleming had been born in Yester, Haddingtonshire, in 1630. His family had strong links within the Church of Scotland. His father was a minister, and his mother's cousin, John Livingston, was one of the most prominent and well-travelled ministers in the kirk. Livingston had been ordained in north-east Ireland, and, familiar with a number of the clergy referred to in Fleming's work, is a probable source for a number of its anecdotes. Fleming himself followed the family tradition and was ordained into the ministry. Although he had an unusual call—hearing an audible voice "call to me...make haste"—his commitment to radical Presbyterianism drove him into exile in Rotterdam, where, it was alleged, he had sheltered some of the murderers of Archbishop Sharp (Mullan, 2004). In exile, Fleming turned to publication, and *The Fulfilling of the Scripture* was his most enduring work (see Gribben, 2007).

The Devil is a principal character in Fleming's text. He appears to mock the godly. Robert Blair, once Livingston's colleague in northeast Ireland, had an earlier teaching appointment at the University of Glasgow. While he was "a Regent in the colledge," he "had been once troubled with an appearing of the Devil...who like a crooked boy that waited on him stood up and laughed him in the face, whilest he was serious in his chamber, and immediatly disappeared" (Fleming, 1693: 379). But Satan was also attempting to deceive and destroy. Fleming recorded another incident from Blair's ministry, in which a merchant from Bangor, in County Down, travelled to Scotland with the purpose of selling horses. At a fair he met a man who was willing to purchase them all, "but he pretending he had not all that money at present gave him bond until Mertimess." Around that time, "going homeward from Bangor one night," the vendor was met by the buyer:

> now said he, you know my bargain, how I bought you at such a place, and I am come as I promised to pay you the price. Bought me, said the other trembling, you bought but my horses, nay sayes the Devil I will have you know I bought your self, and to the poor man confounded with fear said, he must either kill some body, and the more excellent the person were the better it would be for him, else he would not free him, and particularly charged him to kill Mr Blair.

The vendor was "overcome with terror, and through the violence of that temptation, determined the thing, and went to Mr Blair's house with a dagger in his right hand hid beneath his cloak," but found himself providentially unable to commit the deed. He confessed his intention to Blair, who took command of the situation to exhort the merchant to a life of repentance. But the Devil did not give up on his attack: Blair "was after threatened and much terrifyed by the Devil but nothing more followed" (Fleming, 1693: 379–80).

This incident, with its obvious parallels to Gil-Martin's inciting Wringhim to the murder of Revd Blanchard, is followed by another anecdote with specific verbal parallels to Wringhim's memoir. Fleming records "a strange passage of judgement" concerning "a Noble man in our own countrey, whose name with respect to his house, I forbear to mention." This nobleman had managed his estate with "blood, cruelty and oppression," but was brought temporarily to his senses when his second son,

> who after succeeded to that house, by the death of his brother, found a latter sealed and directed to his father, bearing the stile of his house, and without any suspicion whence it came carried it up to his chamber, which, that Lord breaking up, found of a strange stile for it had these words, I summond you—to appear before the tribunal of God, and there answere for your murthers, oppressions, &c. Subscribitur Diabolus

The nobleman, enraged, attempted to murder his son, whom he suspected was behind the practical joke, and who fled the house to return, months later, only after the "intercession of friends." But immediately upon his return, "a letter from the roof of that chamber drops down upon his [father's] hands, sealed and directed as before, which being opened had the were [sic] same words of the former letter with that dreadfull subscription Diabolus." The nobleman was "strucke with a remarkable infatuation," fled all human society, "and in this case shortly dyed, having been made a terrour to himself" (Fleming, 1693: 393–94). There are obvious parallels in the novel. In the *Justified Sinner*, Robert is a second son whose control of the Dalcastle estate, which he inherits after the death of his older brother, could certainly be characterized by "blood, cruelty and oppression." But the anecdote also anticipates distinct verbal patterns in the *Justified Sinner*, which also refers to the Devil as "Diabolus" (Hogg, 2002: 137) and which also describes Wringhim's death as that of a haunted landowner who had become a "terror to myself" (Hogg, 2002: 156). Of course, it is important not to overstate the relationship between the Fleming and Hogg texts. There are distinct thematic and verbal echoes, but it is likely that Hogg was drawing on a wider oral culture, a store of occult tales that Fleming's text had come to consolidate. The Scottish Calvinist tradition had argued that evil could never be entirely externalized; but the oral tradition of Presbyterian culture contained many examples of individuals meeting evil incarnate. Nevertheless, whether in the anecdotes or in the novel, the demon comes to take advantage of cultural uncertainties associated with the value of radical Presbyterianism in the wider cultures of early modern Scotland.

The *Justified Sinner* and Demonic Style

The novel's form also suggests that the sinister is not confined to the contents of Wringhim's tale. On the run from Edinburgh, Wringhim gets a job in a "printing office." "It was here that I first conceived the idea of writing this journal, and having it printed," he explained, and Wringhim gained his employers' permission for the project by describing the memoir as "a religious parable such as the *Pilgrim's Progress*" (Hogg, 2002: 152). But Wringhim's enthusiasm for the project led to his violation of the Ten Commandments:

> I put my work to the press, and wrote early and late; and encouraging my companion to work at odd hours, and on Sundays, before the press-work of the second sheet was begun, we had the work all in types, corrected, and with a clean copy thrown off for farther revisal (Hogg, 2002: 153).

His printing-partner might have realized that Wringhim's encouragement to break the Sabbath—one of the staple markers of godlessness in early modern Scotland—was indicative of the contents of his treatise. Only days later, Wringhim's plans were blasted: "my hopes and prospects are a wreck. My precious journal is lost! consigned to the flames!" (Hogg, 2002: 153). At the beginning of one week—presumably, shortly after an occasion of Sabbath-breaking—"my fellow-lodger came home, running in a great panic, and told me a story of the Devil having appeared twice in the printing house, assisting the workmen at the printing of my book." Wringhim's employer, "who till that time had never paid any attention to the treatise," now took a great deal of interest in its contents. Reading it in a rage, he dismissed the memoir as "a medley of lies and blasphemy, and ordered the whole to be consigned to the flames" (Hogg, 2002: 153). But the most serious indication of his danger, Wringhim's fellow-lodger informed him, was that the Devil had particularly inquired for him. Wringhim's initial response mirrored the skepticism of Enlightenment Presbyterianism:

> "Surely you are not such a fool," said I, "as to believe that the devil really was in the printing office?"

> "Oo, gud bless you sir! saw him myself, gave him a nod, and good-day. Rather a gentlemanly personage—Green Circassian hunting coat and turban—Like a foreigner—Has the power of vanishing in one moment though—Rather a suspicious circumstance that. Otherwise, his appearance not much against him" (Hogg, 2002: 154).

And from that moment, Wringhim began to realize that "my elevated and dreaded friend" was in fact the Devil himself (Hogg, 2002: 154).

But why was the devil overseeing the publication of "a religious parable such as the *Pilgrim's Progress*"? Looking past the contents to the form of the memoir, it becomes obvious that Gil-Martin's influence is actually pervasive in the text. The demonic influence on the narrative is evident in its use of purposefully slippery language and subtle reversions of biblical allusions. Biblical quotations are represented as inherently flexible texts. When Penpunt describes the revival of religion that swept across Auchtermuchty, for example, he noted that the "rigid righteousness" of the town was reflected in the popular appropriation and re-contextualization of biblical texts. Throughout the town, "there was nought to be heard, neither night nor day, but preaching, praying, argumentation, an' catechising... The young men wooed their sweethearts out o' the Song o' Solomon, an' the girls returned answers in strings o' verses out o' the Psalms" (Hogg, 2002: 137). But while these widespread citations of Scripture indicated the grip it now exercised on the public imagination, it also suggested that individual texts could find meaning in contexts radically other than those from which they emerged. While the language of the Song of Solomon could be readily accommodated into courtship, the Psalms do not serve to celebrate human love in anything like the same way. The girls' answers to their sweethearts were turning the intentions of the biblical writers on their heads, using their words, divested of original context, for purposes quite different from their intentions.

But flexible citations of biblical texts also evidenced the unreliability of the preacher through whose work the revival of religion had commenced. The "good people of Auchtermuchty" had been "in perfect raptures with the preacher," and had ridiculed the testimony of the one individual who realized that the preacher was in fact the Devil in disguise (Hogg, 2002: 138). But his evidence eventually won the day, and the people of Auchtermuchty became more skeptical than ever, more resistant to preaching than ever, always suspecting "the cloven foot peeping out frae aneath ilka sentence" (Hogg, 2002: 140). That cloven foot is evident throughout the length of Robert Wringhim's memoir.

The pervasive influence of this diabolism makes the editor-character's role powerfully ironic. Introducing and commenting on the memoir from a position of Enlightenment skepticism, and dismissing its claims of demonic influence, he is actually completing the task that the Devil, assisting Robert Wringhim, set out to accomplish. It is Gil-Martin—rather than Robert Wringhim—that is actually responsible for the publication of the text. For all the editor-character's Enlightenment moderation, the Devil is having the last laugh, and readers become the victims of a diabolical trick.

Demonology in Scottish Fiction after Hogg

Hogg's powerful articulation of demonic influence in form and content developed motifs that were readily appropriated in Scottish Gothic texts. As the Gothic form became increasingly diffuse, and as it moved from the anti-Catholic and anti-European themes of its earliest and most influential advocates, it maintained its interest in demonic "others." In Scotland, as elsewhere, this occult preoccupation continued after the collapse of the earlier religious consensus. As the nineteenth century developed, demonology in Scottish writing evolved into something of a barometer of the cultural standing of religious faith. Scottish writers repeatedly turned to demonic themes in order to describe and locate the focus of evil within their cultural worldview. Tracing the location of evil from the early nineteenth century to the present day, it is possible to see Scottish authors developing Hogg's ambivalence about the external-ity of evil. Reflecting wider trends in Gothic literature, and the growth of secularization, Scottish writers in the nineteenth and early twenti-eth centuries found evil in social and scientific concerns. By the end of the twentieth century, after the global horrors of holocaust and ethnic cleansing, Scottish writers had abandoned the earlier projection of an external evil, and were again suggesting the possibility of a demonic other within the divided self.

Two of the best-known examples of nineteenth-century trends were published at the end of the nineteenth century. Robert Louis Stevenson's *Dr Jekyll and Mr Hyde* (1886) dressed its parable in terms that located exactly the secularization of late Victorian life. Late one night, returning home from "some place at the end of the world," Enfield witnessed a horrible accident while the streets were, significantly, "as empty as a church." Mr Hyde, the "juggernaut" responsible for the accident, is dis-covered, eventually, to be the demonic other of one of London's most respectable physicians (Stevenson, 2003: 9). But Stevenson's London is very like Edinburgh, and the potion that effects the transformation is very like a chalice. But this Eucharist has no redemptive value: science is creating a demon after the failure of popular Victorian faith. This is an anti-Eucharist, and its terrible transformation would suggest the success-ful externalization of evil—were it not for the fact that Jekyll had admit-ted the potion merely satisfied the longing for anonymous sin that had long plagued him beneath his pious exterior. The collapse of religious faith does not rid the world of evil, these novels suggest—it just creates new demons, dogs disguised as diabolical hounds, and men transformed by the removal of all goodness.

The Hound of the Baskervilles (1902), by Arthur Conan Doyle, another son of Edinburgh, saw its hero, Sherlock Holmes, re-appear after his literary death as a spectral detective rubbishing the possibility of a demonic dog—but only after a close encounter that rocked his rational worldview. Holmes' sympathy for the Devil is surprising, for his world is radically ordered, and it is that ubiquity of order that makes possible his famous techniques: Holmes' world can be read, and its order is always predictable. Yet Conan Doyle plays with this idea of rationality, constructing Holmes as a detective who is able to "hover" over Devon by reading maps in his Baker Street flat (Conan Doyle, 1993: 27). Arguably, Holmes' propensity for smoking—and not always only tobacco—provides him with a drug-fuelled access into an alterior state. In this state, his spectral qualities provide keys to the ultimate closure of the case and the reaffirmation of order in the confusion of urban life in the late Victorian world. Holmes, the spectral detective, exposes the fraud of the demonic hound. The landscape of the chase, and the Celtic phrenology of its victims, is charged with profoundly Scottish and Irish themes. But for all his protagonist's preference for rationality, Arthur Conan Doyle, the Edinburgh-born son of Irish parents who devoted the last years of his life to the promotion of spiritualism, was decidedly ambivalent about the possibility of non-material evil.

Almost one century later, Iain Banks' *The Wasp Factory* (1984) continued to narrate fear of the demonic other in Scottish literature. Banks' Gothic masterpiece is set in the militaristic Britain of the early Thatcher years. The island that is the location for most of the novel's plot is overflown by military jets and is the site of the totemistic religion of Frank, the protagonist whose gender confusion is at the root of the plot development. *The Wasp Factory* describes a world where Scotland's traditional religion cannot impinge. The church spires are in the distance, and Frank's faith is a mixture of bizarre ritual and *Lord of the Flies* horror. It is a world haunted by evil—by the murders for which young Frank is responsible, and by the lies that trap him in confusion about his own identity and past.

But Frank becomes the demon who haunts the island, driven from his own secure gender identity into a destabilized murderer for whom evil has become normality. Banks' novel is more fiercely introspective than the romance-adventure fictions of Stevenson and Conan Doyle. In *The Wasp Factory*, the demonic is internalized, no longer projected onto doppelgängers or mysterious potions, as in previous Scottish fiction, but now reflecting the profoundly uncertain identity of modern individuals—and the Scottish nation they represent. Banks, arguably, turns back to Hogg, past the externalizing of evil in crime and science, to argue instead that modern, technological society is creating the monsters that are attempting to destroy it.

In summary, since the publication of Hogg's *Private Memoirs and Confessions*, Scottish authors have repeatedly turned to the image of the demonic "other" to articulate their sense of the proper location of evil. Demonology has provided metaphors that writers have used for social and cultural critique, as means of pin-pointing their sense of the origins of evil. James Hogg drew self-consciously on the demonology of popular Calvinism, and the myths of the Covenanters, to argue that his society faced the danger of those driven by unquestioning religious zeal. As the nineteenth century progressed, Conan Doyle and Stevenson developed demonic motifs in which to play with ideas of uncertain materiality in an increasingly secular world, but they continued to use a lingering demonology in their post-Calvinist alternative Scotlands. Throughout the twentieth century, Scottish writers have turned away from a merely external evil, focusing, in the aftermath of mass genocides and unprecedented holocaust, on the evil that modern history has shown cannot simply be projected to an external other. From James Hogg to the present day, demonology has acted as a cultural barometer of social threat in the literary culture of Presbyterian and post-Presbyterian Scotland.

Chapter 11

Voldemort, Death Eaters, Dementors, and the Dark Arts:
A Contemporary Theology of Spiritual Perversion in the Harry Potter Stories

Colin Duriez

The Harry Potter books are perceived in strikingly different ways. Some who are Christians, for instance, see them as promoting the occult and Satanism, and have tried, sometimes successfully, to ban them from libraries and schools. With the help of an article from the online *The Onion* magazine, the satire of which went unnoticed, this negative stance created a major urban myth.[1] Other Christians, such as Jerram Barrs of The Francis Schaeffer Institute of Covenant Theological Seminary, St Louis, see them as morally unambiguous about the nature of good versus evil, promoting the good. He writes of J. K. Rowling's "very clear moral universe" (Barrs, 2003). A Pagan witch finds herself bemused by arguments that the Harry Potter stories are full of accurate and true information about witchcraft, and by accusations of Satanism. She writes that the "only 'real' witchcraft elements in the books, are the real stereotypes that have dogged Witchcraft for decades. Flying around on broomsticks, pointed witches' hats, and the shooting of lightning from magic wands, to name a few." She points out that Wicca is a religion with a god and goddess. But "there is no spirituality," she claims, "in these books and movies at all!"[2] In contrast, a Jewish Rabbi, Noson Weisz, asserts that "The 'Harry Potter' books are not just novels. They are modern fairy tales with predominant spiritual themes. They describe the struggle between good and evil and the ultimate triumph of the good through courage and ingenuity of the human spirit, and the power of human love."[3] The same Rabbi points out that "Evil as presented in the Harry Potter books—whose ambition is to destroy the good for the sake of its own hegemony—is not innate to the universe. In reality, evil only comes about through the corruption of the good."[4]

The Harry Potter stories of J. K. Rowling, with the attendant movies, have been phenomenally successful around the globe. Her readership—estimated at over 400 million—is larger than the estimated world population in the first century, and more than that of the USA and Canada today. The fantasies of J. R. R. Tolkien and C. S. Lewis have enjoyed a somewhat similar planet-wide success. Though there are important differences in the fantasies of Tolkien, Lewis, and Rowling there are dramatic similarities in the values embedded in their works. This is no more apparent than in their depictions of evil in story form, in a manner that a contemporary readership and audiences find topical and relevant. This chapter will focus upon the Harry Potter stories, with, I hope, some illuminating references to Tolkien and Lewis.

The hero of J. K. Rowling's stories, Harry Potter, attends Hogwarts School of Witchcraft and Wizardry between 1991 and 1998, and each of the seven books corresponds to a year at that secondary school, even though many of the events of the final book, *Harry Potter and the Deathly Hallows,* take place outside the school. The school and its existence is hidden from "Muggles," that is, non-magical people that make up most of the population. Harry grows from an 11 to a 17 year old (the year of coming-of-age for a wizard or witch). The books cleverly combine a number of established genres: the classic boarding-school story in the tradition of Tom Brown (though Rowling's is a co-educational comprehensive), the Bildungsroman (novel of formation and rites-of-passage), fantasy (perhaps Christian and epic fantasy), and even science-fiction of a sort (given the parallels between the natural magic of the wizarding world, and the applied science or technology of the Muggle-world—the world of materialistic modern people, shaped by the scientific revolution). J. K. Rowling's books also belong firmly to the literary context of the 1990s and end of millennium. According to Colin Manlove, in his recent study of children's literature, the narrative point of view of the stories is significant. The stories nearly always are told from Harry's point of view, even though they are in the third person. This strongly affects the structure, making it rather different from a children's tale told from an adult perspective. This may reflect a general cultural shift over issues of identity and authority. Rowling's narrative stance increases the topicality and relevance of the books for a contemporary reader.

J. K. Rowling's portrayal of evil in the Harry Potter stories is complex and many-layered, reflecting a rich tradition of fantasy literature. Fantasy for both adults and children has become increasingly important in contemporary literature, reflecting the tumult of social change in modern society in the twentieth century, with two global wars and numerous other conflicts with apocalyptic casualties (see, e.g., Shippey, 1993: 217–36). In the Harry Potter stories, people and things are often not what they appear, engaging the reader in reflection on the nature of evil. Evil, focused upon the Dark Lord, Voldemort, contrasts with qualities and virtues like love, self-sacrifice, and courage, prized and defended by Harry and his friends. A society based on fear (the Death Eaters) contrasts with the supportive friendship of Harry, Hermione, Ron, Hagrid, and others. Theologically, Rowling's portrayal of evil is Christian-Augustinian, rather than Manichean, Gnostic or materialistic, demonstrating that this ancient tradition is relevant and applicable to a modern world.

The Rich Tradition of School Story and Fantasy

The Harry Potter stories are school stories, but with J. K. Rowling's skew evident on Harry Potter's first arrival at Hogwarts school of Witchcraft and Wizardry.

> The door swung open at once. A tall, black-haired witch in emerald-green robes stood there. She had a very stern face and Harry's first thought was that this was not someone to cross.
>
> "The firs' years, Professor McGonagall," said Hagrid.
>
> "Thank you, Hagrid. I will take them from here."
>
> She pulled the door wide. The entrance hall was so big you could have fit the whole of the Dursleys' house in it. The stone walls were lit with flaming torches like the ones at Gringotts, the ceiling was too high to make out, and a magnificent marble staircase facing them led to the upper floors.
>
> They followed Professor McGonagall across the flagged stone floor. Harry could hear the drone of hundreds of voices from a doorway to the right— the rest of the school must already be here—but Professor McGonagall showed the first years into a small, empty chamber off the hall. They crowded in, standing rather closer together than they would usually have done, peering about nervously…[5]

It could be any school (if you take out the reference to Gringotts, a bank run by goblins), but it is vast, and the deputy headteacher who welcomes them is a witch. She immediately inducts them into the ritual of the magical Sorting Hat, which will place them in one of four houses. Notice how the narrator has reflected Harry's perception of events, including references to his recent visit to the magical shopping street, Diagon Alley, the location of Gringotts bank.

J. K. Rowling's invented world of wizardry is not a distinct other world of the same kind as Tolkien's Middle Earth or C. S. Lewis' Narnia, but constantly interconnects with and interpenetrates the world we know; in fact, it is part of the same world, but hidden from Muggles, that is, non-wizarding folk. Nevertheless, like a faerie world, it has strict rules of being. Its imaginative creation resides in the existence of magic.

The Moral Compass of the Harry Potter Stories

The stories have a clear moral structure, in which the Dark Arts (representing evil) are explicitly condemned, as well as opposed in the unfolding events, as perceived by Harry. The fantasy of the stories is tied up with the existence of magic. This magic is seen as part of the goodness of reality, but, as in the non-magical world, evil exists as a perversion of good.

The Nature of Magic in the Wizarding World of Harry Potter

The scope of magic in the stories is extensive. It can be illuminated (1) by showing its affinity with the high magic of the pre-Enlightenment sixteenth century and (2) by strong parallels that exist between magical practice in the stories and modern technology—arguably the modern manifestation of magic.

The high magic of the sixteenth century

Magic is a central organizing principle of the Harry Potter stories. Fundamentally the population of the world is divided between the majority Muggles and the Wizarding community. J. K. Rowling is drawing upon a concept of magic that is pre-Enlightenment, belonging to a pre-modernist society. Tellingly a bust of Paracelsus is prominently displayed in a hall of Hogwart's School. Paracelsus (1493–1541) was a prominent alchemist of the sixteenth century. This symbolic presence of an ancient concept of magic is further emphasized by the subject of the first Harry Potter story—*Harry Potter and the Philosopher's Stone* (called "Sorcerer's Stone" in US editions). The philosopher's stone is the distinctive quest of the alchemist, the ingredient that would enable the transmutation of base metals into gold and prolong life. This metamorphosis symbolized a deeper transformation—that of the soul itself. Albus Dumbledore, headmaster of Hogwarts, is a practiced alchemist and friend of the historic alchemist Nicolas Flamell, who is a character in the first Harry Potter book.

In his *English Literature in the Sixteenth Century* (1954), C. S. Lewis gives a vivid picture of this old white or "high" magic, which was sharply distinguished from *goetia* or satanic magic—what is called the Dark Arts at Hogwarts.[6] In the sixteenth century, observes Lewis, there was an "animistic or genial cosmology," where nature was perceived as "a festival not a machine." It was not until towards the end of that century that the beginnings of the scientific movement "delivered nature into our hands" (p. 3). This mechanistic perception of nature, in contrast to a cosmos full of life, impacted on both thought and emotion—effectively, to use different words, creating a different consciousness which lost an essential harmony and wholeness. Lewis argues:

> By reducing Nature to her mathematical elements it substituted a mechanical for a genial or animistic conception of the universe. The world was emptied, first of her indwelling spirits, then of her occult sympathies and antipathies, finally of her colours, smells, and tastes… The result was dualism rather than materialism. The mind, on whose ideal constructions the whole method depended, stood over against its object in ever sharper dissimilarity. Man with his new powers became rich like Midas but all that he touched had gone dead and cold. This process, slowly working, ensured during the next century the loss of the old mythological imagination: the conceit, and later the personified abstraction, takes its place. Later still, as a desperate attempt to bridge a gulf which begins to be found intolerable, we have the Nature poetry of the Romantics (Lewis, 1954: 3–4).

If C. S. Lewis is right, the Muggle was born with the dualism of a mechanized view of nature. It can be argued that J. K. Rowling's vision of wholeness and harmony has its roots in the Romantic movement that Lewis mentions (see Duriez, 2007: ch. 4).

Lewis has fascinating insights into the high magic where, in his words, "there is no Satanism or Faustian compact." This high magic can be studied, he says, in people like Picodella Mirandola (1463–94), Ficino (1433–99), Paracelsus (1493–1541), Agrippa (1486–1535), Dr John Dee (1527–1608) and Henry Moore, in his *Philosophical Works* (1662). They held to a kind of "Platonic theology" where Plato represented a common wisdom of the ancients. Interestingly, Lewis himself made imaginative use of this idea of an ancient common wisdom, focused in a sixteenth-century view of Platonism, in his *The Chronicles of Narnia*, much admired by J. K. Rowling.

Magic in the Muggle world: technology and applied science

For both C. S. Lewis and Tolkien, the modern form of magic is technology. In *The Lord of the Rings*, the central image, the ring, is a kind of ultimate machine. When technology is misused it takes on a life of its own, and a whole society can become technocratic, as argued by Jacques Ellul, in his study, *The Technological Society*. Literary critic Alan Jacobs seems to have been the first to notice an important parallel between the proper use of magic in the wizarding world of Harry

Potter and the proper use of technology in the Muggle world. The ethical lessons in the stories of the proper use of magic are parallel lessons in the crux question of handling technology and its awesome power so that our lives are enriched rather than enslaved and ruined. Following the lead given by Jacobs, Benjamin Lipscomb and Christopher Stewart argue, in "Magic, Science, and the Ethics of Technology," that the categories of bad and evil apply as much to technology as to magic. "This is not merely a matter of ruling out bad 'uses' of essentially neutral powers. The Unforgivable Curses aren't simply hurtful uses of essentially neutral powers. They are bad spells. The basic implication of Rowling's ethic contrast sharply with the conventional piety that 'technologies are neutral between our possible uses of them, and what we must do is use them well; no kind of power should be rejected by people outright'" (Lipscombe and Stewart, 2005: 90). Just because a power exists, does not make it right to use it.

The Nature of Evil in the Harry Potter Stories

Like the fantasies of C. S. Lewis and J. R. R. Tolkien, the Harry Potter stories have evil as a central theme, embodied in plot and a rich symbolism. As with Tolkien and Lewis this easily trivialized theme is treated without sentimentality and triumphalism, in a way that allows a wide and varied application by readers.

The images of evil in the stories are now in the vocabulary of children of the world. In terms of education alone, this must count as a remarkable effect. In a world seemingly dominated by a secular cast, a traditional understanding of good and evil is successfully embodied in a powerful and staggeringly popular story. Rowling was prophetic, it seems, when she wrote at the beginning of the very first story that Professor McGonagall remarks to Dumbledore, headmaster of Hogwarts: "There will be books written about Harry—every child in our world will know his name" (even though it is in the Muggle world too that Harry is now known).

Evil as privation and perversion

J. K. Rowling makes no reference to Augustine, but his seminal Christian view of the nature of evil is strikingly similar to hers.

In his *Confessions*, Book Seven, Augustine looks back to his thirty-first year. He realized then that the cause of sin lies in free will, and rejected the Manichean heresy, with its dualism of good and evil. Though he had abandoned belief in astrology, he was perplexed and miserable about the origin of evil. He found in the Platonists the seeds of the doctrine of the divinity of the Word, but not of his incarnation. Finally he discovered the truth about Christ, he confesses, through the study of Scripture, especially Paul's letters. He saw that it follows from the incarnation— God taking on the flesh of a human being—that the world and humanity is good, and that the evil that exists is a corruption of what is good. Evil cannot exist of itself; it has no substance.

> It was manifested unto me, that those things be good which yet are corrupted... So long therefore as they are, they are good: therefore whatsoever is, is good. That evil then which I sought, whence it is, is not any substance: for were it a substance, it should be good. For either it should be an incorruptible substance, and so a chief good: or a corruptible substance; which unless it were good, could not be corrupted. I perceived therefore, and it was manifested to me that Thou madest all things good, nor is there any substance at all, which Thou madest not; and for that Thou madest not all things equal, therefore are all things; because each is good, and altogether very good, because our God made all things very good.
>
> And to Thee is nothing whatsoever evil: yea, not only to Thee, but also to Thy creation as a whole, because there is nothing without, which may break in, and corrupt that order which Thou hast appointed it...
>
> And I enquired what iniquity was, and found it to be no substance, but the perversion of the will, turned aside from Thee, O God, the Supreme...[7]

Evil understood as corruption and perversion of good is exactly how evil is represented in the Harry Potter stories.

Some images of evil in the Harry Potter stories

Voldemort and the Death Eaters

Lord Voldemort, the Dark Lord of the Harry Potter stories, is a former brilliant pupil at Hogwarts originally called Tom Riddle, who turned to evil, seeking immortality. His main strategy is to divide his soul into parts, embodied in objects called horcruxes. This allows him to survive, albeit at first in a disembodied state, after his death curse against the baby Harry went wrong. Harry quickly recognizes Voldemort as the supreme manifestation of evil and as his enemy. As early as his first year at Hogwarts, Harry realizes that stopping Voldemort is more important than being expelled from school. He spells out to his friends the implications of Voldemort getting hold of the Philosopher's Stone. By the end of his sixth year, he realizes that the task of destroying the Dark Lord must for a while take precedence over his studies at Hogwarts, and Ron and even Hermione agree, standing with him in the task.

Voldemort was originally the handsome star pupil at the school, who became head boy. His inward process of perversion and corruption is expressed in his changing physical appearance. In *Harry Potter and the Philosopher's Stone*, his face that has taken shape at the back of Quirrell's head has red eyes and slits. He has become a "mere shadow and vapour"—a wraith. He gets his strength from drinking the blood of innocent unicorns he has had slain. After Quirrell's death Voldemort re-forms into a hideous embryonic figure, a perversion of human birth, who is sustained by the milk of his monstrous pet serpent, Nagini, who apparently is a living horcrux, carrying a portion of his severed soul. After he re-embodies with Wormtail's help he is terrifying and inhuman in appearance. From early in his life he displayed instincts for "cruelty, secrecy and domination." According to Dumbledore he is "the most dangerous Dark wizard of all time."

Voldemort surrounds himself with his Death Eaters. These are his close circle of followers, prepared to torture and kill for him. They carry a mark on their arm, which magically indicates their Dark Lord's summons. The group have a cult of the pure-blood, i.e. wizards and witches that have no Muggles in their family or ancestry.

The Dark Mark that appears on the forearm of Death Eaters becomes active at Voldemort's summons. It is a sign of a skull with a serpent issuing from its mouth. The mark was distinctively put into the sky above a place the Death Eaters have entered or the scene of a killing of theirs. One appears during the Quiddich World Championship in *Harry Potter and the Goblet of Fire* and another is raised above the Astronomy Tower in *Harry Potter and the Half-Blood Prince* to lure Dumbledore to his death.

> And then, without warning, the silence was rent by a voice unlike any they had heard in the wood; and it uttered, not a panicked shout, but what sounded like a spell. "MORSMORDRE!" And something vast, green, and glittering erupted from the patch of darkness Harry's eyes had been struggling to penetrate; it flew up over the treetops and into the sky. "What the—?" gasped Ron as he sprang to his feet again, staring up at the thing that had appeared. For a split second, Harry thought it was another leprechaun formation. Then he realized that it was a colossal skull, comprised of what looked like emerald stars, with a serpent protruding from its mouth like a tongue. As they watched, it rose higher and higher, blazing in a haze of greenish smoke, etched against the black sky like a new constellation.[8]

Later in *Harry Potter and the Goblet of Fire* Harry has a direct confrontation with Voldemort. Wormtail is a faithful Death Eater, one of his band of followers. Voldemort has managed to re-embody himself by the Dark Arts, using horrible means, including employing part of his father's remains, a hand of Wormtail's and some of Harry's blood. Now he is ready to make himself known to his scattered Death Eaters.

> Voldemort bent down and pulled out Wormtail's left arm; he forced the sleeve of Wormtail's robes up past his elbow, and Harry saw something upon the skin there, something like a vivid red tattoo—a skull with a snake protruding from its mouth—the image that had appeared in the sky at the Quidditch World Cup: the Dark Mark. Voldemort examined it carefully, ignoring Wormtail's uncontrollable weeping. "It is back," he said softly, "they will all have noticed it...and now, we shall see...now we shall know..." He pressed his long white forefinger to the brand on Wormtail's arm. The scar on Harry s forehead seared with a sharp pain again, and Wormtail let out a fresh howl; Voldemort removed his fingers from Wormtail's mark, and Harry saw that it had turned jet black. A look of cruel satisfaction on his face, Voldemort straightened up, threw back his head, and stared around at the dark graveyard. "How many will be brave enough to return when they feel it?" he whispered, his gleaming red eyes fixed upon the stars. "And how many will be foolish enough to stay away?"[9]

Boggarts

Harry and his friends first encounter boggarts in *Harry Potter and the Prisoner of Azkhaban*. The events take place in the staff room at Hogwarts, the unlikely site of a lesson in defense against the Dark Arts, a key part of the curriculum.

> "Now, then," said Professor Lupin, beckoning the class toward the end of the room, where there was nothing but an old wardrobe where the teachers kept their spare robes. As Professor Lupin went to stand next to it, the wardrobe gave a sudden wobble, banging off the wall.
>
> "Nothing to worry about," said Professor Lupin calmly because a few people had jumped backward in alarm. "There's a boggart in there."
>
> Most people seemed to feel that this was something to worry about.
>
> Neville gave Professor Lupin a look of pure terror, and Seamus Finnigan eyed the now rattling doorknob apprehensively.
>
> "Boggarts like dark, enclosed spaces," said Professor Lupin. "Wardrobes, the gap beneath beds, the cupboards under sinks—I've even met one that had lodged itself in a grandfather clock. This one moved in yesterday afternoon, and I asked the headmaster if the staff would leave it to give my third years some practice.

"So, the first question we must ask ourselves is, what is a boggart?"

Hermione put up her hand.

"It's a shape-shifter," she said. "It can take the shape of whatever it thinks will frighten us most."[10]

Lupin explains that no one knows the shape of a boggart when he is alone. When it is released it will "immediately become whatever each of us most fears."

The existence of a boggart is tied up completely with fear. It feeds entirely on someone's fear, and only that fear allows it to take shape. Ron sees it as a spider, Harry a Dementor, and Lupin himself as a full moon presaging his dreaded transformation into a werewolf.

Dementors

The following passage is also from *Harry Potter and the Prisoner of Azkabhan,* but earlier in the story. The events take place on the Hogwarts Express, as Harry and friends travel to begin their third year at school. They share the compartment with a sleeping Professor Lupin, who is awakened suddenly.

Standing in the doorway, illuminated by the shivering flames in Lupin's hand, was a cloaked figure that towered to the ceiling. Its face was completely hidden beneath its hood. Harry's eyes darted downward, and what he saw made his stomach contract. There was a hand protruding from the cloak and it was glistening, grayish, slimy-looking, and scabbed, like something dead that had decayed in water…

But it was visible only for a split second. As though the creature beneath the cloak sensed Harry's gaze, the hand was suddenly withdrawn into the folds of its black cloak.

And then the thing beneath the hood, whatever it was, drew a long, slow, rattling breath, as though it were trying to suck something more than air from its surroundings.

An intense cold swept over them all. Harry felt his own breath catch in his chest. The cold went deeper than his skin. It was inside his chest, it was inside his very heart…

Harry's eyes rolled up into his head. He couldn't see. He was drowning in cold. There was a rushing in his ears as though of water. He was being dragged downward, the roaring growing louder.

And then, from far away, he heard screaming, terrible, terrified, pleading screams. He wanted to help whoever it was, he tried to move his arms, but couldn't…a thick white fog was swirling around him, inside him—

"Harry! Harry! Are you all right?"

Someone was slapping his face.[11]

The Dementors are a particular powerful image of perversion, feeding directly on the human soul, particularly on a distressed person. Harry in this case is remembering the screams of his mother before Voldemort killed her. The Dementors also provide a vivid image of radical depression.

The unforgivable curses

Central to the plot of the stories are the unforgivable curses, used exclusively as Dark Arts. A wizard or witch is unable to use such a curse without truly meaning to inflict it. The *Cruciatus curse* causes excruciating pain and torture. The *Imperius curse* completely controls another so that they do absolutely everything you want. The *Death curse* (*Avada Kedavra*) instantly kills—Harry is the only known survivor of such a curse.

The master story-line of the Harry Potter sequence of books springs from the imaginative possibilities of the failure of this invincible curse. Only a deeper magic, the power of the self-sacrificial love of Harry's mother, averts it. Harry is the Boy who Lived. His survival of the curse allows him to be the prophesied "Chosen One," destined to confront Voldemort in a final and decisive fight.

Images of goodness in the stories

Harry and friends

Like the Fellowship in Tolkien's *The Lord of the Rings*, opposed to the Dark Lord, Sauron, Harry and his friends stand implacably against the Dark Arts, and Voldemort in particular. The friends exemplify bedrock virtues and values. Four values in particular are exemplified: love, courage, loyalty, and self-sacrifice. In the adult world, the Order of the Phoenix (a Christ-symbol) led by Dumbledore stands for the same values.

Hogwarts

Hogwarts school reinforces the values and virtues Harry and his friends believe in and fight for. Hogwarts in particular represents wholeness and goodness, and serves to educate young wizards and witches in good practice of magic and opposition to the Dark Arts.

A vision of wholeness is central to the Harry Potter stories, and this vision is focused upon the ideals of a Hogwarts education—which involves learning, preparation for life, and moral education. A Hogwarts education stresses using magic properly, and aims to prepare its pupils for brutal and inhuman attacks from those who have gone over to the dark side.

The Hogwarts vision of wholeness is not simply expressed in its curriculum. It is also embodied in its four houses to which pupils belong. These underline the theme of wholeness, health, and organic harmony. The house structure is prominent in the lives of the students. The school crest reminds them of it—displaying a lion, an eagle, a badger, and a snake, representing the houses. It provokes an image of unity in diversity rather than of discord. The ideal in the school is that the four houses work together to promote wholeness rather than fragmentation, bonded together by friendship and a common purpose. In an interview J. K. Rowling revealed that the houses represent the four elements: Griffindor, fire; Ravensclaw, air; Hufflepuff, earth; and Slytherin, water. Slytherin, which attracts many of the pupils lured by the Dark Arts, is an essential element for completeness. There is a place for Slytherin, with its emphasis on ambition, based on the essential good that has become perverted in many who pass through Slytherin, such as Tom Riddle, or Voldemort, as he later calls himself.

The dominant personality trait that determines which pupil goes into what house corresponds in some way to these four ancient humours. There were several schemes in classical times, relating to the four seasons, regions of the body, and bodily fluids—Hippocrates linked the element air with blood, the season of spring and the liver; earth with black bile, autumn and the spleen; fire with yellow bile, summer and the gall bladder; and water with phlegm, winter and the brain and lungs. The resulting characteristics of a dominant element were, in order, being courageous or amorous; despondent or sleepless; easily angered; and calm or unemotional. These corresponded with Galen's famous taxonomy of type: the sanguine, the melancholic, the choleric and the phlegmatic. More relevant, perhaps, is the alchemical types of Paracelsus, each of which seemed to have a corresponding spirit: changeable (the salamander); industrious (the gnome); inspired (the water nymph or undine); and the curious (the sylph). This is closer to Hogwarts' typology: air as the eagle, championing intellect and wit (Ravensclaw); earth as the badger, encouraging loyalty and diligence (Hufflepuff); fire as the lion, celebrating courage and resourcefulness (Griffindor); and water as the snake, desiring cunning and ambition (Slytherin).

The principle of wholeness and community based on friendship is at the moral center of the stories not only because the Harry Potter books are school stories, but also because the events of the entire wizard world are connected with what happens at Hogwarts. In all the stories Hogwarts, even the last, remains the reference point for events in the wider world, from Voldemort's obsession with the school to Dumbledore's uneasy relation with the Ministry of Magic.

Conclusion: Fresh Metaphors and Renewed Perception

Stories write large the ability of metaphor to help us to see the world in a fresh way, or to restore ways of seeing that have been lost. They create a new consciousness, or felt thought, where abstract concepts are perceived in a concrete form. Good stories are marked by the ability to generalize while remaining particular. The Harry Potter stories, I believe, have given a whole generation of children throughout the world— dubbed Generation Hex by *Time* magazine—a restored vision of ancient virtues and values, and a deeply thought-out traditional understanding of the nature of evil as privation, perversion, and parasite, rather than something that exists independently or has always and inevitably existed, and will exist for ever.

Hogwarts, Harry, and their enemies give concrete expression to the age-old discussion of good and evil, generating fresh metaphors and renewed perception. Rowling is conservative in the sense of restoring and rehabilitating ancient and perennial values, and this allows her work to be subversive in a contemporary context, where the dominant zeitgeist has relativized all values, deeming them merely subjective. Though her narrative reflects post-modern questioning, hers is a universe of moral clarity that does not seem twee or unreal for her readers—not only readers who share her British world, but readers throughout our diverse world.

Notes

  1.   See http://www.snopes.com/humor/iftrue/potter.htm.
  2.   Patti Wigington, "Witchcraft and Harry Potter," http://Paganwiccan.about.com/library/blharrypotter.htm.
  3.   Rabbi Noson Weisz, "Harry Potter and the War Between Good and Evil." http://www.aish.com/societywork/arts/Harry_Potter_and_the_War_Between_Good_and_Evil.asp.
  4.   Ibid.
  5.   *Harry Potter and the Philosopher's Stone* [*Sorcerer's Stone*, in US editions], ch. 7.
  6.   For an analysis and critique of Lewis' exposition, see Shippey, 2007. Tom Shippey's essay explores Lewis' view of magic in relation to his fiction, and that of fellow Inklings, including Tolkien. Shippey points out that Lewis' polemical point

in making this distinction between a mechanical and a spiritual or holistic view of nature, and high and black magic, is represented (not entirely consistently) in his fictional character, Merlin, in his *That Hideous Strength*, where the Arthurian figure from the Dark Ages is awakened in modern England to aid the battle against a dehumanizing evil.

7.   St Augustine, *Confessions,* Bk 7, translated by Edward Bouverie Pusey, 1848.

8.   This extract is from chapter 9 of *Harry Potter and the Goblet of Fire* where many wizards and witches are encamped in order to watch the Quidditch World Cup.

9.   *Harry Potter and the Goblet of Fire*, chapter 33.

10. *Harry Potter and the Prisoner of Azkhaban*, chapter 7.

11. *Harry Potter and the Prisoner of Azkabhan*, chapter 5.

Bibliography

Aichele, G., 2005a. "Jesus's Two Fathers: an Afterlife of the Gospel of Luke," in G. Aichele and R. Walsh, eds, *Those Outside: Noncanonical Readings of Canonical Gospels*. Harrisburg, PA: Continuum/T&T Clark International: 17–41.

Aichele, G., 2005b. "The Politics of Sacrifice." *The Bible and Critical Theory* 1(2). http://publications.epress.monash.edu/loi/bc/index.html(accessed January 15, 2007).

Aichele, G., 2006. "Postmodernism and the Death of 'Man'," in W. Bergen and A. Siedlecki, eds, *Voyages in Uncharted Waters: Essays on the Theory and Practice of Biblical Interpretation in Honour of David Jobling*. Sheffield: Sheffield Phoenix Press.

Aichele, G., 2009. "Jesus Simulacrum, or the Gospels vs. 'the Gospel'," in R. Sabbath, ed., *Sacred Tropes: Tanakh, New Testament, Qur'an as Literary Works*. Leiden: Brill.

Alighieri, D., 1970. *The Divine Comedy: Inferno*. C. S. Singleton, trans. Princeton: Princeton University Press.

Aquino, M., 2002. *The Church of Satan*, 5th rev. ed. San Francisco: Temple of Set.

Auerbach, N., 1995. *Our Vampires, Ourselves*. Chicago: Chicago University Press.

Augustine, 1945. *The City of God*, vol. 2. J. Healey, trans. London: Dent and Sons.

Augustine, 1848. *The Confessions of S. Augustine*. E. Bouverie Pusey, trans. Oxford.

Aulén, G., 1931. *Christus Victor: An Historical Study of the Three Main Types of the Idea of the Atonement*. A. G. Hebert, trans. London: SPCK.

Babington, B., and P. W. Evans, 1993. *Biblical Epics: Sacred Narrative in the Hollywood Cinema*. Manchester: Manchester University Press.

Baddeley, G., 1999. *Lucifer Rising: Sin, Devil Worship, and Rock 'n' Roll*. London: Plexus.

Baddeley, G., 2005. *Dissecting Marilyn Manson*. London: Plexus.

Badley, L., 1995. *Film, Horror, and the Body Fantastic*. Westport, CT: Greenwood Press.

Baker, B., 2007. "Gothic Masculinities," in E. McEvoy and C. Spooner, eds, *The Routledge Companion to the Gothic*. London: Routledge.

Banks, I. M., 1989. *The Player of Games*. New York: Pocket Books.

Barrett, C. K., ed., 1987. *The New Testament Background: Selected Documents*. London: SPCK.

Barrs, J., 2003. "Harry Potter and His Critics." *Perspectives: The Newsletter of Covenant Theological Seminary's Francis Schaeffer Institute*. http://www.covenantseminary.edu/resource/Barrs_HarryPotter_Persp.pdf

Barthes, R., 1986. *The Rustle of Language*. R. Howard, trans. Berkeley and Los Angeles: University of California Press.

Barton, B., 1990. *The Church of Satan*. New York: Hell's Kitchen.

Barton, B., 1992. *The Secret Life of a Satanist: The Authorized Biography of Anton LaVey*. Los Angeles, CA: Feral House.

Barton, S., 2002. "Your Self Storage: Female Investigation and Male Performativity in the Woman's Psychothriller," in G. Turner, ed., *The Film Cultures Reader*. London and New York: Routledge: 311–30.

Bataille, G., 1992. *The Accursed Share. Vol.1*. New York: Zone Books.

Bataille, G., 1993. *The Accursed Share. Vol.2.* R. Hurley, trans. Cambridge, MA: Zone Books.

Beal, T. K., 2002. *Religion and its Monsters.* London: Routledge.

Bendle, M. F., 2005. "The Apocalyptic Imagination and Popular Culture." *Journal of Religion and Popular Religion* 9 (Fall): 1–14.

Berger, H. M., 1997. "The Practice of Perception: Multi-Functionality and Time in the Musical Experiences of a Heavy Metal Drummer," *Ethnomusicology* 41: 464–88.

Berger, P., 1973. *The Social Reality of Religion.* Harmondsworth: Penguin.

Berger, P., and T. Luckmann, 1966. *The Social Construction of Reality: A Treatise on the Sociology of Knowledge.* Harmondsworth: Penguin.

Bietenhard, H., C. Brown, and J. S. Wright. 1976. "Satan, Beelzebul, Devil, Exorcism," in C. Brown, ed., *The New International Dictionary of New Testament Theology.* Exeter: Paternoster: 468–77.

Bindman, D., 1999. "The English Apocalypse," in F. Carey, ed., *The Apocalypse and the Shape of Things to Come.* London: British Museum Press.

Blake, W., 1975. *The Marriage of Heaven and Hell.* Oxford: Oxford University Press.

Boelderl, A. F., and D. F. Mayr, 1995. "The Undead and the Living Dead: Images of Vampires and Zombies in Contemporary Culture." *The Journal of Psychohistory* 23(1): 51–65.

Bonhoeffer, D., 1955. *Temptation.* K. Downham, trans. London: SCM.

Box, G. H., and J. Macquarrie, 1965. "Satan," in F. C. Grant and H. H. Rowley, eds, *Dictionary of the Bible.* Edinburgh: T. & T. Clark: 888–89.

Brewster, B., and Broughton, F. 2000. *Last Night a DJ Saved My Life.* London: Headline Books.

Breytenbach, C., and P. L. Day, 1999. "Satan," in K. van der Toorn, B. Becking, and P. W. Horst, eds, *Dictionary of Deities and Demons in the Bible.* Grand Rapids, MI: Eerdmans: 726–32.

Briggs, R., 1996. *Witches and Neighbours: The Social and Cultural Context of European Witchcraft.* London: Fontana.

Capote, T., 1994 [1965]. *In Cold Blood: A True Account of a Multiple Murder and its Consequences.* New York: Vintage Books.

Capp, B., 1984. "The Political Dimension of Apocalyptic Thought," in C. A. Patrides and J. Wittreich, eds, *The Apocalypse in English Renaissance Thought and Literature.* Manchester: Manchester University Press: 93–124.

Carroll, N., 1990. *The Philosophy of Horror, or Paradoxes of the Heart.* New York: Routledge.

Chastagner, C., 1999. "The Parents' Music Resource Center: From Information to Censorship." *Popular Music* 18(2): 179–92.

Christe, I., 2003. *Sound of the Beast: The Complete Headbanging History of Heavy Metal.* New York: HarperEntertainment.

Christianson, E., P. Francis, and W. R. Telford, 2005. *Cinéma Divinité: Religion, Theology and the Bible in Film.* London: SCM-Canterbury.

Clark, L. S., 2003. *From Angels to Aliens: Teenagers, the Media, and the Supernatural.* Oxford: Oxford University Press.

Clines, D., 1996. "The Significance of the 'Sons of God' Episode (Genesis 6: 1-4) in the Context of the 'Primeval History' (Genesis 1-11)," in J. W. Rogerson, ed., *The Pentateuch: A Sheffield Reader.* Sheffield: Sheffield Academic Press: 33–46.

Cohen, P. A., 1999. "Time, Culture and Christian Eschatology: The Year 2000 in the West and the World." *The American Historical Review* 104: 1615–28.

Conan Doyle, A., 1993. *The Hound of the Baskervilles*, ed. O. Dudley Edwards. Oxford: Oxford University Press [1902].

Cone, J.H., 1972. *The Spirituals and the Blues*. Maryknoll, NY: Orbis Books.

Corbin, C., and R. A. Campbell, 1999. "Postmodern Iconography and Perspective in Coppola's *Bram Stoker's Dracula*." *Journal of Popular Film and Television* 27(2): 40–48.

Cutrofello, A., 2005. *Continental Philosophy: A Contemporary Introduction*. London: Routledge.

Dante, A., 1961. *The Divine Comedy*, vol. 1: *Inferno*. J. D. Sinclair, trans. Oxford and New York: Oxford University Press.

Davies, P. R., 1995. *Whose Bible Is It Anyway?* Sheffield: Sheffield Academic Press.

Day, A., 1996. *Romanticism*. London and New York: Routledge.

Deleuze, G., 1978. "Preface," in D. H. Lawrence, *Apocalypse*, F. Deleuze, trans. into French. Paris: Editions Balland.

Deleuze, G., 1990. *The Logic of Sense*. M. Lester and C. Stivale, trans. New York: Columbia University Press.

Deleuze, G., 1994. *Difference and Repetition*. P. Patton, trans. New York: Columbia University Press.

Deleuze, G., and F. Guattari, 1983. *Anti-Oedipus*. R. Hurley, M. Seem, and H. R. Lane, trans. Minneapolis: University of Minnesota Press.

Deleuze, G., and F. Guattari, 1988. *A Thousand Plateaus*. B. Massumi, trans. Minneapolis: University of Minnesota Press.

Derrida, J., 1978. *Writing and Difference*. A. Bass, trans. Chicago: University of Chicago Press.

Derrida, J., 1994. *Specters of Marx: The State of Debt, the Work of Mourning and the New International*. New York and London: Routledge.

Derrida, J., 1995. *The Gift of Death*. Chicago: University of Chicago Press.

de Waal, E. 1988. *The Celtic Vision: Prayers and Blessings from the Outer Hebrides*. London: Darton, Longman & Todd.

Docker, J., 2001. "In Praise of Polytheism." *Semeia* 88: 149–72.

Douglas, M., 1982. "The Effects of Modernization on Religious Change." *Daedalus* 111(1): 1–19.

Duriez, C., 2007. *The Unauthorised Harry Potter Companion*. Stroud: Sutton Publishing (The History Press). Published in US as *A Field Guide to Harry Potter*. Downer's Grove, IL: InterVarsity Press.

Dyer, R., 1999. *Seven*. London: BFI.

Dyrendal, A., 2004. "Satanisme – en innføring." *Din. Tidsskrift for religion og kultur* 4: 48–58.

Dyrendal, A., forthcoming. "Darkness Within: Satanism as Self-Religion," in J. A. Petersen, ed., *Contemporary Religious Satanism: A Critical Anthology*. Aldershot: Ashgate.

Eckstrom, K., 2004a. "Poll: Belief in Angels, Devil on the Rise." *Biblical Recorder: North Carolina Baptist News Journal*. 26 May. http://www.biblicalrecorder.org/content/news/2004/5_26_2004/ne260504poll.shtml (accessed September 30, 2004).

Eckstrom, K., 2004b. "Two Thirds of Americans Believe in the Devil, Gallup Poll Finds." http://www.beliefnet.com/story/121/story_12192_1.html (accessed September 30, 2004).

Ehrman, B., 2004. *The New Testament: A Historical Introduction to the Early Christian Writings*. 3rd ed. New York: Oxford University Press.

Ellis, B. E., 1985. *Less Than Zero*. New York: Simon and Schuster.

Elwell, W. A., 1988. "Satan," in W. A., Elwell, W. A., ed., *Encyclopedia of the Bible*. London: Marshall Pickering: 1907–1908.

Farren, M., 2006. "The Devil's Advocates." Los Angeles CityBeat. June 15-21. http://www.lacitybeat.com/cms/story/detail/?id=3916&IssueNum=158 (accessed January 16, 2007).

Fine, J., 1998. "The Cradle Won't Rock." *The Village Voice*. November 3: 130.

Fleming, R., 1693 [1669]. *The Fulfilling of the Scripture, or, A Discovery of the Accomplishment of God's Holy Word in his Providential Works*, 3rd ed., n.p.

Flowers, S., 1997. *Lords of the Left-Hand Path*. Smithville, TX: Runa-Raven.

Foerster, W., 2000. "*Daimōn, daimonion, etc.*," in G. Kittel, et al., eds, *Theological Dictionary of the New Testament*, G. Bromiley, trans. and ed. Print edition, Grand Rapids, MI: Eerdmans, 1964–1976. CD-ROM edition, Bellingham, WA: Logos Research Systems.

Forsyth, N., 1987. *The Old Enemy: Satan and the Combat Myth*. Princeton: Princeton University Press.

Foucault, M., 1999. *Religion and Culture*. J. Carrette, ed. London: Routledge.

Frilingos, C. A., 2004. *Spectacles of Empire: Monsters, Martyrs, and the Book of Revelation*. Philadelphia: University of Pennsylvania Press.

Fry, C. L., and J. R. Craig, 2002. "'Unfit for Earth, Undoomed for Heaven': The Genesis of Coppola's Byronic Dracula." *Literature Film Quarterly* 30(4): 271–78.

Fuller, D. P., 1979. "Satan," in G. W. Bromiley, ed., *The International Standard Bible Encyclopedia*. Grand Rapids, MI: Eerdmans: 340–44.

Galloway, A. D., 1951. *The Cosmic Christ*. London: Nisbet.

Gaster, T. H., 1962. "Satan," in G. A. Buttrick, ed., *The Interpreter's Dictionary of the Bible*. New York and Nashville: Abingdon: 224–28.

Gay, P., 1973. *The Enlightenment: An Interpretation*, in 2 vols, *The Rise of Modern Paganism* and *The Science of Freedom*. London: Wildwood House.

Gilmore, D. D., 2003. *Monsters: Evil Beings, Mythical Beasts, and All Manner of Imaginary Terrors*. Philadelphia: University of Pennsylvania Press.

Goux, J., 1990. "General Economics and Postmodern Capitalism," in A. Stoekl, ed., *Yale French Studies 78: On Bataille*. New Haven: Yale University Press: 206–26.

Gribben, C., 2004. "James Hogg, Scottish Calvinism and Literary Theory." *Scottish Studies Review* 5(2): 9–26.

Gribben, C., 2007. "The *Justified Sinner* (1824) and Scottish Presbyterian Demonology." *Studies in Hogg and his World* 17: 127–31.

Hall, J. 1996. "Satan," in J. Hall, ed., *Dictionary of Subjects and Symbols in Art*. London: John Murray: 272.

Hall, S. G., 1991. *Doctrine and Practice in the Early Church*. London: SPCK.

Harrell, J., 1994. "The Poetics of Destruction: Death Metal Rock." *Popular Music and Society* 18(1): 91–103.

Harris, T., 2000. *The Hannibal Lecter Omnibus: Red Dragon, The Silence of the Lambs, Hannibal*. London: BCA.

Harris, T., 2006. *Hannibal Rising*. London: William Heinemann.

Harvey, G., 2002. "Satanism: Performing Alterity and Othering." *Syzygy: Journal of Alternative Religion and Culture* 11: 53–68.

Helland., C. 2000. "Online Religion/Religion Online and Virtual Communities," in J. K. Hadden and D. E. Cowan, eds, *Religion on the Internet: Prospects and Promises*. Amsterdam: JAI: 205–23.

Hiebert, D. E., 1987. "Satan," in J. D. Douglas, and M. C. Tenney, eds, *The New International Dictionary of the Bible. Pictorial Edition*, 899–900. Basingstoke: Marshall Pickering.

Hill, S. J., 2006. "The Daily Disc." *National Post*. 14 November: B2.

Hjelm, T., 2005. "Communication." *Rever – Revista de Estudos da religião* 5(4). http://www.pucsp.br/rever/rv4_2005/t_hjelm.htm (accessed February 27, 2007).

Hogg, J., 2002 [1824]. *The Private Memoirs and Confessions of a Justified Sinner*. P. Garside, ed. The Stirling/South Carolina Edition of James Hogg. Edinburgh: Edinburgh University Press.

Hogle, J., 2002. *The Cambridge Companion to Gothic Fiction*. Cambridge: Cambridge University Press.

Hollier, D., 1990. "The Dualist Materialism of Georges Bataille," in A. Stoekl, ed., *Yale French Studies 78: On Bataille*. New Haven: Yale University Press: 124–39.

Hoover, S. M., and J. K. Park, 2005. "The Anthropology of Religious Meaning Making in the Digital Age," in E. W. Rothenbuhler and M. Coman, eds, *Media Anthropology*. Thousand Oaks, CA: Sage.

Jewish Publication Society. 1999. *Jewish Study Bible*. Tanakh translation, *Genesis*. J. D. Levenson, trans. Oxford: Oxford University Press.

Jolly, K. L., 1996. *Popular Religion in Late Saxon England: Elf Charms in Context*. Chapel Hill: University of North Carolina Press.

Jordan, J., 1999. "Vampire Cyborgs and Scientific Imperialism: A Reading of the Science-Mysticism Polemic in *Blade*." *Journal of Popular Film and Television* 27(2): 4–15.

Kahn-Harris, K., 2007. *Extreme Metal: Music and Culture on the Edge*. Oxford: Berg.

Kane, T., 2006. *The Changing Vampire in Film and Television: A Critical Study of the Growth of a Genre*. Jefferson, NC: McFarland.

Keller, C., 2001. "Eyeing the Apocalypse," in A. K. M. Adam, ed., *Postmodern Interpretations of the Bible – A Reader*. St. Louis, MO: Chalice Press.

Kelly, J. N. D., 1977. *Early Christian Doctrines*, 5th ed. London: A. & C. Black.

Keyworth, D., 2002. "The Socio-Religious Beliefs and Nature of the Contemporary Vampire Subculture." *Journal of Contemporary Religion* 17(3): 355–70.

Kliever, L. D., 1979. "Polysymbolism and Modern Religiosity." *Journal of Religion* 59: 169–94.

Kluger, R. S., 1967. *Satan in the Old Testament*. Evanston: Northwestern University Press.

Kovacs, J., and C. Rowland, 2004. *Revelation*. Oxford: Blackwell.

Kreitzer, L., 1999. "The Scandal of the Cross: Crucifixion Imagery and Bram Stoker's *Dracula*," in G. Aichele and T. Pippin, eds, *The Monstrous and the Unspeakable: The Bible as Fantastic Literature*. Sheffield: Sheffield Academic Press: 181–219.

Kuemmerlin-McLean, J. K., 1997. "Demons (Old Testament)," in *The Anchor Bible Dictionary*. D. N. Freedman, ed. CD-ROM edition, New York: Doubleday.

La Fontaine, J., 1999. "Satanism and Satanic Mythology," in B. Ankarloo and S. Clark, eds, *Witchcraft and Magic in Europe: The Twentieth Century*. Philadelphia: University of Pennsylvania Press: 81–140.

LaVey, A. S., 1969. *The Satanic Bible*. New York: Avon.

LaVey, A. S., 1972. *The Satanic Rituals*. New York: Avon.

LaVey, A. S., 1992. *The Devil's Notebook*. Portland: Feral House.

LaVey, A. S., 1998. *Satan Speaks!* Portland: Feral House.

Leeuw, G., van der, 1986. *Religion in Essence and Manifestation*. J. E. Turner, trans. Princeton: Princeton University Press.

Lewis, C. S., 1954. *English Literature in the Sixteenth Century Excluding Drama*. London: Oxford University Press.

Lindsey, H., 1970. *Late Great Planet Earth*. Grand Rapids: Zondervan.

Ling, T., 1961. *The Significance of Satan: New Testament Demonology and its Contemporary Relevance*. London: SPCK.

Lipscombe, B., and C. Stewart, 2005. "Magic, Science, and the Ethics of Technology," in M. Lackey, ed., *Mapping the World of Harry Potter: Science Fiction and Fantasy Writers Explore the Bestselling Fantasy Series of All Time*. Dallas, TX: Benbella Books.

Lovell Jr., J., 1986. *Black Song: The Forge and the Flame. The Story of How the Afro-American Spiritual was Hammered Out*. New York: Paragon House.

Luckmann, T., 1967. *The Invisible Religion*. New York: Macmillan.

Luther, M., 1955. *Luther's Works*, Vol. 2. St Louis, CO: Concordia Publishing House.

Lyotard, J.-F., 1984. *The Postmodern Condition: A Report on Knowledge*. G. Bennington and B. Massumi, trans. Minneapolis: University of Minnesota Press.

Marberry, J., 2006. *Vampire Universe*. New York: Citadel.

Marcus, G., 2000. *Mystery Train*. London: Faber and Faber.

Marx, K., and F. Engels, 1961. "The Communist Manifesto," in A. P. Mendel, ed., *Essential Works of Marxism*. London: Bantam Press: 13–44.

Marx, K., and F. Engels, 2007. *The Communist Manifesto*. London: Filiquarian.

Massyngbaerde Ford, J., 1995. "Satan," in R. P. McBrien, ed., *The HarperCollins Encyclopedia of Catholicism*. London: HarperCollins: 1163.

Matar, N. I., 1987. "Milton and the Idea of the Restoration of the Jews." *Studies in English Literature, 1500–1900* 27: 109–24.

May, H. G., and B. M. Metzger, eds, 1973. *The New Oxford Annotated Bible with the Apocrypha*. New York: Oxford University Press.

Mäyrä, I., 1999. *Demonic Texts and Textual Demons: The Demonic Tradition, the Self, and Popular Fiction*. Tampere: Tampere University Press.

McGinn, B., 1996. *Antichrist: Two Thousand Years of the Human Fascination with Evil*. San Francisco: HarperSanFrancisco.

McRay, J. R., 1986. "Satan," in W. Gentz, ed., *The Dictionary of Bible and Religion*. Nashville, TN: Abingdon: 934.

Mede, J., 1643. *The Key of the Revelation*. London: n.p.

Medved, H., 1978. *The Fifty Worst Films of All Time*. London: Angus and Robertson Publishers.

Melton, J. G., 1999. *The Vampire Book: An Encyclopedia of the Undead*. 2nd ed. Farmington Hills, MI: Visible Ink Press.

Miéville, C., 1998. *King Rat*. New York: Tom Doherty Associates.

Miles, J., 1996. *God: A Biography*. New York: Vintage Books.

Miller, J. 2000. *Flowers in the Dustbin: The Rise of Rock and Roll 1947–1977*. London: Simon & Schuster.

Miller, T. V., L. J. Veltkamp, R. F. Krause, T. Lane, and T. Heister, 1999. "An Adolescent Vampire Cult in Rural America: Clinical Issues and Case Study." *Child Psychiatry and Human Development* 29(3): 209–19.

Milner, N., 2000. "Giving the Devil His Due Process: Exorcism in the Church of England." *Journal of Contemporary Religion* 15: 247–72.

Milton, J., 1966. *Poetical Works*. D. Bush, ed. Oxford: Oxford University Press.

Mørk, G., 2002. *Drømmer om fortiden, minner for fremtiden. Norsk black metals norrøne orientering 1992–1995*. Unpublished Master's thesis. Department of Religious Studies, University of Tromsø.

Morrow, J., 1996. *Blameless in Abaddon*. New York: Harcourt Brace and Company.

Moynihan, M., and D. Søderlind, 1998. *Lords of Chaos: The Bloody Rise of the Satanic Metal Underground*. Los Angeles: Feral House.

Muchembled, R., 2003. *A History of the Devil: From the Middle Ages to the Present*. J. Birrell, trans. Cambridge: Polity Press.

Muir, K., 2003. "Fraught and Social." *The Times: Features* (March 22): 7.

Mullan, D. G., 2004. "Fleming, Robert (1630–1694)," in H. C. G. Matthew and B. Harrison, eds, *Oxford Dictionary of National Biography*. Oxford: Oxford University Press.

Murrin, M., 1984. "Revelation and Two Seventeenth Century Commentators," in C. A. Patrides and J. Wittreich, eds, *The Apocalypse in English Renaissance Thought and Literature*. Manchester: Manchester University Press: 125–46.

Nielsen, K., 1998. *Satan: The Prodigal Son? A Family Problem in the Bible*. Sheffield: Sheffield Academic Press.

Nietzsche, F., 1974. *The Gay Science*. W. Kaufmann, trans. New York: Random House.

O'Donnell, K., 2000. "Fall, Redemption and Immortality in the Vampire Mythos." *Theology* 103(813): 204–12.

Opie, I., and M. Tatem, eds, 1993. *A Dictionary of Superstitions*. Oxford: Oxford University Press.

Ostwalt Jr, C. E., 1995. "Hollywood and Armageddon: Apocalyptic Themes in Recent Cinematic Presentation," in J. W. Martin and C. E. Ostwalt Jr, eds, *Screening the Sacred: Religion, Myth and Ideology in Popular American Film*. Oxford: Westview Press).

Owen, A. S., 1999. "Buffy the Vampire Slayer: Vampires, Postmodernity, and Postfeminism." *Journal of Popular Film and Television* 27(2): 24–31.

Partridge, C., 2004. *The Re-enchantment of the West: Alternative Spiritualities, Sacralization, Popular Culture and Occulture*, Vol. 1. London: T&T Clark International.

Partridge, C., 2005. *The Re-enchantment of the West: Alternative Spiritualities, Sacralization, Popular Culture and Occulture*, Vol. 2. London: T&T Clark International.

Petersen, J. A., 2005. "Modern Satanism: Dark Doctrines and Black Flames," in J. R. Lewis and J. A. Petersen, eds, *Controversial New Religions*. Oxford: Oxford University Press: 423–57.

Phillips, K. R., 2005. *Projected Fears: Horror Films and American Culture*. Westport, CT: Praeger.

Powell, M. A., 2004. "Satan and the Demons," in K. E. Corley and R. L. Webb, eds, *Jesus and Mel Gibson's The Passion of the Christ. The Film, the Gospels and the Claims of History*. London and New York: Continuum: 71–8.

Praz, M., 1954. *The Romantic Agony*. A. Davidson, trans. London and New York: Oxford University Press.

Price, G. 2005. "The Portrayal of Satan in *The Greatest Story Ever Told* (Stevens, 1965) and *The Passion of the Christ* (Gibson, 2004)." Unpublished essay submitted for the Bible in the Cinema module (module leader, Dr Colin Crowder), MA in Theological Research, Durham University.

Ramsland, K., 1989. "Hunger for the Marvellous: The Vampire Craze in the Computer Age." *Psychology Today* (November): 31–35.

Reinhartz, A. 2007. *Jesus of Hollywood*. Oxford: Oxford University Press.

Richardson, J. T., J. Best, and D. G. Bromley, eds, 1991. *The Satanism Scare*. Hawthorne: Aldine De Gruyter.

Rickels, L. A., 1999. *The Vampire Lectures*. Minneapolis: University of Minnesota Press.

Riess, J., 2004. *What Would Buffy Do: The Vampire Slayer as Spiritual Guide*. San Francisco: Jossey-Bass.

Rogers, M. R., 1981. "Rehearings: Chopin, Prelude in A minor, Op. 28, No. 2." *19th-Century Music* 4(3): 244–50.

Roth, L., 1979. "Dracula Meets the *Zeitgeist*: Nosferatu (1922) as Film Adaptation." *Literature Film Quarterly* 7(3): 309–13. http://rockdetector.com/artist,1928.sm.

Russell, J. B., 1977. *The Devil: Perceptions of Evil from Antiquity to Primitive Christianity*. Ithaca: Cornell University Press.

Russell, J. B., 1981. *Satan: The Early Christian Tradition*. Ithaca: Cornell University Press.

Russell, J. B., 1992. "Devil," in D. L. Jeffrey, ed., *A Dictionary of Biblical Tradition in English Literature*. Grand Rapids, MI: Eerdmans: 199–202.

Sanders, J. A., 1984. *Canon and Community*. Philadelphia: Fortress Press.

Schilbrack, K., 2004. "The Next Pluralistic Philosophy of Religion." Unpublished paper, delivered at Southeastern Commission for the Study of Religion meeting, Atlanta.

Schmidt, J., 1992. *Satanismus – Mythos und Wirklichkeit*. Marburg: Diagonal Verlag.

Schock, P., 2003. *Romantic Satanism: Myth and the Historical Moment in Blake, Shelley and Byron*. Basingstoke: Palgrave.

Schreck, Z., and N. Schreck, 2002. *Demons of the Flesh*. Tokyo: Creation Books.

Schwartz, R. M., 1997. *The Curse of Cain*. Chicago: University of Chicago Press.

Shelley, P. B., 2000a. "Preface to *Prometheus Unbound*," in M. H. Abrams and S. Greenblatt, eds, *The Norton Anthology of English Literature*, 7th ed., vol. 2. New York: W.W. Norton: 733–36.

Shelley, P. B., 2000b. "Prometheus Unbound," in M. H. Abrams and S. Greenblatt, eds, *The Norton Anthology of English Literature*, 7th ed., vol. 2. New York: W.W. Norton: 736–62.

Shippey, T., 1993. "Tolkien as a Post-War Writer," in K. J. Battarbee, ed., *Scholarship and Fantasy*. Turku, Finland: University of Turku: 217–36.

Shippey, T., 2007. "New Learning and New Ignorance: Magia, Goeteia, and the Inklings," in E. Segura and T. Honegger, eds, *Myth and Magic*. Zollikofen, Switzerland: Walking Tree Publishers.

Snoop Dogg, with Davin Seay, 1999. *The Dogg Father: The Times, Trials, and Hardcore Truths of Snoop Dogg*. New York: William Morrow and Company, Inc.

South, J. B., 2003. *Buffy the Vampire Slayer and Philosophy: Fear and Trembling in Sunnydale*. Peru, IL: Open Court.

Spencer, J. M., 1993. *Blues and Evil*. Knoxville: University of Tennessee Press.

Stern, R. C., C. N. Jefford, and G. Debona, 1999. *Savior on the Silver Screen*. New York: Paulist.

Stevenson, R. L., 2003. *Strange Case of Dr Jekyll and Mr Hyde*. K. Linehan, ed. New York: W. W. Norton and Co. [1886].

Stone, B., 2001. "The Sanctification of Fear: Images of the Religious in Horror Films." *The Journal of Religion and Film* 5(2). http://www.unomaha.edu/jrf/sanctify.htm (accessed February 27, 2007).

Straw, W., 1990. "Characterizing Rock Music Culture: The Case of Heavy Metal," in S. Frith and A. Goodwin, eds, *On Record: Pop, Rock, and the Written Word*. New York: Pantheon: 97–109.

Telford, W. R., 1997. "Jesus Christ Movie-Star: The Depiction of Jesus in the Cinema," in C. Marsh and G. Ortiz, eds, *Explorations in Theology and Film. Movies and Meaning*. Oxford: Blackwell: 115–39.

Thistlethwaite, S., 2004. "Mel Makes a War Movie," in J. Burnham, ed., *Perspectives on The Passion of the Christ*. New York: Miramax Books: 127–45.

Thomas, K., 1973. *Religion and the Decline of Magic: Studies in Popular Beliefs in Sixteenth and Seventeenth Century England*. Harmondsworth: Penguin.

Tolkien, J. R. R. 1966. *The Tolkien Reader*. New York: Ballantine Books.

Tolkien, J. R. R., 1994. *The Lord of the Rings*. 3 vols. New York: Ballantine Books.

Trachtenberg, J., 1943. *The Devil and the Jews: The Medieval Conception of the Jew and its Relation to Modern Antisemitism*. New Haven: Yale University Press.

Trachtenberg, J., 1970. *Jewish Magic and Superstition: A Study of Folk Religion*. New York: Athenium.

Victor, J., 1993. *Satanic Panic: The Creation of a Contemporary Legend*. Chicago: Open Court.

Waldman, S., 2004. "Who Believes in the Devil" http://www.beliefnet.com/story/121/story_12197_1.html (accessed October 1, 2004).

Walker, J. 1995. *Halliwell's Filmgoer's Companion*. London: HarperCollins.

Walker, M., 1996. *Scottish Literature Since 1707*. London: Longman.

Walser, R., 1993. *Running with the Devil: Power, Gender, and Madness in Heavy Metal Music*. Hanover: Wesleyan University Press.

Walsh, R., 2000. "Recent Fictional Portrayals of God, or: Disney, Shirley MacLaine, and Hamlet," in G. Aichele, ed., *Culture, Entertainment, and the Bible*. Sheffield: Sheffield Academic Press.

Webster, J. H. D., 1950. "Golden-Mean Form in Music." *Music and Letters* 31(3): 238–48.

Weinstein, D., 1991. *Heavy Metal: A Cultural Sociology*. Lexington: Lexington Books.

Wenham, G. J., 1987. *Genesis 1–15*. Waco: Word Books.

Werner, C., 2000. *A Change is Gonna Come: Music, Race and the Soul of America*. Edinburgh: Payback Press.

Westermann, C., 1994. *Genesis 1–11: A Continental Commentary*. J. J. Scullion, trans. Minneapolis: Fortress Press.

Wilcox, R. V., 1999. " 'There Will Never Be a "Very Special" Buffy': *Buffy* and the Monsters of Teen Life." *Journal of Popular Film and Television* 27(2): 16–23.

Wilcox, R. V., and D. Lavery, eds, 2003. *Fighting the Forces: What's at Stake in Buffy the Vampire Slayer*. Lanham, MD: Rowman and Littlefield.

Wright, R., 2000. " 'I'd sell you suicide': Pop Music and Moral Panic in the Age of Marilyn Manson." *Popular Music* 19(3): 365–85.

Wyman, L. M., and G. N. Dianisopoulos, 1999. "Primal Urges and Civilized Sensibilities: The Rhetoric of Gendered Archetypes, Seduction, and Resistance in *Bram Stoker's Dracula*." *Journal of Popular Film and Television* 27(2): 32–39.

Young, C. R., ed., 1966. *The Book of Hymns*. Nashville: The United Methodist Publishing House.

Zuckerman, M., 1996. "Sensation Seeking and the Taste for Vicarious Horror," in J. Weaver and R. Tamborini, eds, *Horror Films: Current Research on Audience Preferences and Reactions*. Mahwah, NJ: Lawrence Erlbaum Associates: 147–60.

Zwick, R., 1997. "The Problem of Evil in Contemporary Film," in J. R. May, ed., *New Image of Religious Film*. Kansas City, MO: Sheed & Ward: 72–91.

Filmography

Alien. Ridley Scott (dir.). 20th Century Fox, 1979.

Angels in America (television series). M. Nichols (dir.). Los Angeles: HBO Home Video, 2003.

Blade. Christopher Norrington (dir.). Amen Ra Films/New Line Cinema, 1998.

Blade II. Guillermo del Toro (dir.). Amen Ra Films/New Line Cinema, 2002.

Blade Trinity. Stephen S. Goyer (dir.). Amen Ra Films/New Line Cinema, 2004.

Bram Stoker's Dracula. Francis Ford Coppola (dir.). American Zoetrope/Columbia Pictures, 1992.

Buffy the Vampire Slayer (television series). J. Whedon, *et al.* (dir.)., writer. Beverly Hills, CA: 20th Century Fox Television, 1997–2003.

Buffy the Vampire Slayer (movie). F. R. Kuzui (dir.). Beverly Hills, CA: 20th Century Fox, 1992.

Dracula has Risen from the Grave. Freddie Francis (dir.). Hammer Films, 1968.

End of Days. Peter Hyams (dir.). Touchstone Home Video – DVD, 1999.

The Exorcist. William Friedkin (dir.). Warner, 1973.

The Fearless Vampire Killers. Roman Polanski (dir.). MGM Pictures, 1967.

The Greatest Story Ever Told. George Stevens (dir.). United Artists/MGM Pictures, 1965.

Hannibal. R. Scott (dir.). Universal Pictures, 2000.

Interview with the Vampire. Neil Jordan (dir.). Geffen Pictures, 1994.

The King of Kings. Cecil B. DeMille (dir.). DeMille Pictures Corporation, 1927.

The Last Temptation of Christ. Martin Scorsese (dir.). Universal, 1988.

Lust for a Vampire. Jimmy Sangster (dir.). Hammer Films, 1970.

Manhunter. M. Mann (dir.). Optimum, 1986.

The Omen. Richard Donner (dir.). 20th Century Fox – DVD, 1976.

The Omen. Richard Donner (dir.). 20th Century Fox – DVD, 2006.

The Passion of the Christ. Mel Gibson (dir.). Icon, 2004.

The Prophecy. Gregory Wilden (dir.). Dimension Home Video – DVD, 1995.

Revelation. Stuart Urban (dir.). Romulus Films – DVD, 2001

Rosemary's Baby. Roman Polanski (dir.). Paramount, 1968.

The Seventh Sign. Carl Schultz (dir.). Columbia Tristar Home Video – DVD, 1988.

The Silence of the Lambs. J. Demme (dir.). Orion Pictures Corporation, 1991.

Underworld. Len Wiseman (dir.). Lakeshore Entertainment, 2003.

Underworld Evolution. Len Wiseman (dir.). Lakeshore Entertainment, 2006.

Wings of Desire. W. Wenders (dir.). Los Angeles: MGM/UA Home Entertainment, 1987.

Discography

2Pac, *Untouchable*, 1997. Interscope.

Akercocke, *Rape of the Bastard Nazarene*. Goat of Mendes, 1999. Peaceville.

Cradle of Filth, *The Principle of Evil Made Flesh*, 1994. Cacophonous.

Cradle of Filth, *Vempire* or *Dark Faerytales in Phallustein*. EP, 1996. Cacophonous.

Cradle of Filth, *Dusk and Her Embrace*, 1996. Music for Nations.

Cradle of Filth, *Cruelty and the Beast*, 1998. Music for Nations.

Cradle of Filth, *From the Cradle to Enslave*. EP, 1999. Music for Nations.

Cradle of Filth, *Midian*, 2000. Sony BMG.

Cradle of Filth, *Bitter Suites to Succubi*. Mini-LP, 2001. Peaceville.

Cradle of Filth, *Lovecraft and Witch Hearts*. Retrospective anthology, 2002. Music for Nations.

Cradle of Filth, *Live Bait for the Dead*, 2002. Peaceville.

Cradle of Filth, *Damnation and a Day*, 2003. Epic.

Cradle of Filth, *Nymphetamine*, 2004. Roadrunner.

Cradle of Filth, *Thornography*, 2006. Roadrunner.

Infernaeon, *A Symphony of Suffering*, 2007. Prosthetic.

Marilyn Manson, *Portrait of an American Family*, 2003. Polydor.

Mayhem, *De Mysteriis Dom Sathanas*, 1994. Back on Black.

Mayhem, *In the Nightside Eclipse*, 1994.

Monstrosity, *Spiritual Apocalypse*, 2007. Metal Blade.

Nine Inch Nails, *The Downward Spiral*, 1994. Island.

Scarface, *Last of a Dying Breed*, 2000. Rap-A-Lot Records.

Scarface, *The Fix*, 2002. Def Jam South.
Scarface, *Balls and My Word*, 2003. Rap-A-Lot Records.
Scarface, *The Diary*, 2004. Rap-A-Lot Records.
Snoop Dogg, *Doggystyle*, 1996. Death Row Records.
Vomitory, *Terrorize, Brutalize, Sodomize*, 2007. Metal Blade.

Index of Subjects

Index of Names

Breinigsville, PA USA
11 December 2009
229044BV00003B/5/P

9 781845 533106